STAYING
THE
COURSE

About the author

William S. (Bill) Moody, a longtime program officer and later a program director with the Rockefeller Brothers Fund (RBF) in New York City, managed grantmaking programs for 40 years, first in economic development and natural resources management in Latin American, in community action and conservation in sub-Saharan Africa, race relations in South Africa, and eco-development in the Caribbean; later, in sustainable development and civic engagement/democratic practice in Central and Eastern Europe and the Western Balkans; and, along the way, in international relations and human rights. Bill was educated at Northwestern University (BA); University of Geneva, Switzerland; University of Michigan Law School (JD); and the Institute of European Studies of the Free University of Brussels, Belgium (licence spéciale). He is a member of the governing boards of International House, New York, the Belgian American Educational Foundation, and the Woodstock Foundation in Vermont. Bill has two sons, Scott and John; a daughter, Megan; and four grandchildren. He lives with his wife Susan in Princeton, NJ.

"Should be required reading for foundation staffs and board members, as well as for international development professionals and NGO leaders."
Brent Mitchell, senior vice president, Quebec-Labrador Foundation

"There will be many in the foundation and NGO worlds for whom this book will be a surprise and pleasure to read and a learning experience as well. I could imagine that future philanthropists would be energized by the book and benefit from its many lessons."
Marianne Ginsburg, former program officer for environment,
German Marshall Fund of the United States

"A good program officer needs to be knowledgeable, respectful, open to new opportunities, and able to build trust – the glue that keeps societies and communities together. Those qualities are on ample display here."
Jiří Bárta, executive director, Via Foundation (Czech Republic)

"The approach to grantmaking described here – Bill's and the RBF's – helped us make the transition to a democratic society and a market economy. The effects of this work are visible today and will be visible for years to come."
Andrzej Kassenberg, a founder and longtime president, Institute for Sustainable Development (Poland)

"Offers a wonderful description of the way in which a program officer learns, evolves, and matures and of the institutional context that encouraged this process."
Russell A. Phillips, former executive vice president and former acting president, Rockefeller Brothers Fund

STAYING THE COURSE

REFLECTIONS ON 40 YEARS OF GRANTMAKING AT THE ROCKEFELLER BROTHERS FUND

WILLIAM S. MOODY

WITH PRISCILLA LEWIS, EDITOR

ALLIANCE PUBLISHING TRUST

Published by Alliance Publishing Trust

Copyright © 2014 William S. Moody

ISBN 978 1 907376 21 4

Alliance Publishing Trust
15 Prescott Place, London SW4 6BS

publishing@alliancemagazine.org
www.alliancemagazine.org

Registered charity number: 1116744
Company registration number: 5935154

A catalogue record for this book is available
from the British Library.

Typeset in Akzidenz Grotesk
Design by Benedict Richards

Cover photo: Susan Taylor Moody, 12 September 2010
A wooden planked path across a boggy section of the
Jordan Pond Shore Trail, Mount Desert Island,
Acadia National Park, Maine

Printed and bound by Hobbs the Printers, Totton, Hampshire, UK

This book is printed on FSC approved paper.

To Susan, my beloved wife, who constantly steadied the course for me.

To countless people who have more impact than they might imagine through their continuing efforts to inspire and to participate in lasting and beneficial change in their communities.

Contents

Preface

Retrospectives by program officers of major American foundations are few in number and, among those, longtime Rockefeller Brothers Fund program officer Bill Moody has written one that stands out. *Staying the Course: Reflections on 40 Years of Grantmaking at the Rockefeller Brothers Fund* brings to mind the classics in this genre: the books written by Warren Weaver of the Rockefeller Foundation and Forrest P 'Frosty' Hill and Frank Sutton of the Ford Foundation. In their books, these three legendary foundation executives skillfully explained the powerful and positive impact that well-conceived and thoughtfully implemented philanthropic grants and broad programs had on the process of social change and development in South and East Asia and Latin America during the 25 years following the end of the Second World War.

The lessons Bill imparts are equally valuable, although his career covered a different time span (1968–2007) and branched off from an early focus on developing countries in Latin America, Africa, and the Caribbean to a focus, in the early 1980s, on Central and Eastern Europe. The Cold War was still raging when the board of the Fund decided to explore the possibility of working in that region, but there was deep restlessness in the Soviet-controlled nations of the Warsaw Pact, which suffered from failing economies, rampant corruption, and severe environmental degradation. Beginning with an emergency grant to support Polish scholars stranded in the United States when the Polish government took measures to suppress the Solidarity movement, the RBF's involvement broadened to include efforts to help local people meet economic and environmental challenges. When the Cold War ended, the program grew to incorporate a number of impressive initiatives in a wide variety of fields, including new initiatives aimed at consolidating democracy. Bill took an active role in all of these efforts, and his recounting of the trials and tribulations, the many successes and occasional failures is both thoughtfully objective and totally engrossing – as is his account of the RBF's involvement in other regions. In the end, Bill and the RBF were trying to help bring into being and then nurture the elements of civil society in a group of nations (Poland, the Czech Republic, Slovakia, Hungary, and, eventually, several new states in the Western Balkans) in which the rights of individuals and local communities – the essential elements of an effective democratic polity and a sustainable and environmentally conscious free-market economy – had been absent for more than 50 years.

Today's media are so focused on celebrity and the evanescent that stories of slow and sustainable change unfolding over the course of years or even decades are missed. Bill Moody has ensured that this process as it evolved in Central and Eastern Europe (and in Latin America, Africa, the Caribbean, and the Western Balkans) over the last 40 years will be understood and remembered. It is a wonderful book, well worth reading and pondering the lessons it contains.

David Rockefeller
New York City
March 2014

A Foreword in Two Voices
Ambassador William H Luers and Wendy W Luers

I

My wife Wendy and I first met Bill Moody in the spring of 1986 when we were living in Prague, where I served as US Ambassador. That meeting with Bill began a nearly 30-year association for both Wendy and me with the Rockefeller Brothers Fund and with Bill.

Communist Czechoslovakia then was still probably the most tightly buttoned-up nation in the Soviet bloc. Outside of the field of human rights, American foundations and non-governmental organizations saw little value in visiting or learning about – much less supporting or partnering with – the few small non-governmental organizations that were operating then in Czechoslovakia, mostly focusing on environmental issues or the arts. As Wendy and I discovered, the Rockefeller Brothers Fund (RBF) was among the few exceptions to that rule, and Bill was in Czechoslovakia to meet with some of the civil society leaders whose work the RBF was supporting and to scope out new grantmaking opportunities.

Bill was the Fund's pioneer and innovator in Central and Eastern Europe, deeply engaged there well before the fall of the Berlin Wall. The RBF had already established a record of leadership, collaboration with other foundations, and close cooperative relationships with grantee organizations in the United States and in other parts of the world. In Central and Eastern Europe, Bill ultimately positioned the relatively small RBF at the cutting edge of efforts to help post-communist societies.

I enjoyed an insider's perspective on these developments. Not long after meeting with Bill in Prague, I left the State Department to become president of the Metropolitan Museum in New York. Colin Campbell, then president of the RBF, invited me to become a member of the Fund's board of trustees. I became deeply engaged in and admiring of the way the RBF, its program officers, and its board focused intently on learning what the citizens of Central and Eastern European nations in transition wanted and needed, then acting flexibly and creatively to help address those needs. Bill listened to those exciting new voices on the ground and dedicated himself to helping the emerging civil societies in free Poland, Czechoslovakia, Hungary, and elsewhere to take on the many and diverse challenges they faced. All the while, Colin Campbell and his leadership team, recognizing the unique talents and decades of experience that Bill brought to the community of funders and grantees, encouraged him to range broadly and boldly in that new world.

In this book, Bill invites the reader to explore with him his four-decade career at the RBF and his involvement in the philanthropy of the Rockefeller family, pacesetters in the field for generations. He provides invaluable personal insights into and advice on the work of a program officer – how foundation philanthropy works and what he came to believe was the wisest way to make grants. He is persuasive in his message throughout the book. Three lessons stood out for me in particular: (1) be an engaged grantmaker and seek to build relationships of trust with grantees; (2) help grantees build capacity for the long term, including through staff training and the development of a strong administrative structure; and (3) always seek collaborative approaches with other funders and like-minded organizations – a long tradition of Rockefeller family philanthropy.

With all their prior experience and learning about how to help strengthen civil society, the RBF and Bill Moody were ready when the communist structure crumbled. With contacts and friends developed throughout the region, the RBF was poised to engage, build capacity, and seek out new collaborators throughout the world to help bring resources to those changing societies. Bill enjoyed the strong support of the RBF's leadership, staff, and board; his own tenacity and enormous range of friends and associates in the former Soviet bloc nations gave him an inside track to learn what was needed to help Central and Eastern European societies make the transition to democracy.

I hope you will read on for Wendy Luers' somewhat different per-spective on Bill's work and that of the RBF in the 1990s – the period of Bill's greatest impact as a grantmaker and the period in which the RBF made some of its most far-reaching philanthropic contributions.

William H Luers
Director, The Iran Project
Adjunct Professor, Columbia University

II

This is a very personal introduction to an important book that is particularly meaningful to me because it memorializes the exciting and pivotal days of the 1990s in Central and Eastern Europe and the role of Bill Moody and the Rockefeller Brothers Fund in that region.

When my husband, William Luers, was the American Ambassador to Czechoslovakia in the mid-1980s, we befriended Vaclav Havel and the Charter 77 activists (an informal civic initiative critical of the commu-nist government), including many writers, curators, and artists – some of whom were stoking coal in the metro or doing other menial work under the oppressive communist regime. On returning to New York in 1986, we stayed in close contact with our friends stuck behind the Iron Curtain with no passports. After the Velvet Revolution in November 1989, when our friends suddenly became the new government of free Czechoslovakia, we returned to host Havel's inaugural dinner on 28 December 1989. At his inauguration the next day, President Havel wore my husband's tie and his wife Olga wore my blouse!

It was one of the most exciting days of our lives – but then what? No one in the new government had any experience whatsoever in governing a nation; many had not been out of the closed country since 1968. The new Deputy Prime Minister, Jan Carnogursky, and others in the govern-ment asked us to help. Upon our return to the United States, we briefed a group of interested foundation and US government officials at the Ford Foundation. Everyone recommended creating a single point of contact with the Czech government. Since my husband and I were among the few Americans who knew and were trusted by members of the new Czech government, it was decided that I should try to create such an organiza-tion. With the blessing of George Soros, I picked up his existing Charter

77 Foundation (a human rights organization), re-registered it, and opened offices in New York and Prague.

The first people I turned to were Colin Campbell, president of the RBF, and Bill Moody. They introduced me to other funders, helped design programs, and were available whenever I or any of us needed them (which was very often). From the outset, Bill's modus operandi was to be encouraging and engaged; he was never negative, even when he had to turn down funding requests. He was the most empowering funder I have ever encountered.

Bill describes his approach in this book as 'responsive and proactive, serendipitous and systematic.' The description is right on target. Bill was constantly flying to the region, visiting grantees, and opening new vistas. As the Foundation for a Civil Society grew (we changed the name when the original Charter 77 organization closed its doors) and established new offices in the region, Bill trusted us and all the young people who worked with us to reach deep into those semi-broken societies. He was always available for advice, and always with a smile. He believed in the local people and encouraged them to take hold of their own destinies. He collaborated with other funders, private and public, to increase significantly the amount and quality of their investment.

I know that Bill is still beloved by all who worked with him in Central and Eastern Europe. I urge anyone who wants to help empower people to improve their lives, in any region or community, to read Bill's book. Pay particular attention to his 'top ten' principles and practices. They are a wonderful summary of an engaged, trusting, and trust-building approach to promoting positive social change.

Wendy W Luers
President, The Foundation for a Civil Society
Co-chair and Co-founder, Beyond Conflict (formerly the Project on Justice in Times of Transition)
New York
April 2014

Introduction

This book is about helping local people in their communities around the world make lasting, positive change. Drawing on insights from my 40-year career as a program officer at the Rockefeller Brothers Fund (RBF), a grantmaking foundation in New York City, I try to show how relatively modest contributions of money, time, and energy can have big impacts on the economic, cultural, and environmental challenges that face transforming societies. I describe practical strategies and broad principles for effective philanthropy, bringing those principles to life through stories from all stages of my long professional journey – a journey that took me to newly independent countries in Africa and the Caribbean; to Latin American countries that were facing basic challenges in resource management and job creation; to countries in Central and Eastern Europe that were emerging from communist rule; and finally to countries in the Western Balkans that were attempting to rebuild their societies after the violent ethnic conflicts of the 1990s.

The important philanthropic principles and practices illustrated here are not unique to my work or to the RBF's; but they are often neglected, honored only rhetorically, or considered within too short a time frame. Aspiring grantmakers, students of philanthropy, and other readers who want to know more about foundations will find here a personal perspective, informed by extensive experience, on the work of 'giving away' money – including how to gauge the likely impact of intended beneficial actions; how to get maximum impact from relatively modest philanthropic investments; and what pitfalls and obstacles can get in the way of positive change. Colleagues in the foundation community who share some of the broad grantmaking goals of the RBF, and non-profit leaders and emerging leaders around the world whose work the RBF supported, will get a glimpse of the 'big picture' as it looked from the point of view of an actively engaged program officer. Policymakers, issue advocates, scholars, and students who want to help create a more just, sustainable, and peaceful world will recognize the perennial questions raised here: how to empower people to improve their lives and communities; how to build trust across sectoral, cultural, and other divides; how to nurture a viable civil society; how to confront large and complex problems with finite resources; and how to help nations and societies in transition make far-sighted choices – about economic development and resource use, for example, or about governance.

Substantively, the book concentrates on the two major economic and societal issues that were a continuing focus of my four decades of work at the Fund: (1) the need for wise use of natural and cultural resources,* what is now called sustainable development; and (2) the importance to a healthy democracy of an engaged citizenry and an active non-profit/voluntary sector. Two other big concerns – the protection of human rights and the pursuit of peace and security – weave through the book as well.

Geographically, the focus is on Africa, Latin America, the Caribbean, Central and Eastern Europe, and the Western Balkans. While my career at the RBF was spent as an 'international' program officer, I believe that essentially all of the principles and practices identified in this book would also be relevant and important in the context of domestic grantmaking.

Stylistically, I have relied heavily on stories about particular grant relationships (interspersed with some contextualizing chapters) to paint a picture of my work and to describe the goals, strategies, and outcomes of the Fund's grantmaking. Necessarily, I have been selective in deciding which stories to tell, choosing from among many possibilities (the RBF board approved nearly 1,000 grants in my program areas between 1968 and 2007) those that best illustrate broadly applicable models and lessons.

* Our use of this terminology is not to be confused with the so-called 'Wise Use Movement' that emerged in some Western states in the 1970s, as a reaction against the Endangered Species Act.

In discussing outcomes, I have tried to provide a sense of the 'ripple effects' of some investments and involvements – asking where things stood several years after the RBF's engagement had come to an end, and whether impacts are being felt in the present day. For me, discovering some of those ripple effects was an unexpected benefit of working on this book!

That said, it is important to acknowledge that this book does not offer formal assessments of major projects or programs. It is more in the nature of a retrospective, in the preparation of which I supplemented my memory by reviewing a great deal of archival material – including at the remarkable Rockefeller Archive Center, where the records of the Rockefeller family and their philanthropic endeavors are preserved, together with materials from numerous non-Rockefeller foundations and non-profit organizations. I also consulted as fully as possible with former colleagues and project leaders. That said, all of the views of issues, events, individuals, and organizations expressed here are my own and do not necessarily represent the opinions of others previously or presently associated with the foundation or its history.

Organization of the book

Part One focuses on my arrival and early years at the Fund, from 1968 well into the 1980s. Developing countries in Africa, Latin America, and the Caribbean were my primary focus during this time span. Initially, my work and that of the Fund was still very much influenced by the Rockefeller brothers' individual charitable interests. But this period also saw the death of three brothers and their sister, and a gradual shift at the RBF toward greater leadership from staff and a more structured philanthropic approach.

Part Two picks up in the early 1980s, as family leadership on the RBF board was transferred to a new generation. This shift led to the articulation of a new programmatic framework for the RBF's grantmaking, which shaped our work until 2000. During this period, when communism imploded and the Berlin Wall finally came down, my work focused on the transforming states and societies of Central and Eastern Europe. This was truly grantmaking 'in the thick of history,' as the RBF tried to anticipate and respond to the political and social currents and cross-currents that were buffeting the region.

In 2000 a change in leadership at the Fund and a major program-matic review led to the development of a revised program architecture, within which I worked until my retirement in 2007. This period is treated in Part Three. When the new program architecture was adopted, I was already engaged in exploring whether the Fund might usefully apply les-sons from its long experience in Central and Eastern Europe to some of the problems facing the Balkans, which were then emerging from the bloody conflicts of the early 1990s. Ultimately, countries in the Western Balkans were formally incorporated into the new program structure as one of sev-eral 'pivotal places' for RBF grantmaking, and I spent the remainder of my time at the Fund working on that region.*

In the third section I also reflect on the non-monetary contributions that a program officer can make by becoming personally involved in the creation or governance of institutions which have the potential to outlast even the long attention span of a foundation like the RBF. A concluding chapter offers my overall perspective on the 'legacy' of the four decades and several strands of RBF philanthropy in which I was privileged actively to participate, and summarizes key principles and practices for promoting positive change.

* Lists of grants made in each of these regions, and internationally, are provided at the back of the book (pages 280–300).

Primary focus of grantmaking

Reached through regional and exploratory grantmaking

Over the course of 40 years at the Rockefeller Brothers Fund, my geographical areas of responsibility included Africa, Latin America, the Caribbean, Central and Eastern Europe, and the Western Balkans.

Part One

CHAPTER ONE

My Introduction to Rockefeller Philanthropy

I BELIEVE in the SUPREME WORTH OF THE INDIVIDUAL and in his right to life, liberty and the pursuit of happiness.

I BELIEVE that every right implies a responsibility; every opportunity, an obligation; every possession, a duty.

I BELIEVE that truth and justice are fundamental to an enduring social order.

I BELIEVE in the sacredness of a promise, that a man's word should be as good as his bond; that character – not wealth or power or position – is of supreme worth.

From Credo of John D Rockefeller, Jr, 8 July 1941

A phone call from New York

In the early spring of 1968, shortly after my 29th birthday, I heard the phone ringing in my office at Warner, Norcross & Judd, in Grand Rapids, Michigan, as I was leaving a meeting down the hall. Only six months before, I had returned to my law firm after a year in Europe pursuing a postgraduate degree in European Studies (with an emphasis on legal considerations and issues) from the Free University of Brussels, Belgium, so I was trying to dig back into life and work in Michigan. I picked up the phone on the third or fourth ring, and heard a man say, 'This is James Hyde of the Rockefeller Brothers Fund in New York City. I'm calling because I am looking for a young lawyer to fill the position of international staff associate for the Rockefeller Brothers Fund and Rockefeller Family & Associates. I was given your name by William Bishop and Eric Stein [two of my international law professors at the University of Michigan Law School]. Would you be interested in discussing this position?'

I recognized the caller's family name because a Charles Cheney Hyde had written a classic text on international law that I used in law school and still have in my library today – and indeed, the Jim Hyde who called me was the author's son. But I had never heard of the Rockefeller Brothers Fund, a foundation created in 1940 by the grandsons of the legendary John D Rockefeller. Moreover, my then wife Katie and I had just bought our dream house, with good schools and a lake nearby. We had a two-year-old son, Scott, and Katie was six months pregnant with our second child. My first reaction was to say I was not interested. It took only a few moments of honest reflection for me to recognize that, down deep, I was yearning for an opportunity to spend professional, weekday time – not weekend volunteer time or future possible weekday time – on international issues such as economic development, environmental challenges, and the protection of human rights. I told Mr Hyde that I was interested in learning more about the foundation and the job opening.

Before that day, I could not in my wildest dreams have imagined that such an opportunity was out there and that a lawyer working in a relatively provincial town in the Midwest could compete for a position at a prestigious philanthropic foundation in New York City. Yet, less than four months later – two months after my second son, John, was born – my family and I were on our way to a new life on the East Coast; and I began an extraordinary 40-year career at the Rockefeller Brothers Fund (RBF).

* * * *

I was born and raised in Michigan, and I felt proud to be a Midwesterner; I still do!

My father, Carl Edwin Moody, grew up poor near Battle Creek, Michigan, and was the first of ten children to achieve a university education. My mother, Isobel Louise Moody, had a middle-class upbringing in Chicago and Detroit, where her father was in the piano business and was an excellent pianist, too. My father was my primary mentor and hero in my growing-up years. To this day, 25 years after he died at age 85 after working 54 years for the Penn Mutual Life Insurance Company, I still hear people say about my dad, 'You could always trust and count on Carl Moody. Your best interests were always in the forefront of his thinking, and you could be sure that Carl would follow through on whatever he agreed to do!' My mother chafed at being a 'stay-at-home mom'; but she was a generous and caring person throughout her life. In my early teenage years, she returned to college to become an elementary school teacher – the beginning of the happiest period of her life. My only sibling, Jodie (named Josephine after my great aunt Josephine Shorter, the wife of my namesake), inherited my maternal grandfather's musical talent and my mother's good looks. She was and still is lively, curious, and engaged in various community activities – she is wonderful company, although we disagree with one another about most political issues!

My childhood was a pretty happy one. As a teenager, I had a newspaper route, worked as a cashier at the supermarket, and took other part-time jobs. I wish I had been a better athlete! I had more success in student government, eventually getting elected president of the Detroit High School Student Council, which served as a voice for all the public high schools in the city. From an early point in my life, however, I had an interest in other countries and peoples. Perhaps it started when I was seven or eight, when my namesake and great uncle, William J Shorter – home on leave from his management roles in Uruguay for Swift & Co of Chicago – would sit with me on the sofa and tell me about riding to work on a horse, about people speaking different languages, and about how happy and 'at home' he and his wife Josephine felt in a place where people with different backgrounds all worked and socialized together.

During my childhood, Uncle Bill and Aunt Jo were my only relatives who had traveled to or lived in a foreign country – except for relatives who had served in the Second World War in Europe or the Pacific. As a kid, theirs were the stories I mainly heard. Frankly, I wonder if those war stories might have contributed to my early curiosity about other parts of the world and the people who lived there. Why did people want to shoot and kill each other? How could this make any sense?

Of course, growing up in Michigan, I had visited Canada many times, which did not feel very foreign. My mother's family spent several generations in Ontario before seeking jobs in the US, and I had cousins there. But for whatever cause or reason, there was something inside of me that pulled me as a youth towards maps, geography, world history, and foreign affairs.

That fascination came into focus for me in 1956, when I spent the summer as an American Field Service exchange student in Germany. I was 17, and the experience was galvanizing; it awakened in me an insatiable desire to learn everything possible about people and places all over the world. My summer living with two German families in the industrial heartland, the Ruhr region, just 11 years after the end of the Second World War, brought me into daily contact with people who had supposedly been my enemies not very long before but who had interests and dreams similar to mine.

Besides my experience in Germany as a high-school student, two other foreign experiences were highly important in shaping my thinking and outlook in the years leading up to my joining the Rockefeller Brothers Fund. The first of these was my junior year abroad at the University of Geneva, Switzerland, and its affiliated Graduate Institute of International Studies. The second was my postgraduate year at the Institute for European Studies of the Free University of Brussels, Belgium, which I had completed shortly before receiving that phone call from Jim Hyde. In addition, there were several professors at Northwestern University in Evanston, Illinois, where I received my BA, and at the University of Michigan Law School, where I received my law degree, who played critical roles in expanding my horizons. In fact, as Jim indicated in his initial call, it was two of my international law professors who had passed along my name.

* * * *

As I pondered that phone call from New York, my first instinct was that Katie would not want to move. She was an exceptional elementary school teacher, widely respected in the local educational system. We had good friends in Grand Rapids and our families were less than three hours away in the Detroit area, where we both grew up.

I was wrong. Katie listened intently and calmly to my analysis, which increasingly favored accepting the job, if I received an offer. Ultimately, even though she would have preferred to stay in Grand Rapids, she urged me to explore this new possibility fully, since it was so consistent with my interests and since I had found living overseas and learning about other cultures so rewarding. I could not have asked for a more open-minded and heartfelt encouragement. My parents also listened closely and attentively to my story. They suggested that either decision – going to New York or staying in Grand Rapids – could have big benefits; they told me to follow my heart as well as my head.

In late spring, after a round of interviews with officers and staff at the RBF, I received an offer to join the Rockefeller Brothers Fund and Rockefeller Family & Associates. On 8 August 1968 I began my new career.

Arrival at the RBF

It was a hot, humid day when I arrived to start my new job at 30 Rockefeller Plaza, captivated by the extraordinary murals on the ceiling of this tallest building in Rockefeller Center. My soon-to-be-favorite elevator operator, George (an immigrant from Poland), greeted me and took me to the 54th floor, which I had already visited in the spring, as part of the interview process. Entering the reception area, I realized I was no longer a visitor. That day I had become a staff associate for international affairs at the Rockefeller Brothers Fund and Rockefeller Family & Associates (RFA), the office that provided family members with investment, legal, and accounting services in addition to managing their philanthropic activities.

As I waited for Jim Hyde, my new boss and head of the RBF's International Program, I looked at my surroundings. The furnishings were sturdy and comfortable, neither antique period pieces nor flashy, modern design statements. The reception room was quiet and friendly, without distinguishing features. You might imagine that the Rockefeller family, one of the wealthiest families in the world, would have chosen a more assertive or costly décor. But in fact, I felt totally at home in the understated ambiance.

Within minutes, Jim walked through the door to greet me and introduce me to the receptionist as a new member of the staff. Jim and I then walked along a corridor to his office – modest, like the reception area, but with a sweeping view of Lower Manhattan and the Hudson and East rivers. After some welcoming words, Jim ushered me to my own small office, next to his (and fortunately, with the same remarkable view).

I was joining the RBF at a tumultuous time for the United States, with young people protesting against the Vietnam War and rejecting other aspects of the cultural and political status quo. The position I now filled had become available as an indirect consequence of intergenerational tensions in the Rockefeller family itself. My predecessor, Robert W Scrivner, had been selected by members of the Rockefeller family to become the first director of a new family philanthropy, called the Rockefeller Family Fund (RFF). I was not the only program staff to be hired in 1968; in fact, several new professional staff members were being brought on, as the

Bill Moody, new member of the RBF team, at work on the 54th floor of 30 Rockefeller Plaza.

RBF endowment grew and its activities began to expand beyond the immediate range of the brothers' personal philanthropic interests. The other three new hires were Richard A Salomon, Russell A Phillips, Jr, and Thomas W Wahman. Rick was the youngest, in his mid-20s; the rest of us were around 30.

None of us was a specialist in the fields in which we would be working. As Jim told me in our first phone conversation, he was looking for a young, broadly educated, team-playing generalist, with some overseas experience, who would be 'trainable' in the areas in which the RBF would be active. Trainable we all proved to be – and with encouragement from our more experienced colleagues, we all quickly began to grow professionally in ways that enabled us to influence and ultimately to help shape the phil anthropic work of the family and the Fund.

Rick, who had just received his MBA from Columbia University, was hired to help Robert Bates, Secretary of the Fund, with a range of administrative responsibilities, including preparations for board of trustee meetings. In less than two years, Rick's role had evolved to helping David and Peggy Rockefeller with their grantmaking in Maine, where they had a home and longtime interests, and helping David with his leadership roles in such organizations as the Council on Foreign Relations and the Museum of Modern Art (MOMA). Over the years, Rick became a senior adviser to David, especially in the management and allocation of resources and assets, while simultaneously occupying important independent positions in the financial sector.

Russell was a young lawyer from North Carolina, who had worked for Wilmer Cutler & Pickering in Washington, DC. He was hired primarily to assist Dana Creel, the director of the Fund, with special projects and a range of other matters. Not long after his arrival and with Jim Hyde's encouragement, Russell took responsibility for the RBF's grantmaking in Asia. Russell would eventually become corporate secretary and vice president of the RBF, and later the executive vice president, meanwhile continuing to direct the Fund's programs in Asia. Now retired, Russell remains an invaluable asset, trusted and confided in by RBF staff and Rockefeller family members, as well as by foundation leaders across the philanthropic sector.

Tom was from Minnesota; he attended (and played hockey for) Dartmouth, and later graduated from Union Theological Seminary. During his 20-year career at the RBF, Tom would emerge as one of the boldest, most creative, and far-sighted program officers in the US foundation community, working primarily on social justice and poverty reduction in the southern states as well as natural resource challenges. Subsequently, Tom formed the Resources Development Foundation, which led the way in developing new approaches to seemingly mundane but critical environmental challenges, such as waste disposal.

That first day, Jim took me around to meet Rick, Russell, and Tom, as well as most of the other staff at the RBF – fewer than two dozen, in total. I briefly met Dana Creel, a pipe-smoking lawyer from Georgia who was director of the Fund and soon to become its president; Robert Bates, the corporate secretary and 'utility infielder,' so to speak; and Gene Setzer, senior staff associate for conservation and soon to be vice president of the RBF as well as senior philanthropic adviser to Laurance Rockefeller. Even at this very early stage, I could sense the devotion of staff members at all levels to the mission of the RBF and to the Rockefeller family.

What I could not yet imagine, on that first day, was my great good fortune in having Jim Hyde as my boss. Born in Chicago, Jim moved east as a teenager when his father accepted a position as professor of international law at Columbia University Law School, where Jim would receive his law degree. During the Second World War, Jim was a lieutenant commander and international law adviser to the commander of the Pacific Fleet, Admiral Chester W Nimitz. In 1951 he was named deputy US representative to the United Nations General Assembly. Jim worked nearly full time at the RBF from 1959 until 1977; he also taught and consulted, and he contributed articles on international law to professional journals until 1980, when he retired more fully.

What I remember most about Jim was how he took me under his wing in my early years at the Fund, giving me regular 'tutorials' about international issues, with particular attention to anything that might be of interest to the Rockefeller family or the RBF. He carefully reviewed the initial memos that I prepared, especially those for board and family members. We sometimes had differing views about an issue or about appropriate next steps, but Jim encouraged me to speak up and defend my analysis, and to take the initiative in bringing my ideas forward. Nine years later, Jim

The Rockefeller Brothers Fund was created in 1940 by the sons of John D Rockefeller, Jr. Pictured (left to right): John 3rd, Winthrop, sister Abby, Laurance, David, and Nelson. (© Ezra Stoller/Esto)

would retire and I would be given the opportunity to grow into his shoes, which I attempted to do in my own ways.

But as I came back to my new office after that round of initial introductions, all I could do was pinch myself. Less than one year earlier, I had been planning to spend my professional life as a lawyer in Grand Rapids, Michigan. What a difference a phone call can make!

Rockefeller 'family headquarters'

I knew that I was going to be working both for the Rockefeller Brothers Fund (80 per cent of my time) and for the Rockefeller family office (20 per cent). In fact, I soon realized that I was *surrounded* by Rockefeller family activities, which occupied three full floors of 30 Rockefeller Plaza – the flagship building of Rockefeller Center. The RBF offices on the 54th floor were linked by an internal staircase to the 55th and 56th floors, where four of the five Rockefeller brothers had offices and where a few organizations in which the brothers and other family members played critical roles were headquartered. RFA staff provided a range of services to the brothers and other family members on all three floors.

Legal interpretations of the US Tax Reform Act of 1969 brought an end to the intermingling of all of these activities and, ultimately, to my split payroll arrangement, which was terminated in 1976, not long before the RBF and the RFF moved to a separate building across the street. But those initial years spent in 'family headquarters' gave me a remarkable opportunity to interact with a range of colleagues and to appreciate the value of the Rockefeller family's unique tradition of service and sharing. As I would see repeatedly during my career, the Rockefeller name and the family's longstanding involvement in philanthropy – not to mention business and politics – were important assets that enhanced the impact of the RBF's grantmaking, even when the dollar amounts of our grants were modest by comparison with those of much larger foundations (the fact that we played in the 'big leagues' also meant that we had to become adept at stretching and leveraging our limited funds!).

Scholars and biographers have told the Rockefeller story elsewhere, in rich detail, but a few key points of reference will provide a sense of the family's philanthropic tradition.

John D Rockefeller, Sr (1839–1937), who made the original family fortune in the second half of the 19th century in the petroleum industry (he founded Standard Oil and turned it into a powerful monopoly), began contributing regularly to charity in his youth, when his income was quite modest. As his fortune grew, he became a controversial figure, envied and admired as well as despised and feared; but he also emerged as a respected philanthropist, establishing the University of Chicago, supporting pathbreaking biomedical research at Rockefeller Institute in New York City, funding healthcare and hospital services in Beijing (then Peking), and establishing other important initiatives and institutions in the US and around the world.

JDR, Sr passed on his commitment to philanthropy to his only son, John D Rockefeller, Jr (1874–1960). After a long personal struggle – fueled by anguish over the 'Ludlow Massacre' of 1914, in which the Colorado National Guard and mining camp guards attacked a tent colony of coal miners on strike against a Rockefeller-owned company, killing some two dozen men, women, and children – JDR, Jr decided that he would not remain in his father's company, but would devote his life to managing the family fortune and overseeing its philanthropic institutions. Over time, he drew on his considerable wealth to make major contributions to education, healthcare, arts and culture, conservation of nature and protection of cultural heritage, and employment generation. In 1913 he helped his father create the Rockefeller Foundation, which further extended and consolidated the management of Rockefeller interests in medicine and public health, education, agriculture, economic issues, and several other fields. The Rockefeller Foundation was one of the earliest expressions of a new approach to giving – philanthropy, as distinct from charity – that aimed for more systemic impacts on social problems. The Rockefeller Foundation was also one of the earliest and largest American foundations to adopt a worldwide orientation.

JDR, Jr instilled strong service and stewardship values in his own children, and in 1940, with their father's encouragement, JDR, Jr's five sons – John 3rd, Nelson, Laurance, Winthrop, and David – established the Rockefeller Brothers Fund as a vehicle through which they could coordinate their individual giving and amplify its impact. Their sister Abby joined them shortly thereafter; but she chose to follow separate paths for most of her philanthropic endeavors. The brothers each contributed about $100,000 per year to the RBF from 1940 to 1951; the Fund analyzed requests and distributed the money on behalf of the brothers (and sometimes other family members) to a variety of civic, cultural, and service organizations. JDR, Jr was so impressed by the positive effects of the active engagement of his sons in charitable undertakings that he contributed about $59 million in Rockefeller Center notes to the RBF endowment in 1951. He left another $150 million to the endowment upon his death in 1960, considerably strengthening the RBF's financial underpinnings. During these years, the brothers were also receiving distributions from 'skipping generation' trusts their grandfather had established, so their individual philanthropic capacities were growing as well. Gradually, the RBF developed a grantmaking program that was broader than the brothers' philanthropic interests, a process that was well under way when Rick, Russell, Tom, and I joined the staff. An administrative vehicle was becoming a real foundation, with influence on New York, national, and international affairs.

While the Rockefeller Foundation has long been independent of the Rockefeller family, family members (now including members of the fourth and fifth generations) make up about half of the RBF board, and a member

The mission of the Rockefeller Brothers Fund

The fundamental mission of the RBF has never changed, although its articulation has evolved. Always, a primary emphasis has been on empowering people to solve their own problems. Always, there has been a respect for the dignity of individuals everywhere, a concern about the well-being of our planet and its resources, and a desire to prevent violent conflicts.

From the start, the brothers saw themselves as citizens of and responsible to three communities – global, national, and local (New York City) – and the RBF's grantmaking programs have always reflected that awareness. In fact, when I joined the Fund, those were the titles of our major programs: International, National, and New York City.

In keeping with changing times and challenges, specific programmatic goals and strategies have evolved. But the Fund's current mission statement is entirely consistent with its history: 'The Rockefeller Brothers Fund advances social change that contributes to a more just, sustainable, and peaceful world.'

For additional information, see www.rbf.org/content/about-fund.

of the family always chairs the board. Some of the brothers' children – the generation known as the 'cousins' – became deeply involved in guiding the work of another family foundation that was established in 1967, called the Rockefeller Family Fund.

Other wealthy industrialists of the late 19th century created foundations and endowed institutions that remain active to this day. But the Rockefellers have been especially deliberate about instilling philanthropic values in each succeeding generation of the family, and encouraging each generation to participate fully in the conduct of philanthropy – including by forming new philanthropic institutions.

The internal staircase

What did my being situated in the Rockefeller family headquarters – and having access to that 'internal staircase' between floors – mean for my education as a grantmaker?

When I arrived at the RBF and RFA in 1968, all of the Rockefeller brothers were at or near the peak of their careers. John 3rd, at 62, had followed in his father's footsteps and was dedicating most of his energies to philanthropy; he was playing leadership roles in efforts to address international population and family-planning issues, US relations with Asia, and the needs of the 'third sector' (non-profit and non-governmental organizations) in the United States. Nelson, aged 60, was in the middle of his third term as governor of the State of New York, and six years later would become Vice President of the United States; he had a particularly deep interest in Latin America. Laurance, 58, was already recognized as a leading conservationist and venture capitalist; the chair of the RBF (he held that position longer than any other family member), he was also a longtime chair of Memorial Sloan Kettering, the famous cancer treatment center. Winthrop, 56, had left New York years earlier for Arkansas, where he made a lasting, positive impact as a philanthropist and politician; he had recently been elected the first Republican governor of the state. David, the youngest Rockefeller brother at 53, would become chairman and CEO of the Chase Manhattan Bank the following year; he had already distinguished himself in international affairs and was playing leadership roles in the Council on Foreign Relations and other institutions that were addressing challenges around the world.

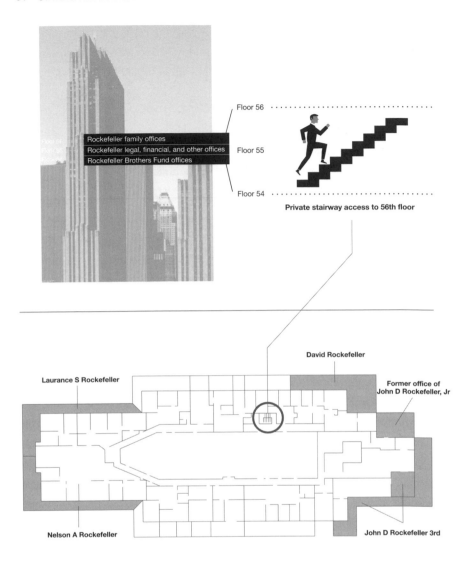

Floor 56 ·

Rockefeller family offices
Rockefeller legal, financial, and other offices   Floor 55
Rockefeller Brothers Fund offices

Floor 54 ·

Private stairway access to 56th floor

David Rockefeller

Laurance S Rockefeller

Former office of
John D Rockefeller, Jr

Nelson A Rockefeller

John D Rockefeller 3rd

30 Rockefeller Plaza, 56th Floor

Regular on-the-job exercise that I greatly enjoyed early in my career: walking up (and down) an internal staircase from the RBF offices on the 54th floor to attend meetings with Rockefeller family members and/or their staff on the 56th floor and, occasionally, on the 55th floor.

While Winthrop rarely visited New York City, the other brothers all had offices and staff on the 56th floor (Room 5600) of 30 Rockefeller Center. Of course, Russell Phillips worked most closely with John 3rd, on the Asia-related aspects of the RBF's International Program and on certain initiatives of the JDR 3rd Fund, which was incorporated in 1963 and focused on encouraging East–West cultural understanding; making the arts an integral part of education at all levels; and promoting collaborative efforts between youth and business and professional leaders. But during my years on a joint RBF/RFA payroll, I benefited greatly from my close contact with Nelson, Laurance, and David, and with their advisers. These relationships did not end when my split payroll arrangement was terminated, but they were formed and nurtured in those early years, when I was up and down that internal staircase every few days, for meetings – both formal and informal – with my colleagues on staff as well as with the brothers themselves.

At an almost unconscious level, as I became familiar with family members' giving practices, I absorbed elements of the philanthropic 'philosophy' of this wealthy family. They were in it for the long haul; they articulated ambitious goals, knowing full well that those goals could not be reached quickly. They were willing to make long-term commitments to effective organizations and institutions – a decade or two or more, long enough to 'make a difference,' as Andrew Carnegie said. They were also prepared to work with partners from different sectors and from a variety of political and ideological camps, in order to achieve progress. They were acutely aware of the need to preserve vital human, natural, and institutional assets – in New York City, the United States, and around the world.

Other kinds of learning were going on as well. In Nelson's office, John Camp – a longtime adviser – became an important mentor and friend. John was completing more than two decades of assignments in Latin America, which was one of the regions for which I would soon have responsibilities. A forester with considerable experience in agriculture and ecology, John spoke excellent Spanish and knew the history, geography, politics, economics, and cultures of every country in South and Central America – plus a wide range of local people in all walks of life. He was a consummate listener, a straightforward communicator (he had a gentle demeanor but could be tough when necessary), and a thoughtful team member. I was fortunate to make my early field trips to Latin America with him, before he retired. In meeting after meeting, I studied his line of questions and his sincere way of relating to people in all stations of life, from government ministers to hotel doormen.

An adviser to Laurance Rockefeller, William H (Holly) Whyte, would also have a considerable impact on me, which complemented and

A photograph on the mantel

On my second trip with John Camp, we traveled to the southern cone of South America to meet with the leaders of organizations that had submitted grant requests and to participate in a worldwide 4-H conference in Argentina (4-H is a youth development and empowerment organization). En route, I made my only brief visit to Uruguay, to see the widow, Josephine Shorter, of my great uncle Bill (William Shorter) – my namesake, who had lived overseas most of his adult life and whose stories helped to spark my youthful interest in other countries and cultures.

Imagine my surprise when I saw a picture of Nelson Rockefeller in Aunt Jo's living room, with the inscription, 'To Bill Shorter with best wishes and many thanks for a swell job – Nelson A Rockefeller.' I learned that during the Second World War, when Nelson was Coordinator of the Office of Inter-American Affairs under President Roosevelt, he had asked business leaders posted abroad to help him stay abreast of war-related developments in various South and Central American countries. Apparently, my uncle Bill was part of Nelson's team in Uruguay.

Aunt Jo left the picture to me when she died, and I still treasure this record of a remarkable coincidence.

deepened what I was learning from John Camp. By 1968 Holly had already become a respected urbanist and was noted for his well-known book *The Organization Man*. From a small office on the 54th floor, Holly led an initiative called the Street Life Project that was supported by the RBF and by Laurance. The project took Holly to neighborhoods throughout NYC to film what actually happened on street corners and in public parks. He was accompanied by a young staff associate, Fred Kent, who went on to head the Project for Public Spaces, successor to the Street Life Project and a frequent ally of the RBF in later years. When I could, I would tag along to see what they were learning. The time-lapsed footage that Holly and Fred shot – thousands of hours – revealed that people instinctively preferred to gather with friends and colleagues at certain kinds of places. Yet public spaces and private buildings were not often designed to take account of what the people themselves wanted. Too much planning was done in a vacuum or 'top down' – not bottom up. This work exemplified for me the importance of listening and watching and giving full respect to what people want for their own communities.

Through my interactions with both of these advisers to the brothers, I was reminded that I was not the expert – on Latin America, or urban life, or any number of other issues. If I was going to help people help themselves, I would need to learn their own views – even as I sought out expert opinions in order to better understand the context and the risks the RBF might be taking when 'betting' on the best local people and projects. I also realized that the very process of listening to people's needs and priorities could help to nurture cooperation and trust, both among local community leaders and communities, and between a foundation and the communities it is trying to assist.

Of all the brothers, I had the most direct contact in those early years with David Rockefeller. While he had a special interest in Latin America, as did his brother Nelson (both owned substantial properties in that hemisphere at the time), David was a global thinker and actor in both the business sphere – through his leadership of the Chase Manhattan Bank – and in the field of international relations – through his leadership in non-governmental organizations such as the Council on Foreign Relations, the Trilateral Commission (which he helped to found), and the Center for Inter-American Relations (now the core of the Americas Society).* He was also an active supporter of the Overseas Development Council. David saw that I was eager to learn from him and responded to my eagerness. In my initial years at the RBF, he would include me in meetings – not only in NYC but also in other countries – with dignitaries from all over the world. His office would let me know when he was traveling to a country in which the RBF's International Program was active, so I could help him make contact with our grantees. I studied his ways with people; his humility, naturalness, and sincerity. I embraced his vision of 'constructive engagement' – even with regions and countries that had not necessarily been friendly to the United States – and admired his commitment to trying to find common ground, even with adversaries.

Laurance S Rockefeller also offered me opportunities and experiences I will never forget. He was a towering figure in environmental protection and historic preservation by the time I reached the RBF in 1968. I felt fortunate in my early years to be included in some of his field activities,

* The Trilateral Commission, a non-governmental, non-partisan discussion group, was founded in 1973 to foster closer cooperation between North America, Western Europe, and Japan. The think-tank draws its participants from the business, academic, and political sectors (excluding current holders of public office).

such as a Hudson River study tour, by boat and helicopter, and visits to non-profit groups in New York and New Jersey that were addressing water, energy, and other environmental issues. Laurance's efforts in the 1980s to help establish the 'greenway' movement – which aimed to create routes, trails, or natural corridors that preserve natural and cultural heritage and provide options for recreation and tourism – would have a major impact on the RBF's programs in Central and Eastern Europe a decade later.

The style and approach of these and other early mentors – which were shared by the RBF program staff as a whole and many of the Fund's board members – aligned with my own basic orientation and helped to shape the grantmaking principles and practices that will be illustrated in the coming chapters.

My work begins

From the start, I found the subjects and geographic areas in which I was involved to be absolutely fascinating, and I was eager to learn everything possible about them. My boss, Jim Hyde, quickly brought me into all aspects of the International Program – meetings with important applicants, grantees, family members and their staffs. Within the first two years, I had traveled to the two main continents for which I had grantmaking responsibilities – Latin American and Africa – and reported extensively on my trips. As I earned Jim's confidence and gained my own, our professional relationship evolved and we began to function as colleagues who each had his own work responsibilities.

My inbox began to fill with a wide variety of materials to address. In addition to reviewing and responding to new requests for funding – from US-based as well as foreign applicants – I was reading reports from grantees, meeting with grantseekers, performing due diligence on promising proposals, and preparing grant recommendations for board meetings. As I built networks of contacts overseas and accumulated insights from my on-the-ground experiences in regions of interest to the Fund and family, I was asked to draft strategy papers and contribute to decision-making about the directions that our International Program should take, and I began to play a more active role in collaborations with other foundations. Soon the brothers and their advisers were sending me an interesting array of requests for funding that had come directly to them and were related to international affairs. After reviewing the proposal and doing my usual due diligence, I prepared a memo to the brother or his personal staff member with my analysis and recommendation, and sometimes a draft letter for the brother's reply.

As I said to my wife with some regularity, I could not wait to get out of bed in the morning and go to the office! Compared to many people I knew who were in their late 20s and early 30s, I had an exceptional degree of freedom and responsibility, combined with careful mentoring and monitoring of my progress. Soon I was on a first-name basis with everyone in the offices, including the brothers as well as senior staff. I and the other young professional staff also had occasional opportunities to interact with board members. This conscious personalization of organizational relationships was important to me and affected how I felt about my job: these people cared about me; I wanted to give all that I could to carry out my work with distinction. I think most of my colleagues on the RBF staff felt much as I did.

The proposals I was reviewing – taken together with the literature I was reading, the in-office discussions, and the workshops and conferences I attended – played a critical role in my on-the-job education. They enriched my thinking about the RBF's mission, overall strategies, and program goals. Through reviewing proposals, I also learned about the various methods available for inspiring and motivating local people and helping them to take action themselves. I read about fascinating efforts to create training programs, to engage communities in collaborative problem-solving, to develop and carry out action plans for grass-roots initiatives or national advocacy campaigns. I also read about strategies for promoting policy change at the national and international levels. Clearly, lots of good people were trying to solve difficult, often intransigent, problems and make the world a better place; and many of them did not need a great deal of funding in order to do a great deal of good work.

Like many foundation program officers, I found it difficult to balance the work of reviewing incoming proposals with the work of investigating promising projects, making a compelling case for the projects I wanted to recommend to the board, monitoring existing projects, and helping to assess and develop new strategies for the Fund's international grantmaking. From the beginning, I felt that the RBF's non-profit, tax-exempt status and philanthropic role obliged me to respond to all inquiries in as thoughtful a way as possible. Paying careful attention to unsolicited proposals, I thought, was both the right and the smart thing to do, because it helped the RBF to understand what was going on in the field and because it could lead us to remarkable individuals and projects. Of course, we were also obliged to respond to inquiries as promptly as possible! All of our incoming (work-related) mail was logged, and there was a rule that every inquiry had to be dealt with in a month, if not sooner. If you hadn't answered an inquiry in two weeks, the office manager's deputy would come by to ask – nicely but firmly – about the status of that proposal.

In that age before the internet, several service organizations existed to which I could turn for basic information about non-profit organizations, the primary applicants to the RBF; the National Information Bureau, for example, served as an information clearing-house before GuideStar was established in the 1990s. Moreover, even by the end of my first year, I had developed the beginnings of a network of colleagues and friends, including within other foundations and non-profit organizations, whom I could contact for a 'reading' or, at least, comments on a particular organization or project. Some grant requests were clearly outside our areas of activity and thus could be answered in a more 'summary' way. In other cases, the response would describe either next steps in the proposal consideration process or the reason(s) for declining the proposal. For me in those early years, even drafting a declination letter was an education, since it sharpened my own understanding of the RBF's objectives and strategies.

Little by little, I began to establish criteria for proposals that appeared promising. As important as the project itself were the people involved and their qualities. If the applicant or team of applicants impressed me with their on-the-ground credibility, experience, knowledge, and passion – if their egos were 'in place,' so they could learn as well as lead – I would have extra incentive to probe further. I also looked closely at whether the project would be operating out of a stable, appropriate institutional framework – or one the capacity of which could be strengthened. In order to make these kinds of judgments, it was essential for me to develop a sufficiently broad and deep familiarity with the region or country and its people. I valued the mantra of the Peace Corps volunteers I often met in the field: 'Know your site!' These early criteria evolved into principles for effective grantmaking that guided me throughout my career.

I did not review proposals in a vacuum. When I arrived, the RBF was in the process of becoming a professionally managed foundation, not only an administrative mechanism for the brothers' giving. The staff was being expanded, the board would be enlarged to include distinguished non-family members, and the categories, strategies, and guidelines that governed the RBF's grantmaking were being reformulated. These evolving strategies and guidelines provided the broad parameters within which I began my work. As I became more knowledgeable and able to advance my own observations, analyses, and recommendations, I would play a more active role myself in helping to shape and reshape the Fund's broad program objectives.

Naturally, the grants and program strategies I advocated did not always produce the desired results – although many did, and a few of the avenues we pursued led to significant, lasting achievements, of which the Fund is justly proud. Many of the organizations that we helped to launch have matured and become leaders in their fields. But some projects and approaches in which we invested were only partly successful or success-ful in ways (or on a timeline) that we did not anticipate; some of our grants proved to be premature or simply less effective than we had imagined they would be, for a variety of reasons. Some of the judgments I made – I hope and trust, not too many! – seem in hindsight to have been mistaken or flawed or incompletely thought out. Sometimes, unforeseen events and rapidly changing circumstances on the ground would undermine a grant-ee's chances for success – though occasionally such shifts opened up unexpected opportunities. All of these possibilities are illustrated in the pages that follow.

Rockefeller Brothers Fund Board Chairs and Presidents 1968–2007

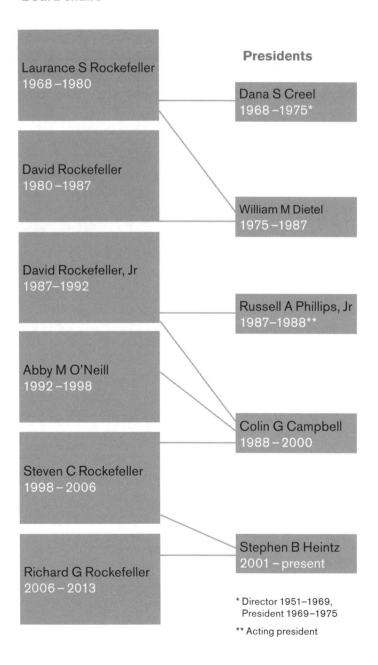

Board chairs

Presidents

Laurance S Rockefeller
1968–1980

Dana S Creel
1968–1975*

David Rockefeller
1980–1987

William M Dietel
1975–1987

David Rockefeller, Jr
1987–1992

Russell A Phillips, Jr
1987–1988**

Abby M O'Neill
1992–1998

Colin G Campbell
1988–2000

Steven C Rockefeller
1998–2006

Stephen B Heintz
2001–present

Richard G Rockefeller
2006–2013

* Director 1951–1969,
  President 1969–1975

** Acting president

CHAPTER TWO

Setting the Stage
1968 to late 1980s

When I began my grantmaking career in 1968, the Cold War provided a tense framework for international relations. The Soviets and the Americans were competing for control of developing countries in Latin America and in newly or soon-to-be independent nations across Africa and the Caribbean. This complicated the already steep challenges facing many African countries, whose people desperately needed jobs, healthcare, and education if they were to improve the quality of their lives. In Latin America, Cuba had become a staunch ally of the Soviets, and Fidel Castro was helping to stir up revolutionary unrest in the Andean countries, Central America, and the Caribbean.

Aside from Cold War-related concerns, the mismanagement and destruction of natural resources was looming as a worldwide challenge, with problems already evident in Latin America and emerging for African nations as well. Mutual suspicion dominated relations between Asian and Western countries, and in China the inhuman Cultural Revolution was under way. In South Africa the policies of apartheid were separating the races in more and more insidious ways.

Not all of the news was bad. I was excited to see that the European Economic Community (EEC) was showing promise of becoming more than a free-trade area. After centuries of warfare among European nations, former adversaries had begun to negotiate economic policies that would eventually become law in much of Western Europe, and initial steps towards political unification were going forward. The principle of self-determination was being articulated and honored, at least rhetorically, in international forums, as former colonies in Africa, the Caribbean, and elsewhere gained their independence throughout the decade and into the 1970s.

I knew that international dynamics such as these had important implications for the United States and for Americans, and I believed that some global problems ought to have a moral claim on our attention as well. But as I soon discovered, in the US foundation world almost all grant funds were applied to domestic needs and opportunities. Only five cents on a US foundation dollar was allocated to grants for international or foreign purposes. What this meant for the RBF was that even with a modest endowment (in the late 1960s) of $250 million and an overall annual operating budget of $10–15 million, we ranked among the top five to ten largest US foundation donors engaged in making grants for international purposes (including, for example, the Ford and Rockefeller foundations, the Carnegie Corporation of New York, and the Mellon Foundation).*

Of course, the RBF's interest in international issues was nothing new for the Rockefeller family. When John D Rockefeller and his son JDR, Jr established the Rockefeller Foundation (RF) in 1913, its mission was to improve 'the wellbeing of mankind throughout the world.' JDR, Jr's philanthropic interests were broad and reached well beyond the borders of the United States. I knew that the Rockefeller brothers and their sister had traveled extensively in their younger years; as adults, John 3rd, Nelson, Laurance, and David each maintained strong interests in some region of the world or some aspect of global affairs. It was not surprising that the RBF had had an international program for some time.

But what did this program look like in the 1970s, when I was becoming deeply engaged in my new job as an international program officer? What was the institutional context for my work?

The 1970s at the RBF

When I joined the staff of the RBF, a gradual intergenerational shift in Rockefeller family philanthropy was already under way. In the late 1960s

---

* In the late 1970s and early 1980s, as described in chapter 11, I played an active role in encouraging more US foundation attention to international and global issues in a world that was becoming increasingly interdependent.

and early 1970s the founding brothers were still active, but Abby O'Neill, the oldest of the next generation (the 'cousin's' generation), was beginning to play a more visible role, including at the RBF, as were other cousins from all branches of JDR, Jr's family.

Sadly, by the end of the 1970s three of the Rockefeller brothers and their sister had passed away. Winthrop, then governor of Arkansas, died in 1973 from cancer. Abby Mauzé died in 1976, also from cancer. John 3rd died in 1978 in a car accident. Nelson died in 1979, of a heart attack.

The 1970s also brought an end to that intermingling of family activities at 30 Rockefeller Plaza which I described in the previous chapter. The US Tax Reform Act of 1969 – enacted in response to some high-profile instances of unduly close relations between foundations and their controlling individuals – eventually led, in 1978, to the RBF moving its offices out of 'family headquarters' at Rockefeller Center. Since the joint payroll system that had permitted me to work both for the RBF and, occasionally, for individual family members violated the spirit, if not the letter, of the act, it was eliminated after a serious review of options. This was a change that I understood but regretted, since I thought our joint payroll practices were sufficiently transparent, and I believed it was beneficial for RBF program staff to be familiar with and to learn from the philanthropic activities of family members.

Also in the 1970s, the RBF weathered a crisis that left it reduced in size but still able to go forward, including with its international work. The story is both a family drama and a foundation drama – which is not uncommon at family foundations! When Nelson returned to New York City in 1977, after his term as US Vice President had come to an end, he expressed a desire to see the RBF endowment spent down completely during the lifetime of the brothers. He argued that the money should be used to provide long-term financial stability to certain organizations that had become special interests of one or more of the brothers – ranging from major institutions such as Lincoln Center, Colonial Williamsburg, and the Museum of Modern Art, to the Maine Coast Heritage Trust – or with which family members had had a long and significant association. His proposal sparked strong disagreement among the brothers. Arguments were advanced for keeping the foundation endowment intact; compromise positions were also proposed and debated. John 3rd was concerned about the perception of undue family control of foundation giving, and one

My first boss, Jim Hyde (far left), and Grant Schrum, former president of the National 4-H Council, with Dana Creel, then RBF president, shown accepting a plaque awarded to the RBF around 1970 in recognition of the Fund's long interest in 4-H efforts. Next to Dana is John Camp, one of my mentors. I am on the far right.

non-family trustee, John Gardner (founding chairman of Common Cause and previously president of the Carnegie Corporation of New York), eventually resigned in protest.

Ultimately, compromise prevailed. Some of the Fund's $250 million endowment would be used for 'tie-off' grants, leaving the remainder for the RBF to draw upon.* Dana Creel, the outgoing RBF president, assembled a committee to review the options and to recommend a set of big, one-time grants to selected institutions; in the future, such institutions and programs would be treated like any other applicant. These so-called Creel Committee grants amounted to more than $100 million, which left about $150 million in the RBF endowment by the end of the 1970s.

During this protracted and tense debate, the RBF staff could not be certain that the Fund had a future; then the Creel Committee grants resulted in significant cuts to the budgets of all our grant programs. Through it all, Bill Dietel, president of the RBF in the second half of the decade, did a heroic job of keeping our spirits up and keeping things on an even keel. To be honest, I was less affected by the crisis than some

* A tie-off grant is a final grant marking the end of a long period of support. It is typically designed to help buffer the effects of defunding.

of my colleagues, partly because most of the tie-off grants being negotiated were for national or New York City institutions. But I had very strong
feelings about not letting the RBF go out of existence. Quite apart from
concerns about my own position and work, I knew that the RBF would be
greatly missed by people in many parts of the world who were trying to
address some of the fundamental social, economic, and environmental
challenges of our time. I was deeply relieved and grateful that the Fund's
work – including its international work – would continue.

The basic International Program framework in the 1970s*

During the 1970s, the core of the first phase of my career, the RBF's
International Program addressed a set of interrelated development challenges in several specific geographic regions of the world, while at the
same time focusing on key aspects of international relations. Two broad
themes ran through our work: (1) conservation and employment generation, i.e. the wise use of natural and cultural resources (what is now often
called sustainable development); and (2) international cooperation, which
we sometimes referred to simply as 'international relations,' and at one
point described as 'structuring interdependence.' Even at this fairly early
date, the RBF and many Rockefeller family members were attuned to
the ways in which the nations and societies of the world were becoming
increasingly interconnected, and to the need for cooperation and shared
rules and norms in order to address shared problems. The protection of
human rights emerged as a dimension of our international cooperation
work in the late 1970s, and for a time this theme was a distinct focus of
some of our grantmaking.

Geographically, our work on conservation and employment generation was concentrated in developing countries in Africa, Latin America,
and the Caribbean. The Fund's grantmaking related to Asia straddled the
two big themes, focusing both on sustainable-development challenges

---

* The RBF's grantmaking strategies and guidelines were (and still are) reviewed periodically
and adjusted, if necessary, to reflect changes in the contexts in which the Fund is active. At
much longer and less regular intervals, there have been more significant but still evolutionary
reformulations of the Fund's overall 'program architecture.' The three main sections of this
memoir mark those larger shifts – but nowhere have I attempted to track all of the interim
adjustments to the categories and headings we used to organize our grantmaking over
the years. Instead, in the stage-setting chapters that introduce each section, I have tried
to convey the big themes and geographic focuses that shaped the Fund's international
grantmaking during that phase of my career.

(primarily in Southeast Asia) and on regional and US–Asia relations. My hands-on responsibilities – first as staff associate in the RBF's International Program and then, when my boss Jim Hyde retired, as head of the program – never included the Asia component of the program, which Russell Phillips managed.

I devoted approximately 70 per cent of my time and effort to challenges facing developing countries in Africa, Latin America, and the Caribbean, and about 30 per cent of my time to international cooperation initiatives, especially those that might complement and reinforce the on-the-ground work that I was encouraging the Fund to support in developing countries. While not underestimating the importance of those initiatives, I noted that a number of other, larger funders were already quite active in the area of international relations. I felt the RBF could make a big contribution with its modest resources (although the Fund was still among the top 20 foundations at the time) by dedicating a substantial share of its grant dollars – and the majority of my time – to projects addressing the problems that local people in developing countries faced, and to helping to create the local capacity that would enable people to continue to make progress on those issues in future years. I was delighted that the officers and board of the Fund agreed with this assessment.

For most of the 1970s the International Program had an annual budget of approximately $1.5 million (out of a total grantmaking budget that averaged $9 to 12 million per year), allocated more or less as follows:*

....

Conservation/employment/sustainable development

Africa	$250,000–300,000
Latin America/Caribbean	$300,000–350,000
Asia	$350,000–400,000

....

International cooperation	$550,000–650,000

....

(Some of these grants were directly relevant to one or another of the geographic regions listed above.)

* Actual dollar amounts are used throughout this book; figures have not been adjusted to reflect inflation. A $1.5 million annual budget in 1970 would be the equivalent of close to $9 million today – although the inflation-adjusted value of the Fund's endowment and total grantmaking budget would also be higher today, of course, and the International Program's share of the total would be the same.

After the Creel Committee grants, the budget for international grantmaking was reduced to about $1.2 million. The consequences of that reduction are mentioned at several points in the coming chapters – although fortunately the growth of the Fund's endowment compensated for those cuts within a few years.

During that same decade, the US government spent roughly $100 billion on defense and $3 billion on development assistance every year. By comparison, the $1.5 million annual budget of the RBF's International Program appears inconsequential. But the Fund's experience by then – and the brothers' own experiences – had demonstrated the critical need for private, non-governmental initiatives that were not stifled by politics or bureaucracy.

To this day, the Fund's work is guided by the belief that the imaginative and thoughtful placement of modest amounts of foundation money can advance the cutting edge of progress in international cooperation and development assistance, and contribute an element of pluralism to US global engagement.

The next three chapters paint a picture of the Fund's work in developing countries from roughly 1968 through the mid- to late 1980s.

International cooperation

While I have not chosen to devote a full chapter to the international cooperation component of the Fund's International Program, no picture of this phase of my career would be complete without at least a sketch of our work under this heading. Looking at what was a very diverse array of grants from the 1970s, I would highlight three types of activity that were supported by the Fund.

- We supported initiatives designed to improve communications
  and relations within and between regions, primarily through
  grants to high-level, mostly US-based policy centers that focused
  on the regions in which the Fund was active: for example, the
  African-American Institute, the Center for Inter-American
  Relations (now the Americas Society), the International Union for
  Conservation of Nature, the Caribbean Conservation Association,
  the Overseas Development Council, the Woodrow Wilson Center
  for Scholars, and (under Russell's management) the Asia Society

and the Japan Society. I viewed these grants as worthy in their own right, and important opportunities to combine action on the ground with policy analysis and policy advocacy at the national and international level.

- We also supported programs to facilitate greater collaboration and exchange (of ideas and talent and technology) among nations. This work is exemplified by our longstanding support of Volunteers in Technical Assistance (in fact, I served on the VITA board for many years – a form of program officer engagement that will receive attention later in this book). VITA utilized volunteer American engineers and scientists to improve the prospects for small businesses and farms – thereby creating jobs – in developing countries, including those countries in which the Fund was already working. The RBF also made the first foundation grant to Technoserve, which provided expert support for entrepreneurs in developing countries. Again, this was an example of how the RBF's support of a US-based group could complement the work we were doing on the ground.

- In addition, we became active in efforts to promote human dignity around the world, through our support of a broad range of human rights initiatives (the Fund's support of efforts to defend the rights and promote opportunities for blacks in apartheid South Africa is described in chapter 3). Unfortunately, the scope of our human rights-related efforts had to be curtailed after the Creel Committee grants; nonetheless, the Fund was able to make some important contributions. For example, the RBF joined the Ford, MacArthur, and Revson foundations in providing start-up support for the Lawyers Committee for Human Rights, which has since evolved into Human Rights First, a recognized leader in this field, with offices in New York and Washington. The RBF also helped to establish public-interest human rights law projects in New York, Geneva, Washington, DC, and Johannesburg – all under the aegis of local bar associations and other associations of lawyers and judges. Together with Bruce Bushey of the Ford Foundation, I played a small but active role in helping a group of law professors to design and launch an international human rights organization that would serve as an information resource for scholars, activists, lawyers, and policymakers around the world. This organization, now called Human Rights Internet, is still active today. Much of the RBF's human rights work was carried out in collaboration with other foundations, illustrating the importance of horizontal relationships among program officers at different foundations – another theme that will emerge in future chapters.

Closing reflections

As I wrap up this scene-setting chapter and plot out the chapters to come, I am powerfully aware of how much I learned from my work in the 1970s that helped me in later years.

Some of the lessons apply to the process of grantmaking. I learned to do my homework in advance, so I could interact more confidently and productively with applicants, even though I was not an expert on their subject matter or country. I realized time and again that grantor and grantee need each other for both to succeed; we were on the same team, so I needed to work hard to build relationships of mutual understanding and trust. I learned that grantseeking is often a laborious, time-consuming, and even degrading experience; I resolved to help make the process less onerous for grantseekers, and I was grateful that the RBF as an institution shared my preference for less rather than more bureaucracy. I could act fast in most cases, with grant payments made six months or less (when necessary) from the time of proposal submission.

I realized that small investments could make a significant impact if well placed, and that the RBF had the stature to leverage its investments by encouraging contributions in cash and in kind from other foundations. I saw that the RBF's ability to provide multi-year, unrestricted support was vital to many organizations, giving them the ability to plan ahead, make commitments to good staff, and take advantage of special opportunities for action. I learned that I could help in small ways from my base in New York, by putting grantees in touch with other institutions and organizations in my network. And I realized that the organizations we supported wanted us to pay close attention to their progress reports, to ask tough questions about important programmatic and institutional challenges. Time after time, I heard expressions of appreciation for my own and the RBF's willingness to demonstrate this kind of sustained interest and to encourage such honest conversations. Many other donors, I learned, were not able or willing to engage in this way.

Finally, during those first years of my career I was gaining confidence in myself as a grantmaker – confidence that would serve me well as I began to play an active role and even to take the lead in some major collaborative initiatives in the 1980s and 1990s. But that is a subject for future sections of this book.

Having grown up in Michigan, with its icy winters, how could I resist ice-skating at lunchtime, with the rink just around the corner in Rockefeller Center? With me are Theodore (Ted) Smith, former president of the Agriculture Development Council, and Lynn Anderson, an RBF staff member whose office was next to mine during the 1980s. (photo: Robert Stone)

Tunisia

Morocco

Western
Sahara

Algeria

Libya

Egypt

Mauritania

Mali

Niger

Chad

Sudan

Eritrea

Djibouti

Senegal

Somalia

Gambia

Burkina
Faso

Guinea-Bissau

Guinea

Nigeria

Central African
Republic

South
Sudan

Ethiopia

Sierra Leone

Ivory
Coast

Liberia

Ghana

Togo

Benin

Cameroon

Equatorial Guinea

Kenya

Rwanda

São Tomé
and Príncipe

Gabon

Congo

Democratic Republic
of the Congo

Uganda

Burundi

Tanzania

Angola

Malawi

Zambia

Zimbabwe

Mozambique

Botswana

Madagascar

Namibia

Swaziland

South
Africa

Lesotho

Primary focus of grantmaking

Reached through regional grantmaking

CHAPTER THREE

The Importance of Collaboration
Africa, 1968 to mid-1980s

Indeed development is becoming, and must increasingly become, a path chosen by developing countries for themselves . . . Aid-givers will have to talk less, listen more and think more creatively if they are to find channels to help bring about widespread, indigenous, self-sustaining growth.

Guy Hunter, 'The New Africa'
Foreign Affairs (July 1970), page 724

Everyone learns on the job; the process is so common it hardly seems worthy of notice.

But the phrase takes on real significance when, as a very new grant-maker, you are sent out into the field – and when 'the field' is a continent as unfamiliar as Africa. That was my experience shortly after arriving at the RBF. The sudden immersion was challenging and sometimes disorient-ing, but I wouldn't have wanted it any other way. I reminded myself that Jim Hyde told me he wanted to hire a generalist, not an expert, and that he must have valued the curiosity and willingness to learn that a generalist might bring to bear on the Fund's international work.

I knew when I arrived at the RBF that one of my priorities as a staff associate would be to help the RBF make an impact on some of the chal-lenges that faced the newly independent countries of sub-Saharan Africa. Because I followed international news, I had a general sense of conditions in that region. But as soon as I was settled in my new office, Jim Hyde wasted no time sending me relevant proposals; he also gave me informal 'seminars' on relevant topics, and of course I was doing my own reading and research. Soon a clearer picture emerged.

The 1960s had been an historic period, during which three-quarters of the sub-Saharan African countries (more than 30 out of more than 40) gained their independence. Sadly, the decade was also one of great politi-cal instability. The colonial powers had carved out African countries to suit their own interests with little respect for tribal boundaries or long-term economic prospects. These arbitrarily created nations were expected to follow Western parliamentary practices; with very few exceptions, classical democracy did not take hold. Competition among tribal groups for power and resources was a persistent source of tension.

Development assistance policies in the 1960s and the 1970s tended to reinforce the dual economies that had been fostered during the colonial era. Typically, infrastructure development and industrialization benefited urban areas, which became centers of production and consumption, while rural areas were left to stagnate at the edge of the cash economy. By the end of the 1960s concern about this unsatisfactory situation was growing, but by then the pace of population growth was compounding the problem. Unemployment and under-employment in the countryside produced increased migration to urban centers, where already there were not enough jobs to go around. While many of the new African countries were rich in natural resources, little attention was being paid to ensuring the wise use of those resources or the fair distribution of income from their use. In southern Africa in the 1960s and 1970s, the wars for independence in Rhodesia (formerly Southern Rhodesia and now Zimbabwe) and Mozambique became entangled with the Cold War between the United States and the Soviet Union, and with other conflicts in Angola and Namibia. In South Africa the government was becoming increasingly harsh and inhumane in its efforts to maintain white rule.

Clearly, there were many issues and places on which a concerned foundation might focus its attention. When I joined the RBF staff in 1968, the Fund was already engaged in grantmaking to address economic development and natural resource management challenges in East Africa and (on a smaller scale) race relations in South Africa. Those were my initial areas of responsibility. In 1975 an internal review of the International Program showed good basic progress being made in East Africa, where a number of other donors were already active or becoming interested in the region. Jim Hyde and I made a number of recommendations that were approved by the board: the RBF would shift its focus to southern Africa, especially Botswana, and also increase its nascent involvement in West Africa, one of the world's poorest regions, where we had already been doing some exploratory grantmaking. At the same time, the RBF would maintain its involvement in the growing effort to eliminate apartheid in South Africa.

Early lessons: flexibility, patience, and finding the right partners
I had been at the Fund for less than two years when I made my first trip
to Africa, with Jim Hyde, to see some of the projects we were already
supporting and to explore new possibilities. The RBF had embraced a
pioneering approach to conservation and job creation in East Africa. Our
strategy was to help protect wild and natural areas for all time in ways that
could generate jobs and income for indigenous people. Figuring out how
to advance this goal was my first big grantmaking challenge.

For a young grantmaker from the American Midwest who had never
traveled to the global South, that first visit to Africa was eye-opening. The
impressions and contrasts were unforgettable: the beauty of the sunrise
in Africa's national parks and that feeling of being able to see forever; the
brilliant colors of the women's clothing; the struggle to eke out a subsist-
ence living; the power of tribal traditions and the lure of new possibilities
introduced via radio and television; the desire for change and a better life.

I could see there were initiatives under way in each country – some
of them sponsored by governments, others by bilateral or international aid
programs or by foundations and non-profit organizations – that sought to
help local communities improve their lives. Sensitized by what I had learned
from John Camp and Holly Whyte, I could also see that while good work
was being done, the operating assumption often was that 'we are bringing
the knowledge, experience, and money they need.' Local people had lots
of experience and savvy of their own, but it was not always factored into aid
programs. Donors often introduced new ideas and approaches without
exploring how they could be blended with the long traditions and practical
experience of local populations.

I resolved that I would find ways to work more collaboratively with
local people – not in the spirit of we/they, but rather, 'all of us together.' It
was clear to me that the RBF could not achieve its goals without the energy
and excitement of local leaders and communities, who in turn could make
faster progress with the help of our resources.

I soon learned that the process was not so straightforward. Among
other things, I was the new kid on the block, and I simply did not know the
territory yet – where to turn for advice, who to contact in order to reach
decision-makers, etc. Nor was I able to spend as much time in Africa
as I would have liked, since I was based in New York and travel to the
region was very expensive (typically, I went once a year, sometimes twice).

While I did my best to find indigenous partners whenever possible, most of the newly independent African nations had not yet developed a formal non-governmental sector, and there were not many locally led initiatives of the sort that an American foundation could fund (although Africans were making significant contributions to assistance projects, and some would go on to become project leaders).* It seemed that I would need to proceed more slowly and less directly than I had imagined.

Indeed, in those early years I often found credible partners and allies among expatriates from Europe or North America who had made their homes in Africa and were passionate about helping local communities. Some development workers also had high credibility on the ground – Peace Corps volunteers, staff of UN agencies, and occasionally even foreign business managers. These 'expats' had earned the trust and respect of the Africans among whom they lived or worked. They not only wanted to do good, but also were committed to building the capacity of Africans to help themselves. As they worked alongside villagers to solve immediate problems, they trained local leaders and modeled good project and financial management practices, helping to lay the foundation for sustainable local initiatives and institutions. And they stuck around; they knew that problems are not solved – and skills are not learned – overnight.

A good example is Ned Seligman, a Peace Corps volunteer who ended up guiding a project we funded in Upper Volta (now Burkina Faso), helping villagers build earthen dams to collect desperately needed water during the rainy season. On my annual visits, I went to the work sites with Ned, met volunteers from the villages, and rolled up my own sleeves to help out. At night, I slept on Ned's front porch, trying to catch some cooling breezes. Ned has never really left West Africa. He became Peace Corps Director in São Tomé, a tiny volcanic island 200 miles off the west coast of Africa, at the equator. There he established a non-profit organization called Step Up, which helped villagers construct health clinics and libraries and address environmental issues. Today, many years later, Ned continues to live in São Tomé among his extended 'family' – despite having lost both legs below the knees and most of his fingertips from a staphylococcus infection he contracted on a trip to the United States nearly a decade ago.

---

* Not all civic groups are eligible to receive charitable contributions directly from US foundations, according to Internal Revenue Service rules. I return to this topic in some detail in chapter 5.

I realized that good on-the-ground partners were not defined by their nationality, gender, diplomas, religion, or skin color. Especially in the initial phases of my work in Africa, I often recommended support for 'foreign' organizations that had staff living in local communities for extended periods of time. In some instances, we funded these organizations for many years, since their experiences in one location could often be transferred or adapted to other contexts (including in West Africa and Botswana, when the Fund's focus shifted to those locations).

On the left, William M (Bill) Dietel, president of the RBF from 1975 to 1987, with one of the leaders of the African Wildlife Leadership Foundation, during a field trip in Kenya. As an experienced farmer himself, Bill had no qualms about getting up close to herd animals.

The African Wildlife Leadership Foundation, for example – which eventually shortened its name to the African Wildlife Foundation (AWF) – was an ally in numerous efforts to establish and enhance national parks and other protected areas, train local staff to manage those areas, and educate local communities about the value of what some then called wildland areas (national parks, watersheds, marginal lands) as sources of income and jobs. With RBF support, AWF's outstanding field team in Kenya provided leadership in the creation of the Voi Education Center in Tsavo East National Park, one of the oldest and largest of the nation's parks (with Tsavo West, it covers 4 per cent of Kenya's land). An equally strong AWF team in Tanzania helped to establish the RBF-supported College of

African Wildlife Management in Mweka, in central Tanzania. Today, AWF is active in nine sub-Saharan countries through an 'African Heartland Program' that works with local stakeholders to design conservation strategies, protect endangered species, and empower people through training and economic development.

As time went on and I began to look beyond natural resources management per se for job creation opportunities, I was referred to the Partnership for Productivity Foundation (PfP), a Pennsylvania-based Quaker initiative which was then active in Kenya, helping people to establish and strengthen their own small businesses. The RBF rarely funded American faith-based organizations working in developing countries, because of the difficulty in ascertaining the extent to which proselytizing might be a priority, but the PfP met all my criteria for an expatriate partner in this kind of job creation effort: its staff members were able to motivate local leaders to make lasting commitments to PfP projects; those projects represented sensible, realistic concepts for generating income, not pie in the sky; the PfP had experienced board members and advisers, including Quaker business people; PfP project leaders knew how to prepare a business plan, even if the details were understandably sketchy at times; and the organization was determined to make wise use of natural resources. So effective and trusted was the PfP's country director in Kenya, George Butler, that the Kenyan government asked him to become the head of a regional government agency tasked with creating small businesses and jobs, and to train local people to staff the agency. Although the PfP would not let him go, George dedicated time anyway to help the new agency get started. The PfP went on to become involved in other parts of Africa and elsewhere in the developing world, and operated through the early 1990s.

I also discovered through my early trips to East Africa that I had some very special opportunities because I worked for a private foundation. I did not have to please shareholders, in the traditional sense, nor did I have to win renewed support from voters or constituents every two or four years. Instead, I could imagine helping people step by step, over a period of many years. The RBF could contribute not only to solving problems but also to building the capacity of local communities, organizations, and leaders. Moreover, in those days I did not think an annual budget of $150,000 or a grant of $5,000 or $10,000 was small; I had seen how far such amounts

Maintaining an on-site presence

For a foundation like the RBF, which is active internationally but whose resources are modest, the question of whether or not to maintain an office 'on site' is a challenging one. The RBF had conducted a short-lived economic development program in West Africa in the early 1960s, before I arrived at the Fund; business creation in the region was a special interest of Nelson Rockefeller. The director of this West Africa program was based full time in Nigeria. The program lasted only four years – in large part, because of the high cost of maintaining an RBF presence on site (including staff salaries, office expenses, housing, etc.).

I quickly learned from my own work in Africa how important it was to spend time on the ground, getting the lay of the land, talking to local people, and making first-hand observations about challenges and opportunities. But whenever I raised the subject of establishing some kind of RBF presence on site, even if only a part-time staff person who was already in residence, someone on the staff or board would admonish me to 'remember the old West Africa program.'

I couldn't let go of the idea, however, and eventually I had some success. In 1987 I was granted a sabbatical year that enabled me to live in the Central European countries where I was working at the time; that experience helped to prepare me for the expansion of our efforts in the region after the Berlin Wall came down. And by the time I retired in 2007, the Fund's new president (Stephen Heintz, who had directed the Prague office of the EastWest Institute for many years) agreed with my recommendation that the new program officer for the Western Balkans, which was my focus then, should be based in the region or at least hale from the region and be able to spend a significant amount of time there each year.

could be stretched in local villages and provinces.* And I could contemplate making multi-year commitments to our grantees, once sufficient trust had been established, thereby enabling organizations and programs to plan ahead and hire new staff.

When the RBF shifted its attention to Botswana and ramped up its work in West Africa, after the program review of 1975, I tried to build on

* The purchasing power of a $10,000 grant made in 1975 is more than $40,000 today (2014); likewise, a $150,000 grant made in 1975 would be equivalent to a $600,000 grant today.

these experiences, observations, and relationships (my fluency in French was especially helpful in the Francophone countries of West Africa). I sought out on-the-ground partners from local communities when possible – it was easier in Botswana, for reasons that will be described below – and from the network of expatriates who had made long-term commitments to improving the lives of local people. In addition to the kinds of governmental and non-governmental agencies that I had found working on the ground in East Africa, I soon discovered that the Ford Foundation had several offices in West Africa, with staff members who were willing and able to advise me. I was very grateful for their input, which helped to fill the gaps between my own visits to the region.

Taken from my window aboard the Ougadougou Express in the mid-1970s, during what was then a 24-hour trip from Ouagadougou, desert capital of Upper Volta (now Burkina Faso), to Abidjan, coastal capital of Ivory Coast. I loved the experience of meeting people on the train, buying goods from local people at stations along the way, and taking in the expansive vistas as I traveled from very dry to very humid surroundings. (photo: author)

Up close and personal

My work in East and West Africa confirmed for me that I liked being the kind of program officer who closely follows the activities of his grantees and tries to be helpful and engaged in ways that go beyond providing money. But there's such a thing as too much engagement!

En route to Cameroon in late 1975, I stopped in Fort Lamy (now N'Djamena), the capital of Chad, for an overnight stay. I woke the next morning to find that a rebel group had carried out a coup d'état, killing most of the government leaders in the process. The rebels had also chosen to base themselves in the hotel where I was staying! We non-Chadian guests (a handful of Europeans and myself) were not sure of the intentions of the rebel troops toward us, and watched with trepidation as they moved about with machine-guns in hand, depleting all of the food and alcohol in the hotel. Thanks to the steadying role of the French military mission in Fort Lamy, the city became calm in a few days, and I could leave the country within a week, unharmed.

In the course of my travels to Africa, I also contracted hepatitis and, later, leishmaniasis – a parasitic disease that is transmitted by the bite of a certain type of sandfly. Both diseases, fortunately, were treated early and cured. On one memorable occasion, an African wolf spider crept into my ear while I was sleeping. He (or she) traveled free to the United States with me, before being removed and sent for analysis – the first such spider to be identified by the New York State Health Department in many years.

In some cases in West Africa, we worked with familiar partners – organizations with which we had already established good relationships. For example, in Ghana and elsewhere, we again funded the Partnership for Productivity, together with Technoserve, to help incubate business concepts for small agricultural and non-agricultural ventures. Then, encouraged by those initiatives, we made grants directly to the University of Science and Technology in Kumasi, Ghana, for a technology consultancy center, where technology-based business ideas could be developed and tested. In Burkina Faso we worked closely with the Peace Corps – and with Catholic Relief Services (CRS) based in Switzerland – to support projects that helped local people secure water for their villages by building earthen dams to capture flash flood waters.

In other cases, we looked to our experience in East Africa for models of projects that might be funded in West Africa. With the French government and the United Nations Development Program, for example, we helped to establish the School for the Training of Wildlife Specialists in Garoua, Cameroon – the first such facility in Francophone West Africa – modeled on the training center we had supported in Mweka, Tanzania.

Our annual budget for grantmaking in West Africa was modest, less than $120,000; we made an average of three or four grants per year. Yet, just as in East Africa, this relatively modest amount could have quite an important impact, thanks in large measure to the highly effective and committed indigenous and expatriate individuals who staffed the projects we funded.

The RBF in Botswana: transferring knowledge and experience

In the early 1970s, when the RBF began exploratory grantmaking in the southern nation of Botswana, it was an opportunity for me to apply some of what I was learning about problem-solving and capacity-building within a very different context than that provided by West or even East Africa.

Why did we choose to work in Botswana? I believed, and my colleagues agreed, that it would be useful and important to focus attention on one newly independent African country that was evolving in very positive ways and that could be a model for the troubled southern region and beyond. Like many other African nations, Botswana was blessed with raw materials (mainly diamonds and copper), beautiful wildlands and wildlife, large open spaces (Botswana is the size of France), and a population of only 800,000 in the 1970s – with nearly 2 million cows, an important economic resource (Botswana's herds were almost free of hoof-and-mouth disease and therefore in demand in Europe as a source of meat). But unlike many other African countries, within less than a decade of achieving independence (from Britain), Botswana was functioning as a constitutional democracy with considerable government transparency, little mismanagement, and virtually no corruption. At the time, it was the only African country without an army (the Botswana Defense Force was created in 1977). I was intrigued that few US or European foundations had singled out Botswana for regular attention (the Ford Foundation provided advisers to government ministries). And I thought that a relatively small foundation with modest resources might be able to help Botswana meet

Botswana in the 1970s

The first president of Botswana, Sir Seretse Khama, had been a leader of the independence movement and was a legitimate claimant to the chieftainship of the Bamangwato, one of Botswana's principal tribes. Married to a white British woman he had met when studying in the UK, Sir Seretse set the tone for an open, tolerant, multiracial society in which blacks and the minority whites would be comfortable with each other – and from what I could observe, this was most often the case. Undoubtedly, it helped that most of the population spoke the same language, Setswana. I felt safe walking anywhere in Gaborone, the capital, and in small villages as well – even on dirt paths after dark. People didn't even lock their doors.

Sir Seretse Khama died in 1980 at the age of 59, having served 14 years as president. He bequeathed to his successor, Vice President Quett Masire, a healthy multi-party democracy and little or no government corruption. Throughout the 1970s Botswana's economy expanded beyond agriculture to include mining, tourism, and various light industries. The biggest challenge in recent years has been the HIV/AIDS epidemic, which hit the country hard. Today, access to new drugs and an aggressive public education program are helping to counter the spread of this dread disease in Botswana. At the same time, Botswana's democracy has become frayed around the edges, with a still lively press but corruption in the public and private sectors growing.

the urgent challenges of building a sustainable economy and creating jobs for the increasing numbers of young Batswana who were not content with the farm life of their ancestors.

Over the course of a dozen years, from 1972 to 1984, the RBF made grants for Botswana in the fields of vocational training, small-business development, job creation, and protected areas management. Bill Dietel, the president of the Fund, became an ardent advocate for our work in Botswana (and elsewhere in Africa), especially after his first trip to Africa in 1975. On that trip, he accompanied me to Botswana and Kenya, visiting RBF-supported projects and meeting local people in both countries. He was so impressed by what he saw in Botswana that he returned three times, with members of his family – and persuaded his alma mater, Princeton University, to give an honorary degree to Sir Seretse Khama, Botswana's first president.

Our annual budget for this work averaged between $75,000 and $100,000. As a rare US foundation active in a sustained way in Botswana, we were asked to support efforts to improve the educational system and strengthen model schools – which we viewed as a long-term contribution to sustainable economic development. (After several years of working closely with the government and non-profit leaders in Botswana, I was asked to consider becoming the country's Director of Tourism for the next several years – which I suppose could have represented a different kind of contribution to economic development and an exciting adventure! While the RBF was willing to give me a leave of absence, a serious talk with my wife and sons, who were deeply involved in their lives in the US, led me to decline.)

When the RBF began to support economic development work in Botswana, the country relied on advisers from the UK and other countries to help manage the various government ministries and train civil servants (sometimes the ministers themselves). In the early days of independence, the UK actually supplied at least half of the annual budget of the government; this subsidy was, understandably, decreasing every year, placing pressure on the government and the Batswana people to figure out how to achieve economic independence. In most ministries, there were good, productive relations between the indigenous senior government officials and the foreign advisers. This is not to say that everything went according to plan or that everything succeeded. Nevertheless, Botswana was one of the rare African countries in which we were comfortable making a grant to the government itself – for the Botswana Wildlife Training Institute in Maun. In the case of two other RBF-funded training centers – those in Mweka, Tanzania, and in Garoua, Cameroon – we would only make grants directly to the centers themselves or to foreign NGOs or international agencies that we could trust to spend (and account for) the grant funds as we had agreed.

In addition to being able to work directly with the Botswana government, we found that a network of indigenous non-profit groups (often called 'brigades' or associations) had already begun to emerge in Botswana, with recognition from the government. Some of these non-profit groups worked closely both with tribal leaders in villages and with government authorities. Many had attracted foreign volunteers from the UK, the Netherlands, and other countries as well as the Peace Corps. In almost every corner of Botswana, I met locals and expatriates working hard and effectively, side by side, to help train and educate young people and to create institutions that would provide practical knowledge and experience for those Batswana who were seeking jobs outside of traditional farming and cattle-raising.

As a result, in Botswana I was able to come closer to my initial vision of funding and working directly with local people through grants to such groups as the Ngamiland Youth Training Centre (to help young people find work in rural and village areas); Pelegano Village Industries (for small-business development); and Kanye Brigades Development Trust (for a revolving loan fund).

Visiting one of the job-creation and community-development efforts the RBF was supporting in the 1970s and early 1980s in Botswana (and other African countries). (photo: author)

In fact, the RBF's largest grant recipient during our 14 years of activity in Botswana was the Kweneng Rural Development Association (KRDA), which was headquartered in Molepolole, at the edge of the Kalahari Desert, in the Kweneng district of Botswana. The KRDA was registered as a non-profit trust under Botswana law. A committee of local people, elected annually, managed the organization, which worked in close cooperation with local and central government authorities. The KRDA received a total of $248,000 in grants from the RBF, for self-help, job-creating development projects. The Fund's support played a role in building the capacity of the KRDA, which has evolved and become the Bakwena Community Development Association, which provides programs and services for local people to this day.

But even in Botswana the picture was not a simple one. Take, for example, one of the KDRA's most successful projects. With RBF funding, the KRDA established the first light-industrial employment opportunities in the Kweneng district – a garage and mechanics' training project, called Boikanyo Engineering. Over time, the project expanded to include a petrol and diesel station and a vehicle repair shop, and eventually a light-engineering facility. RBF support also helped train a local person to replace Boikanyo's original expatriate manager, and in 1980, just four years after the project's first full year of operation, Boikanyo generated gross revenues of $849,000.

Behind the scenes, however, the transition to local project leadership was not easy or smooth. Writing about the Boikanyo project in 1981, KDRA Executive Trustee David Inger observed:

> Boikanyo gave us very useful experience on how difficult it is to organize such a program, which by local standards is very sophisticated, in a situation where local technical and managerial skills did not exist. We assumed that one expatriate would be sufficient to help grow the business ... In fact, as many as five expatriates have been required, although all will soon be localized, and the business will soon exceed $1 million.

Many of the projects we funded took much longer than expected to get established, because of the difficulty of hiring appropriate and reliable staff. I learned to be less naïve in my expectations about the pace of change, and more thoughtful about the need to help local people step into new roles by providing training and opportunities for the transfer of knowledge and experience. Some years later, when I was responsible for the RBF's efforts to build civil society in some of the formerly communist countries of Central and Eastern Europe, those lessons would stand me in good stead. While the citizens of Central and Eastern European countries obviously had many advantages over the citizens of the African nations in which the RBF was active, decades of communist rule had prevented people from accumulating experience in creating civil society organizations and institutions with the capacity to be effective over the long haul.

Hollywood beckons!

Given my active grantmaking role in Botswana, I was asked by colleagues at the African-American Institute, in 1976, to help advise Elizabeth Taylor about possible philanthropic opportunities there. Her recent remarriage to Richard Burton had taken place in northern Botswana, and she wanted to express appreciation for the warm welcome they received in that country.

I participated in several meetings with Ms Taylor, but one, at the Waldorf Astoria Hotel, stands out. I was greeted at the door by Ms Taylor's assistant, who showed me into a charming room and seated me on a small sofa. Ms Taylor soon appeared – and out of all the chairs and sofas in the room, she chose to sit right next to me on the sofa. As she looked intently at me with her violet eyes, I confess that for the briefest moment I felt I was a leading man in one of her movies, which no doubt is what she wanted me to feel! Ms Taylor was prepared to contribute $250,000 (from the sale of a ring), specifically for the upgrading of health facilities in Kasane, the town in which the wedding was held. Sadly, it was not to be: at that time the Botswana government felt unable to apply such a large amount to one small clinic project.

Ms Taylor offered the gift, ironically, during the same month in which her second divorce from Richard Burton was finalized.

Combating apartheid in South Africa: collaboration with other funders

The RBF's efforts to assist in the fight against apartheid in South Africa raised a set of grantmaking challenges that were unlike those we faced elsewhere in Africa. South Africa had strong institutions – although many were arrayed on behalf of maintaining white rule – and sophisticated, sometimes highly educated leaders (black and white) who were already working in various ways to combat the apartheid system. But what kind of contribution could the RBF make, with its quite limited resources, to this protracted struggle, which eventually assumed global proportions? Several grant relationships illustrate the possibilities we uncovered.

The RBF had been making a small number of South Africa-related grants since 1965 – for example, we helped to fund an exchange program that brought black and white South African leaders to the United States for discussions about issues related to apartheid; and we supported efforts to assist refugees escaping apartheid and to educate Americans about conditions in South Africa. But in 1974, in an effort to make a more sys-temic impact on the problem, we began a seven-year relationship with an indigenous institution, the Johannesburg-based South African Institute of Race Relations. At a time when people around the world were beginning to deplore apartheid, the Institute researched and published information on what was really happening inside South Africa. Its reports often provided the only reliable information on important aspects of race relations. Even the South African government recognized the thoroughness and balance of the data the Institute gathered. Over the years, the Institute's convinc-ing research and analyses – including its annual report on race relations – helped to arm the anti-apartheid movement with vital facts and figures.

In 1975, as part of the internal review of the Fund's International Program, Jim Hyde and I requested and received a slightly increased budget – $100,000 per year – for expanded activity in South Africa. I began to examine new entry points for RBF involvement in South Africa. I had been trained as a lawyer, and as part of the RBF's 'international cooperation' grantmaking, I had been helping to establish public-interest human rights law projects in New York, Washington, DC, and Geneva. So perhaps it is not surprising that I was drawn to focus on the rule of law and the role of lawyers in helping to fight the inhuman treatment of blacks in South Africa.

In the mid-1970s, leading South African lawyers, black and white, established organizations and programs that defended important test cases, expanded practical training in public-interest law, and improved free legal assistance to the poor. Three such lawyers – Arthur Chaskalson, Felicia Kentridge, and Jeff Budlander – approached the Ford Foundation, the Carnegie Corporation, and the RBF with a proposal for a Legal Resources Centre (LRC) in Johannesburg that would promote the use of law as a peaceful means of redress and progress. The proposed Centre would provide legal representation in important cases, and its attorneys would help to train law students (black and white) to work in storefront legal aid clinics. It was a bold and proactive concept.

Together with Bill Carmichael and Sheila McLean of the Ford Foundation and David Hood of the Carnegie Corporation, I met several times with the project founders to ask questions and provide advice that would help them launch the LRC in the most promising way. These conversations were inspiring, frank, and constructive. Ultimately, the three American foundations provided initial grants totaling $200,000 per year for three years (and Harry Oppenheimer, chairman of the South Africa-based Anglo-American Corporation, committed $25,000 per year for five years) to get this undertaking off the ground in 1978. The RBF continued supporting the LRC until 1984, with grants totaling $195,000; the Carnegie Corporation's support continued to that point as well; the Ford Foundation's involvement was even more sustained.

Arthur Chaskalson, who had left a successful law practice to become a respected human rights lawyer, directed the LRC from its inception until 1993 and attracted outstanding, dedicated lawyers to its staff. When Nelson Mandela became president of South Africa, he selected Chaskalson to be the first president (later, chief justice) of the new South African Constitutional Court. By all accounts, the LRC made a genuinely significant contribution to ending apartheid and went on to advance social justice in a number of other issue areas. In fact, in 2004, long after my grantmaking responsibilities in South Africa had come to an end, the RBF (which had maintained a special focus on that country, under different program guidelines) began to fund the LRC's work to help ensure access to education for poor and vulnerable children. The LRC remains active today, with a staff of 65 and an annual budget of over $3 million. I was moved and proud to see that the RBF is still listed as a 'Partner Investor' on the LRC's website.

Also in collaboration with the Ford Foundation and the Carnegie Corporation of New York, the RBF played a role in the early years of another important human rights organization in South Africa – the Centre for Applied Legal Studies (CALS) at the University of Witwatersrand in Johannesburg – that continues to provide a range of services to people in need today. Founded in 1978 by John Dugard, former dean and professor of the Law Faculty at Witwatersrand, the Centre complemented and cooperated with the Legal Resources Centre in efforts to hold the South African government accountable to the principles of common law that provided some possibility of protection for the oppressed. Detailed research by the Centre, particularly in the area of security legislation and policing, exposed the implications of policies of apartheid. The Centre also offered extensive education programs for members of the legal professions and for the public more generally. Now, more than 35 years later, the Centre continues to use the law to implement and protect the human rights of individuals.

Success has many parents. The RBF cannot claim sole credit for any huge steps forward in the struggle against apartheid, but I believe we made highly useful contributions to key change agents. Importantly, the experience of working so closely on the LRC proposal with colleagues from other foundations – each of us having our own style and priorities, but all of us sharing a common goal – gave me a sense of what was possible when foundations let go of the need to 'do their own thing,' and join forces with one another in true collaborative fashion. In order to tackle big, complex problems, that kind of collaboration is essential. As I went on to work in other regions of the world, I found that such horizontal ties (between program officers at different foundations who are working on similar issues) could be even more important than relationships between the program staff of a single foundation.

Closing reflections

The tendency to make overly ambitious statements about program goals and achievements is an occupational hazard among foundation program officers. I am sure that we at the RBF often described ourselves as 'promoting economic development in East (or West) Africa' – when of course, in a literal sense, we did not have the resources to do any such thing. We were a small piece of the puzzle; our total Africa-related grant expenditures during the period covered by this chapter amounted to slightly more than $5 million over 17 years (through approximately 150 grants), or approximately $300,000 a year. When I reflect on the impact of our grantmaking in Africa from the late 1960s through the mid-1980s (especially in light of the development challenges which still plague much of Africa), I am very aware of that reality.

I do feel that in a number of places in East and West Africa our funding filled voids and enabled new ideas and enterprises to take root. We helped to 'fertilize' local initiatives with expertise from other places – and we left behind a stronger cohort of local leaders and institutions in most of the areas where we were active. Some of the organizations we supported have grown and continue to operate effectively today. The natural resources management programs we helped to launch are now firmly established and contributing to local economies; the process of creating those programs helped to build a local vision for conservation, heritage protection, and sustainable development.

In Botswana, my own inquiries suggest that the new and young organizations we supported 30 years ago later encountered a range of problems that probably called for more sustained engagement from funders than we understood to be needed. While not all of the organizations and programs we funded still exist, some do and others have transformed themselves, such as the Kweneng Rural Development Association (KRDA) into the Bakwena Community Development Association, as mentioned earlier. In broad terms, I think it is fair to say that the RBF's 12-year involvement in Botswana was valuable on a practical level, and I believe our commitment was heartening for national and local leaders who were determined to see Botswana achieve greater economic self-reliance and for many young Batswana men and women who were eager to seize new opportunities.

In South Africa we lent our modest support to a powerful movement, betting on several projects that turned out to be important assets in the struggle against apartheid. Now, many years later, our principal grant recipients continue to address current critical human security challenges in South Africa.

Not every project we funded was successful. As indicated at several points in this chapter, project implementation was often slower and more halting than we imagined it would be. While small grants could go a long way, I think we probably tried to do too much with too little – although we stuck with many projects through two or more grant cycles.

I was often frustrated at not being able to spend enough time on the ground in Africa; among other things, I might have been able to detect some problems at an earlier stage. And in the late 1970s the sharp reduction in the Fund's endowment that resulted from the one-time Creel Committee grants made it impossible for us to pursue some of the new program directions I would have liked to explore. I was particularly disappointed not to be able to spend more time with moderate Afrikaners in South Africa – people like Fred van Wyk, longtime director of the Institute of Race Relations, a gentle renegade who endured death threats from others in the Afrikaner community. It seemed to me that more discussions and initiatives involving moderate Afrikaners could have accelerated progress toward eliminating apartheid. But we did not have the funds to develop this complex and sensitive grantmaking agenda.

One last observation: in retrospect, I regret that we did not pay enough attention to the growing problem of government mismanagement and corruption in the East and West African nations where we were active. This systemic challenge has undermined many efforts to improve people's lives and prospects, and it was a mistake on my part not to urge the Fund somehow to help tackle the problem. At this time, though, there were very few local organizations in Africa that worked on corruption or transparency issues, and corruption had not yet become a high priority for international NGOs. In later years, however, we would have an opportunity to address governance and transparency concerns in Central and Eastern Europe and in the Western Balkans, my geographic areas of focus from the early 1980s until my retirement in 2007.

Belize

Guatemala

Honduras

Nicaragua

El Salvador

Panama

Costa Rica

Venezuela

Guyana

Suriname

French Guiana

Colombia

Ecuador

Brazil

Peru

Bolivia

Paraguay

Chile

Argentina

Uruguay

Targeted grantmaking

Reached through regional grantmaking

CHAPTER FOUR

Investing in Individuals
Latin America, 1968 to mid-1980s

Kenton [Miller] was a gentle lion of conservation. There was
no wilderness so remote that you would not run into a disciple
of Kenton's in a sweat-stained shirt and beaten-up hat, out in
the boonies, trying to learn about and protect nature. One park
ranger in Venezuela gasped, 'I feel like I am meeting the patron
saint of protected areas.' Kenton was, simply, one of the most
wonderful people ever to work here.

Jonathan Lash, President, World Resources Institute,
from 'Honoring the Life of Dr Kenton R Miller' (2011), www.wri.org

When I arrived at the RBF in 1968, the Fund's longstanding interest in Latin
America was at an important inflection point. The American International
Association for Economic and Social Development (AIA) – which Nelson
Rockefeller took the lead in establishing in 1946 – had been the centerpiece of the RBF's Latin America grantmaking program. The AIA aimed to
promote 'self-development and better standards of living, together with
understanding and cooperation in Latin America' and worked primarily in
cooperation with governments. The Rockefeller family had contributed
more than $7 million to the AIA, of which about half came from the RBF.
But in 1969 the AIA closed its doors, as board members felt the organization had achieved significant advances in the fields in which it had been
active for more than two decades. Jim Hyde, John Camp, and I were tasked
with examining how the grant monies freed up by this change – $200,000
to $300,000 per year, at that point – could best be spent.

I was eager and ready to focus on this assignment. Among my
favorite childhood memories were the stories that my great uncle, Bill
Shorter, had told me about the decades he spent living and working in
Uruguay. Several years of high-school Spanish and various college-level
courses had further whetted my appetite for knowledge about the region.

I certainly was not a Latin America expert, but I was keen to help the RBF make a positive impact there.

What follows is the story of how we recalibrated our Latin America grantmaking, introducing a concerted focus on the wise management of natural areas as a strategy for economic development. In the process, we forged a uniquely close working relationship with a remarkable individual – and managed a funding partnership with a major international organization. Both experiences were the source of important lessons and reflections for me as a new program officer trying to understand how a relatively small private foundation could have a meaningful impact on large problems.

It is important to note that even as the Fund's grantmaking in Latin America took on new dimensions, we continued to contribute to a number of US-based policy institutions with programs that focused on US–Latin American relations. Among these institutions were several in which David Rockefeller played a leading role and had encouraged increased attention to inter-American relationships. We viewed our support of such projects at the Council on Foreign Relations, the Center for Inter-American Relations, the Overseas Development Council, and other respected think-tanks and policy centers both as a valuable grantmaking strategy in its own right, since it advanced the RBF's broad goal of promoting international cooperation, and as a significant complement to the work we were funding on the ground in Latin America. This was a deliberate, two-tier approach to international grantmaking that the RBF would implement more fully in Central and Eastern Europe.

A new day for the RBF in Latin America

By the late 1960s the population of Latin America was among the fastest-growing regions in the world, and the demand for food, water, shelter, and other basic necessities was increasing exponentially. Throughout Latin America, economic development goals were being pursued without much consideration for how development strategies would affect the environment or people's long-term well-being. Although some individuals were beginning to recognize the importance of protected areas, there was no general appreciation (among citizens or governments) of the negative consequences of mismanagement and pollution of natural resources – watersheds, grasslands, biodiversity, wildlands – or of how important those resources could be to employment generation, overall economic development, and improving the quality of people's lives.

Such challenges resonated with the staff and leadership of the RBF, given the Rockefeller family's longstanding interests in conservation. Laurance Rockefeller, then chair of the Fund, was particularly involved in conservation and land management issues. My colleagues and I quickly began to look for ways in which the Fund might balance its ongoing focus on economic and social development in the region with new efforts related to the wise use of natural resources.

We were not alone in believing it was time to focus on natural resources management in the region. In addition to the US-based environmental organizations that were beginning to pay attention to challenges in Latin America, the Organization of American States (OAS) had recently decided to consolidate its work on agriculture and forestry within a specialized agency based in Costa Rica that emphasized natural resources management: the Inter-American Institute for Cooperation in Agriculture (IICA).* Moreover, the UN's Food and Agriculture Organization (FAO) had for decades been focusing considerable attention on forestry education and research throughout Latin America and was the main source of assistance for natural resources management in the region. We did not know it at the time, but such international and multilateral initiatives would play important roles in the story of the RBF's involvement in Latin America.

In January 1969 John Camp prepared a memorandum entitled 'How to Start a Conservation Program in Latin America.' This memorandum set us on a course of investigation – reading about the issues and learning what various agencies and organizations were doing, meeting informally with key people in the appropriate fields, listening a lot and making site visits whenever possible in order to get a first-hand sense of what was happening on the ground. But the memorandum also urged us to identify some pilot or demonstration projects that could be supported right away, even before a fully fledged grantmaking program was hatched.

As part of our investigations, John and I made a study trip to Latin America in October and November of 1969. We traveled to Guatemala,

---

* The IICA later changed its name – though not its acronym – from Instituto Interamericano de Cooperación para la Agricultura to Instituto Interamericano de Ciencias Agrícolas.

Costa Rica, Colombia, and Dominican Republic, as well as Puerto Rico.*
We met a cross-section of people in all four Latin American countries and
in Puerto Rico who confirmed the need for sustained attention to improving
the management of natural resources through research, teaching, training,
experimentation, and public outreach. We also discovered that there was
very little money available to underwrite such efforts (the US-based and
international non-governmental organizations working in this area were
already spread thin) and little prospect of significant new monies entering the field any time soon. We kept our eyes open for promising plans
and people in which the RBF could invest a relatively modest amount of
money – $150,000 to $200,000 per year, which represented most of the
funds formerly committed to the AIA and about half of the existing annual
budget for grantmaking in Latin America – and hope for some significant
outcomes and impacts.

In Costa Rica we found an extraordinary individual with the kinds
of ideas, experience, credibility, and management skills we were seeking.
The remainder of this chapter focuses mainly on the body of work that grew
out of that encounter.

My intention in taking such a 'singular' approach here is to call
attention to a particular kind of opportunity that grantmakers may seize
– the opportunity to invest in individuals. No chapter in this book gives
equal attention to all of the projects we supported in a given region or time
period; the grant listings provided at the end of this book are designed
to help address that shortfall. But this chapter is particularly guilty in that
regard. Even as we devoted a substantial share of our resources to a particular, and extended, partnership, we continued to invest in a range of
local projects that were designed to help people in rural and urban areas
create economic opportunities and improve their communities.

In fact, nearly half of the RBF budget for Latin America in the 1970s
was directed toward economic development and job creation, including early efforts at eco-development. For example, with multi-year support from the RBF, the Fundación Nicaragüense para el Desarrollo, in
Nicaragua, established a cooperative that provided technical and financial
assistance to small farmers so they could improve their farming practices
and marketing techniques. RBF support for Acción Comunitaria del Perú

* I would travel to Latin America a number of times over the next 15 years, although I would
never again write such a lengthy trip report – 46 single-spaced pages!

helped local people in poor areas of Lima learn better ways to construct their own homes and to meet other needs of their families.

Given the scale of our resources relative to the scope of economic development challenges in Latin America, we also directed some of our grants to consortia and networks that were comprised of many organizations or projects. RBF support for SOLIDARIOS – a consortium of Latin American 'national development foundations' (some of which the RBF had helped create in the 1960s) – covered management training for foundation staff who were supervising soft loans and technical support programs for local entrepreneurs outside of normal bank channels. RBF support for the National Association of the Partners of the Alliance (later called simply the 'Partners of the Americas') – a network that links US states and communities with counterparts in Latin American and Caribbean countries through technical, educational, and cultural exchange projects – helped participants expand their focus to include projects that emphasized conservation and wise resource use. Modest funding helped PACT (Private Agencies Collaborating Together) in South and Central American countries – and other parts of the developing world – strengthen the capacity of local self-help community groups.

As was the case in Africa, we found that providing funds for staff capacity-building was often an effective way to enhance the impact of these projects. Not many other donors were prepared to respond quickly to urgent requests for small grants from non-governmental organizations and consortia in Latin America. As time went on, we learned that other donors were paying particular attention to our assessments when considering their own, often larger pledges to projects we had helped to kick off or keep alive by filling an unexpected gap. Over the course of my career, I came to view this kind of leverage as a hallmark of RBF grantmaking.

During the period covered by this chapter, the RBF made more than 80 grants related to Latin America, totaling more than $4.5 million. The special story told below should be viewed against that backdrop.

A serendipitous encounter

John Camp and I had traveled to the IICA's Research and Training Center (CATIE – Centro Agronómico Tropical de Investigación y Enseñanza) in Turrialba, Costa Rica, in the autumn of 1969 for a day of meetings and observation. At lunch, I was seated next to a young American, Dr Kenton

R Miller, whose name I had already heard from several people we met on this trip and from the UN Food and Agriculture Organization (FAO) staff in Rome, with whom I had consulted about our Africa program on an earlier trip. Kenton was 30 years old, with a BS in Forestry (Wildland Planning, Ecology) and an MS in Forestry (Management) from the College of Forestry, University of Washington, Seattle, and a PhD from the College of Environmental Sciences and Forestry (Forestry Economics, Wildland Management, Tropical Forestry) at the State University of New York, Syracuse. He had been working in Latin America for more than four years already and was fluent in Spanish.

Kenton Miller, on the right, was a respected field observer who went into remote, rarely visited places to understand local conditions. Here he is shown with David Oliveira Assoreira, a Portuguese biologist who was involved in the development of a management plan for the Brasilia National Park. (photo: Maria Tereza Jorge Pádua, 1976)

In the course of our afternoon at CATIE, I spent a little over an hour with this impressive young man, and during that short period I learned a great deal about his work and his plans for the future. Kenton was actually an employee of the FAO who was sent to CATIE as part of an effort to research suitable locations for the establishment of protected areas in Latin America. He argued persuasively that these 'wildland' areas should be thought of as instruments for the sustainable management of goods and services that benefit society as a whole. He believed that nations should apply a systematic approach to managing these natural resources, creating networks of protected areas that would meet specific objectives: protecting key watersheds; maintaining biological and genetic diversity; providing recreation opportunities and enhancing scenic beauty; ensuring sustainable timber production, grazing capacity, or wildlife harvesting; preserving resource flexibility; and promoting rural economic development.

Kenton distilled his thinking into a draft program consisting of five 'projects' or strands of activity, which he had begun to circulate. The program was designed to help catalyze sector- and region-wide changes by intervening at several strategic points simultaneously. Among the interventions he recommended were improved training in wildlands management; the creation of interpretation programs at national parks to educate the public about the value of natural areas; and the development of methodologies for integrating effective natural resources management into overall national and regional planning processes.

Kenton was making headway in helping his colleagues and peers understand the need to explore some of these avenues. But at a time when the budgets of many international agencies were in decline, Kenton was not sure if the FAO could even continue to loan him to IICA/CATIE, much less support a multi-year program of the sort he had laid out. Kenton asked me whether the RBF could possibly fund his efforts. I responded that we would examine his proposed program carefully and get back in touch with him soon.

I sounded calm and measured at the time, I think – but in fact I was exhilarated. Meeting a young professional with such fully developed ideas and leadership potential was exciting; it was an unforgettable experience, especially coming so early in my own career in philanthropy. Frankly, I already felt in my gut that Kenton was someone the RBF could bet on! But I also knew it was critical to get to know Kenton better myself and to check him out with a range of people. Was he capable of managing such a wide-ranging program? Was his thinking as innovative and 'big picture' as I suspected it might be? And even if I received positive readings on him and his plans, the RBF's grant budget could not possibly cover the entire cost of his five projects. Nor did we have staff in the field who could help us stay on top of such a wide-ranging program. A cooperative venture would be needed, with at least one other donor organization. Which organization might make a good partner for the RBF? Many questions were going through my mind as that day in Turrialba ended.

In the course of our continuing travels in the region, John and I heard resounding praise for Kenton's breadth of knowledge, his on-the-ground experience, his credibility among peers and local leaders, his teamwork skills, his ability to communicate effectively – and to listen effectively – in English and Spanish, and his management skills. Many people mentioned as well his gentle manner, and the fact that he did not have an outsized ego. Upon returning home, I did more due diligence, collecting several additional enthusiastic endorsements of Kenton's abilities and work plans.

Forging an unlikely partnership

Within weeks of returning from that first trip to Latin America, I invited Kenton to come to New York to meet Jim Hyde and some of my other colleagues. Kenton impressed everyone he met, which made it easy for me to keep his plan on a fast track in our office. He and I spent a good deal of time talking about options for funding his program. We considered the pros and cons of a cooperative RBF venture with the FAO, where Kenton was on staff, or with CATIE, where he was on loan. We also explored the possibility of partnering with the Organization of American States or some international environmental organization. Kenton ultimately recommended a partnership with the FAO, because of strong interest among FAO staff at headquarters in Rome and at the Latin American field office in Santiago, Chile. Kenton also noted that he knew how things 'worked' internally at the FAO.

Initially I was skeptical. The FAO was a large and bureaucratic organization; the RBF was small and less rigidly structured. In addition to the differences in organizational culture, I knew that the FAO was laboring under significant financial constraints. Indeed, as we began to explore the possibility of a collaboration, it became clear that the FAO wanted the RBF to contribute a much bigger share of the funding than we were prepared or able to provide. Although there were very few disagreements between us about program goals and strategies, I could see that we would have to negotiate carefully our respective roles and financial responsibilities. Fortunately, almost everyone we dealt with at the FAO was highly professional, committed, and straightforward; the negotiations were not overly laborious.

The issue of overhead charges

Like all international organizations, the Food and Agriculture Organization (FAO) – which would be the official recipient of our grants in support of Kenton's work – expected to take a 14 per cent overhead charge out of each grant. This is not an uncommon practice; many large institutions that host multiple projects (universities, for example) collect overhead fees to cover the administrative support, office equipment, accounting, and other backup services from which the projects housed at the institution benefit. While the logic of this practice is clear, funders tend to grimace when they see a meaningful share of their grant allocated to institutional overhead. And in this case, Jim Hyde and I felt that 14 per cent was simply too much to pay the FAO for program management, since the RBF was going to be such an active partner in the venture. We argued that the overhead fee should be cut in half, to 7 per cent.

The FAO ultimately agreed; but our satisfaction faded when we realized that the FAO had excluded the joint FAO/RBF project from the support services that were offered to projects which had paid the standard overhead rate. The result was more work for Kenton and his team. After a year, we withdrew our objections and allowed the FAO to charge us the standard rate for the remaining years of the cooperative venture.

The RBF also ended up covering more salary costs for this program than I thought should have been the case, since a big part of the FAO's contribution was supposed to be 'people.' Indeed, many of Kenton's superiors and peers in various departments at the FAO became valuable colleagues in our shared endeavor. But because of the FAO's budget crunch, having flexible RBF money to pay part or all of some salaries proved critical to getting and keeping good staff for the program.

Soon the outlines of an agreement began to take shape. Given the scale and the unusual nature of this proposed collaboration, it needed vetting not only by the Fund's president, Dana Creel, but also by Laurance Rockefeller, chair of the RBF board. On 3 May 1971 the RBF executive committee approved a grant of $300,000 over two years (1971 and 1972) to the Food and Agriculture Organization of the United Nations, which FAO matched with the help of contributions and in-kind support from other international institutions – especially the United Nations Development

Program (UNDP) – and from donor country development agencies as well as governments in the region.

Our collaborative effort was known as 'Trust Fund #199' in Rome and Santiago, and the 'FAO/RBF Wildland Management Program' in our offices. RBF funds were used mainly to support on-the-ground activities (such as training), but some of our funds were also needed to pay part of the salaries of Kenton (whose office was in the Santiago office of the FAO) and his deputy. The assumption was that the RBF would contribute another $200,000 to this program for 1973 and 1974. We all expected that project spin-offs would continue after the initial years, and the FAO itself planned to maintain a natural resources management program for some years after our four-year collaboration had come to an end.

Supporting the wise management of natural areas in Latin America

These grants launched more than a decade of RBF engagement in nat-ural resources management efforts in Latin America.* Our grantmaking spanned the full arc, from supporting the implementation of an innovative program, through encouraging the adaptation of that program in new set-tings, to enabling the dissemination of knowledge and insights gleaned from those applied projects.

- During the first phase of our grantmaking, from 1970 to 1974, the focus was on implementing Kenton's program to assist primarily South American countries with the management of national parks and unallocated natural areas, as part of a comprehensive approach to environmental conservation and rural land management. This was the period during which the FAO/RBF partnership was in effect. Most of the fieldwork for the FAO/RBF program was undertaken in Chile and Costa Rica, with additional activities taking place in a few other countries in Latin America. Kenton's exceptional program leadership team, which included outstanding foresters, ecologists, and planning experts from around the world, made significant progress toward meeting

* The term 'wildlands,' which Kenton originally favored, was not widely adopted. Kenton is known as a pioneer in the sound management and utilization of mainly protected areas, such as national parks and forestry preserves.

all program goals: training forestry professors and protected area personnel, conducting demonstration projects on the development of park interpretation materials, and promoting new approaches to protected areas management. Kenton's deputy, Arne Dalfelt (a Norwegian forester on loan to the FAO), would go on to help launch the follow-up program in Central America, described below.

Kenton (in the middle) was also widely appreciated for his listening and assimilating abilities. He is shown here in 1984, again in Brazil, with Marc Dourojeanni (right), then vice president of the IUCN (International Union for Conservation of Nature), and Luiz Fernando Galli (left), then the director of aquaculture in the Companhia Energética de São Paulo. (photo: Maria Tereza Jorge Pádua)

– During a second, follow-up phase of work (1974–9), lessons from South America were adapted and applied in Central America, at the request of national planning agencies throughout the region.* Also, it was during this period that Kenton helped Brazil develop its first park management plans. The RBF's institutional partner for the follow-up program in Central America was CATIE, the research and training center in Costa Rica where I first met Kenton

---

* In this same period, the RBF also responded to requests from several Caribbean nations for assistance with natural area management efforts in the Eastern Caribbean; our work in the Caribbean is the subject of the next chapter.

Miller. The total budget for this four-year program was about
$800,000, toward which the RBF contributed nearly $200,000.
Central American governments, the US government, UNDP, and
other international institutions provided the balance.

In general, it proved to be more difficult than we expected to work in
Central America. We had chosen to focus on the poorest countries at a
time (as it turned out) when political instability and violence – exacerbated
by the meddling of external actors, including the US Central Intelligence
Agency – were beginning to ravage the region. Some of the worst fighting
was going on in the very areas we were trying to protect. Even where work
was possible, program activities were sometimes impeded by delays in
receiving funds or government approvals. But the Central America effort
did succeed in introducing a core group of wildland management personnel to the concepts and principles of conservation and wise resource
use that Kenton Miller had articulated, and the program leadership team
facilitated effective planning processes at the local and national level in
several countries. The program initiated many valuable research projects
that were carried out by local planners and organizations.

- After the FAO/RBF program came to an end, Kenton Miller
  joined the faculty at the University of Michigan's School of
  Natural Resources, where he was appointed to head a Center for
  Strategic Wildland Management Studies and Eco-Development.
  During Kenton's academic tenure (1975–83), the RBF made
  several modest grants to support his work. His efforts during
  this period were among his most important in terms of promoting
  conservation through protected areas management and
  influencing the attitudes of professional foresters and associated
  specialists.
- One multi-year grant to the University of Michigan funded Kenton's
  preparation of a seminal textbook on national parks and protected
  areas management. This textbook, entitled *Planificatión de
  Parques Nacionales para el Ecodesarrollo en América Latina*
  (*Planning National Parks for Eco-development in Latin America*),
  was published in 1980 and had a huge impact in Latin America.
  Now out of print, it was and still is recognized as a benchmark
  contribution.

   – From his base at the university Kenton also helped to conceptualize the Central American follow-up program (given his other responsibilities, he was necessarily less directly involved in that effort) and spearheaded the planning of a spin-off program in the Caribbean, called the Eastern Caribbean Natural Area Management Program (ECNAMP), which is described in the following chapter.

Program outcomes

All of the practical projects we helped to fund in Latin America were designed and implemented on a cooperative basis with local, national, and international agencies, both governmental and non-governmental.

Cumulatively, as a result of the two large wildland programs combined (FAO/RBF and CATIE/RBF), over 60 professors of forestry and resource management from throughout Central and South America received advanced field training and began to incorporate new concepts and methods into their teaching. 'Wildland management' became a program or a course at several major universities in the region; the program at the university in Valdivia, Chile, was particularly strong, and members of the faculty were able to provide technical assistance on resource management initiatives throughout South America. In several Latin American countries and territories, RBF-funded projects provided in-service training for mid-level park and protected areas staff, as well as for mid-level government officials tasked with natural areas management. Kenton's team played a leading role in the region-wide expansion of an existing training facility in Argentina. Interpretation materials created for two national parks (in Costa Rica and Chile) – complete with exhibits, maps, and manuals – were the first such public education materials to be produced in the region, and they inspired other similar efforts throughout South and Central America.

Taken together, these programs facilitated the production of over 30 planning documents that were submitted to government agencies in Latin America, with many of these plans ultimately being implemented. Kenton and his team succeeded in developing a methodology for integrating natural resource conservation and protected areas management into overall national and regional planning; the methodology was taught to forestry professors and used in numerous planning processes; and a manual explaining the methodology was published. In fact, many of these protected areas and other wildland management program activities led to the production of manuals and guides that are still being used in diverse settings across the region as well as elsewhere in the world.

As this last observation suggests, these programs also had significant ripple effects. Years after the RBF's programs ended, Kenton's 'disciples' were playing leadership roles in scores of natural areas management projects throughout Latin America. The principles of management on which our programs were based are the cornerstones of training and research at CATIE, where hundreds of practitioners and future leaders in the field of natural resources management have had an opportunity to develop their skills. And over time, other funders, impressed by the good work that was being done, have stepped in to support specific follow-up projects. In the early 1980s, when the US Agency for International Development, the US National Parks Service, and the World Wildlife Fund–US wanted a current assessment of natural resource management training needs in Latin America and the Caribbean, they recruited Kenton to lead the study, in order to ensure continuity with his earlier efforts.

Closing reflections

The adoption in 1983 of a new program framework at the RBF brought our grantmaking in Latin America (and other developing countries) to a close. Today, three decades later, it is difficult to gauge the overall impact of the natural resource management programs we supported in Latin America. The idea that the management of natural areas should be part of development planning was still very new at the time. While conservationists and development professionals had begun to work more 'on the ground' and in a less top-down fashion, compared to the 1950s and 1960s, the two communities still tended to work in quite separate silos. I had forgotten how true this was until I asked some old friends and colleagues from both disciplines to read a draft of this chapter. Those who had devoted themselves to conservation efforts in Latin America or the Caribbean were thrilled that I was writing about Kenton's groundbreaking work; one or two of the development experts, on the other hand, had not even heard of him. And in the years since, even as the 'eco-development' connection has been more widely embraced, I have become painfully aware of what slow, uphill work it is to advance sustainable strategies for economic growth in the face of

powerful, well-funded corporate interests and the media's relentless pro-
motion of consumerism.

The goals that Kenton and we set for those pioneering resource
management efforts were ambitious, and they were not always achieved.
But as I look back on the full span of our 'wildlands' grantmaking in Latin
America, and at the concrete outputs identified above, there are some less
tangible – but very significant – impacts that I believe the RBF can point to.

- First, these programs modeled a new approach to planning
  for parks and wildlands. Mid-level forestry staff and academics
  learned that rapid economic exploitation is not the only way to
  obtain beneficial goods and services from natural areas – an
  important conceptual shift. Later in his career, as director general
  of the IUCN and at the World Resources Institute, Kenton had
  opportunities to influence decision-making, including that of
  planning agencies. RBF-funded activities also introduced to
  the region the then unfamiliar notion that parks can play a role in
  educating the public about the importance of protecting natural
  areas – and that they should play this role, because building public
  constituencies for conservation is critical. The dissemination of
  such new ideas and conceptual frameworks is not sufficient to
  ensure rapid or lasting progress. But it can be a vital precursor
  to change.

During a field visit to Costa
Rica in the mid- to late
1970s, Alvaro Ugalde,
former director of the
National Parks of Costa
Rica (holding map), explains
our surroundings to me (at
left), John Camp (behind),
and Arne Dalfelt, who was
Kenton's deputy in Chile
and later helped to organize
the follow-up to the FAO/
RBF wildland program – the
CATIE/RBF collaboration –
in Central America.

– Second, I suspect that the whole of those program activities and accomplishments may be even greater than the sum of its parts. By which I mean that the management programs we helped to fund almost certainly contributed, at least in some measure, to strengthening a conservation ethic – among both leaders and publics – in Latin America. I saw the same thing begin to happen in the Caribbean, as a direct consequence, in part, of the spin-off program that was implemented there (ECNAMP), as well as the efforts of the Island Resources Foundation.

– Finally, the concepts Kenton Miller advanced with RBF support in Latin America and at the University of Michigan – about management by objectives, the need to create integrated conservation systems rather than piecemeal preservation projects, the importance of incorporating natural areas management into overall regional planning – have become part of the nomenclature of natural resources management all over the world. Kenton's innovations have become 'common sense.' Through his teaching and writing, Kenton also helped to educate the next generation of planners and conservationists, including scores of Latin American students who flocked to study with him at the University of Michigan.

Of course, when my colleagues and I were asked to recommend a reallo-cation of the grant funds that had been going to the American International Association for Economic and Social Development, I never imagined that we would choose to devote such a big share of those funds, right up front, to a single program, reflecting largely the vision of a single individual, on which we would collaborate with a huge international organization (the FAO). If we had not developed such respect and trust for Kenton Miller, in a rather short period of time, I am not sure we would have proceeded as rapidly as we did. Between my first encounter with Kenton and the launch of the FAO/RBF Wildland Management Program there were only about 18 months, during which time a final proposal was developed and vetted, and complex negotiations with the FAO undertaken and completed. Not long, really, given the size and unusual nature of the initiative.

I noted that my early experiences as a program officer in Africa taught me a great deal about the importance of flexibility and of finding the right on-the-ground partners and project leaders. Those observations are certainly relevant to the Fund's work in Latin America as well. Take the notion of flexibility: our collaboration with the FAO, about which I was initially skeptical, worked well in part because both parties were willing to experiment with an unfamiliar arrangement. While we both were straight-forward about our expectations, we also both were willing to be (selec-tively) flexible in adapting to circumstances. Of course, the fact that we had shared goals for the program and a shared confidence in Kenton Miller made it easier for us to establish mutual trust and respect – which does not mean that we were never challenged by the differences in our ways of operating. The chief downside to this relationship was the FAO's depend-ence on yearly funding pledges from governments and international organ-izations (pledges that were not always honored), which made it difficult for the FAO to plan ahead or stay the course. Key staff were assigned to other positions or they relocated to other organizations, with significant consequences for our work. But overall, our flexibility paid off. There were real benefits for the RBF in working with the FAO; its large staff of experts, its ties with other international and multilateral organizations, and its ability to open doors at the highest levels of government were all valuable assets.

But the notion of 'finding the right project leaders' does not really do justice to the unusually close and extended working relationship, between 1971 and 1983, that we developed with Kenton Miller. Foundations are always investing in individuals, in a sense; projects and organizations are not disembodied entities. The decision to fund or not fund a project is deeply influenced by the donor's level of trust and confidence in the pro-ject's leadership. But betting on an individual, over time and across dif-ferent settings – that is a somewhat different proposition. It can produce enormous payoffs for the issues and fields in which a foundation works, because it gives exceptional individuals additional standing, influence, and convening power, which can help them to attain positions in which they have the ability to shape policy, spearhead change, and build new fields or institutions.

Kenton Miller went on from the University of Michigan, for example, to become director general of the International Union for Conservation of Nature and Natural Resources (IUCN), the world's oldest and largest global environmental organization. He was elected chair (twice) of the prestigious World Commission on Protected Areas – in the 1970s while at

Michigan and later in 2000. During this period the RBF provided modest funding to help cover Kenton's travel to key locations and meetings, ensuring a place at the table for protected areas management. This kind of 'walking around' money can be critical but is rarely provided by foundations. His legacy is honored by the IUCN's Kenton R Miller Award for Innovation in Protected Areas Management, which carries a $5,000 prize (and to which the RBF contributed the first $25,000). Kenton thanked the RBF many times over the years, not only for the grants we made in support of his work, but for the special role we played in his career.*

None of this is to say that an individual with Kenton's abilities and leadership potential would not have 'made it' without foundation support; but helping to advance the career of such an individual is one of the privileges that private funders – even modestly resourced funders – enjoy. I certainly felt that way about Kenton and several other people with whom I established extended working relationships during my career.

Betting on an individual also raises – and should raise – important questions and challenges for funders, however. I believed in Kenton's ideas and plans and their importance, but sometimes, during this long period of working closely with him, I would ask myself if I was channeling too many resources to programs headed by, or influenced significantly by, one person. Did I have a blind spot? Was I causing the RBF to miss other opportunities that should have been given greater attention? I tried to review other incoming proposals carefully, and I gave the grant reporting we received from Kenton's team and related efforts the same kind of scrutiny I would give reports from other grantees.

In the final analysis, I have no doubt that we received value and results beyond our expectations and beyond our monetary investment in Kenton's work. I do believe strongly that grantmakers have a responsibility to be open to new approaches and to ask themselves questions about opportunity costs and favoritism – although I never heard anyone (including any trustee of the Fund) make that accusation about the RBF's support of Kenton Miller. I suspect this is because his work was so clearly innovative and transformative, and because he himself never sought the spotlight.

* It is worth noting that the RBF did not make any grants directly to Kenton. Over the years, all funds were granted to charitable organizations for programs and activities established, directed, and/or implemented by Kenton and his team. US foundations are prohibited from making grants to individuals except through programs with selection procedures approved by the US Internal Revenue Service.

He was a wonderful team player, generous with his praise, absolutely trust-worthy, and indefatigable.

I stayed in touch with Kenton and continued to seek his advice long past the time when the RBF stopped supporting his work; we became friends as well as colleagues. At some point in the 1990s, I learned that Kenton had been diagnosed with a serious illness. After fighting his illness bravely for many years, he died in May 2011.

I miss him still.

Honoring Kenton Miller

From 'Honoring the Life of Dr Kenton R Miller' (2011), by Nels Johnson, Deputy State Director, The Nature Conservancy (formerly with the World Resources Institute):

> I've worked for many people over the years but none finer than Kenton. His impact on me as a person and a professional was profound. He was a giant in the conservation community. He was a teacher, a mentor, a humanist, and a thought leader, but he was absolutely committed to converting ideas into action. Above all else, he was persistent. Kenton had a hard time speaking ill of anyone and it showed. I traveled the world with Kenton from San José, Costa Rica, and Nairobi, Kenya, to Oslo, Norway and Bangalore, India and many other places in between on five continents. Without exception, we met people who knew Kenton or had encountered him in any number of capacities and they uniformly greeted him as one of their most esteemed colleagues and friends. I am but one of many who were fundamentally shaped by Kenton's vision, pas-sion, and commitment for conservation as a foundation for human quality of life.

British Virgin Islands

Antigua and Barbuda

Puerto Rico

St Kitts and Nevis

Guadeloupe

Dominica

Martinique

St Lucia

St Vincent

Barbados

Grenada

Trinidad and Tobago

Turks and
Caicos Islands

Cuba

Haiti

Jamaica

Dominican
Republic

Primary focus of grantmaking

CHAPTER FIVE

A Willingness to Take Reasonable Risks
Caribbean Islands, mid-1970s to late 1980s

Merely to name them is the prose
Of diarists, to make you a name
For readers who like travellers praise
Their beds and beaches as the same;
But islands can only exist

If we have loved in them. I seek,
As climate seeks its style, to write
Verse crisp as sand, clear as sunlight,
Cold as the curled wave, ordinary
As a tumbler of island water . . .

Derek Walcott, 'Islands'

Among the Rockefeller brothers, it was Laurance who had the strongest interest in the tropical islands of the Caribbean. He was deeply committed to the conservation of the region's natural resources; it was in the Caribbean that he launched his 'RockResorts' hotel concept, providing high-quality vacation experiences while protecting the environment and employing local people. In the 1950s Laurance's land donations were instrumental in the creation of the Virgin Islands National Park in St John, US Virgin Islands. In the 1960s Laurance helped to create the BVI (British Virgin Islands) National Parks Trust, the first such land preservation agency in the Caribbean, as well as the Caribbean Conservation Association (CCA), the Caribbean's first regional NGO. By the time I joined the RBF staff in 1968, Laurance was widely known and respected in the region for the several roles he was playing there – as a business person, environmentalist, and philanthropist. He was one of the few American donors active in the Caribbean.

ECNAMP (Eastern Caribbean Natural Area Management Program) team members, pictured around the early 1980s, in the British Virgin Islands for a survey of conservation priorities. From left to right: Ivor Jackson, Tessa Bertram, and Allen Putney.

Despite Laurance's involvement, the Caribbean was not among the regions on which I expected to work when I came to the Fund. To the extent that I had thought about the Caribbean at all, I suppose I shared the widespread perception of the islands as beautiful places to visit in winter – dotted with palm trees, ringed with sunny beaches, lapped by crystal-clear water. Surely these islands were 'better off' than the developing countries in South and Central America that were on my agenda.

But in fact I soon learned from mentors and colleagues at the Fund (and from my own research) that the Caribbean islands had the same kinds of economic, political, social, and environmental problems that faced other newly independent nations and developing countries around the world. Most of the islands had insufficient financial capacity and staggering levels of unemployment and under-employment – more than 35 per cent, on average – that were driving large-scale migration to urban areas and developed countries, including the United States. Island economies faced dramatic increases in the price of oil, while their primary or only export commodities (sugar, bananas, bauxite) were subject to wild price fluctuations. Agricultural development was hindered by colonial-era land distribution and tenure arrangements, poor agronomic standards, and inadequate government support services. In many locations, population and tourism pressures were leading to uncontrolled deforestation and soil erosion, increased air and water pollution, and other unfavorable environmental consequences that worsened problems already created by exploitation during the colonial period.

Even as I learned more about conditions in the Caribbean islands, my early experiences in Africa and Latin America were teaching me that it was possible for the RBF to make a positive difference, with modest amounts of money, in the lives and prospects of people in developing countries. I was becoming more and more convinced that the wise management of natural resources could be a means of improving incomes and creating jobs. And I was absorbing compelling ideas about land-use planning and resource management from Kenton Miller, whose work in Latin America we had begun to support.

It seemed to me that many of the Fund's international grantmaking strategies and experiences would be highly relevant to the Caribbean islands. I also felt that an RBF involvement in the Caribbean would be entirely consistent with the Rockefeller family's traditional willingness to look at parts of the world where fundamental changes were taking place – changes with important human and environmental implications – and to ask, 'Is there something we can do to promote more equitable, peaceful, and sustainable outcomes?' The family's sensitivity to the ethical and practical implications of global interdependence would be articulated more explicitly in the new program framework that was developed for the RBF in the early 1980s, but it animated Rockefeller philanthropy long before that time. Where better to act on this awareness than in the new island nations struggling to take shape on America's doorstep – our neighbors, not our playground?

It wasn't long before Jim Hyde and I proposed that the RBF consider developing a responsive initiative in the Caribbean. We had recently hired a new staff associate for the International Program whom we could see working with me in the Caribbean, so the timing seemed propitious. In the early 1970s the board authorized us to explore the possibilities.

A new program in a new geographic area

As part of this exploratory process, I interviewed many people in the US who were knowledgeable about the Caribbean region (including Kenton Miller, who had traveled and conducted research there), and spent considerable time myself on the islands, learning about the needs, priorities, hopes, and frustrations of a broad cross-section of local people, including government officials, heads of businesses, educators, and community and NGO leaders, as well as taxi drivers and chance acquaintances in public places.

One of the organizations I consulted, for example, was the Inter-American Foundation (IAF), which had been established in 1969 as an independent agency of the US government to focus on the needs of people in Latin America and the Caribbean. IAF staff viewed the 'foreign assistance' process just the way I did, even though IAF was a government agency and I worked for a private foundation: we listened carefully to local people, favored bottom-up strategies, and paid attention to capacity-building. I benefited as well from conversations and collaboration with the World Wildlife Fund, whose Caribbean program ultimately received support from the RBF and whose US branch would later partner with us to support other involvements in the region. Russell Train, then the president of WWF–US, eventually became a trustee of the RBF.

I also sent Allen Putney – a former colleague of Kenton's from the Latin America wildlands management project – to the Eastern Caribbean, for the express purpose of considering how lessons learned in South and Central America might apply to those island nations. The Eastern Caribbean islands had the lowest per capita incomes and highest unemployment rates in the region, in addition to severe environmental problems and virtually no experience with land-use planning or environmental management. Allen came back excited about the potential for developing an Eastern Caribbean resource management program that would be responsive to locally articulated needs and would take full advantage of Kenton Miller's core principles and practices; he started to sketch out what such a program might look like.

Based on these inquiries, I outlined for the board a grantmaking program that would address economic and environmental challenges in the Caribbean within the framework of what we called eco-development (and would later call sustainable development) – an approach that brings together sound resource conservation and management strategies with economic development strategies in order to create jobs while using resources wisely.

The board approved my plan. Unfortunately, our new staff associate left the RBF shortly thereafter! I was on my own. But surrounded as I was by supportive colleagues – who themselves were overextended but nonetheless managed to be remarkably helpful and encouraging – I was tremendously excited to be developing a program 'from scratch,' in a geographic area where the Fund had not previously been active.

Work and family life

During the late 1970s and throughout the 1980s, as my responsibilities grew and I took on additional assignments, I often pondered the balance between work and family life. I loved my job and had lots of energy; I worked long hours and traveled about eight to ten weeks spread over the year – but I felt I was at home most of the time and I tried to play an active role in overall family life and a full role in raising our sons. My wife Katie did not always agree. She, too, was busy, working on her PhD and writing an excellent book, *Growing Up On Television* (New York Times Books, 1980).

At any rate, we grew apart, for complex reasons. While I do not know how much of a role my work style played in that process, I do know that ultimately we were not able to negotiate those and other strains in our relationship. We separated in 1980 and soon divorced.

Between 1977 and 1986 the RBF made approximately 60 grants within the Caribbean program, totaling more than $3.5 million. Our Caribbean grantmaking began in the Windward and Leeward Islands of the Eastern Caribbean, but over time its geographic scope extended to the broader Caribbean area. Approximately one-quarter of the total grant monies went to support the program that Allen Putney developed, which was eventually called the Eastern Caribbean Natural Area Management Program (ECNAMP). ECNAMP was launched in 1977 as a joint project of the Caribbean Conservation Association and the School of Natural Resources at the University of Michigan (Kenton Miller's home base at the time). Responding to local needs and building on lessons from RBF-supported efforts in Latin America under Kenton Miller's leadership, Allen and his team of Yves Renard, Ivor Jackson, and Tighe Geoghegan took some of the first steps in the Caribbean toward developing community-based approaches to the management of natural resources.

The RBF was ECNAMP's largest single donor, providing slightly more than half of the $1.5 million that ECNAMP raised over ten years from a range of donors. During those years, government agencies and NGOs from throughout the region turned to ECNAMP for conceptual guidance as well as practical assistance in implementing both terrestrial and marine resource management initiatives. ECNAMP workshops provided important skill-building opportunities for fisheries and forestry officers as well as staff of protected areas, while ECNAMP consultants helped get projects off the ground – always in collaboration with local governments and grassroots leaders.

ECNAMP team member Yves Renard, in a photo taken in the early 1980s, standing on a promontory overlooking the Savanne Bay area of St Lucia. He is showing Nancy Hammond of the World Wildlife Fund–US the location of rafts being used to grow seaweed, a main ingredient in a traditional local drink.

In the late 1980s ECNAMP evolved into an independent NGO called CANARI (Caribbean Natural Resources Institute), based in Trinidad and Tobago, which still offers some of the same programs that ECNAMP provided and is still a regional and global leader in community-based resource management. In fact, CANARI serves as the Regional Implementation Team for the Caribbean Program of the Critical Ecosystems Partnership Fund of the World Bank, Conservation International, the French Development Agency, the European Union, the Global Environment Facility, the government of Japan, and the John D and Catherine T MacArthur Foundation. As happened many times in different parts of the world over the years, the RBF played a critical role in the early history of what is now an important indigenous NGO.

A formal, independent evaluation of ECNAMP, commissioned by the Fund in 1986, after our Caribbean program made its last grants, showed that ECNAMP had been a vital catalyst for action, while also creating a new awareness in the region of the need for more systematic, far-sighted resource management – and for training of a network of individuals prepared to further that cause.

We also channeled some of our funding through US-based intermediary organizations that were working in the Caribbean, including several of the organizations whose work we had funded in Africa. RBF support helped the Partnership for Productivity Foundation (PfP), for example, to disseminate successful methods of intensive farming that made use of the islands' often scarce arable land without relying on chemical fertilizers, insecticides, or fungicides. The PfP had proved its worth in Africa, and I knew that it met one of my top criteria for recommending a grant to an intermediary organization: it was staffed with individuals who did their homework, who were quick learners and good listeners, who shared their

Site visits: meaningful to donors and grantees alike

At some point in the 1980s, during a stay on Trinidad, I asked to spend a full day tagging along with Father Gerard (Gerry) Pantin, founder of a non-sectarian community development organization called SERVOL (Service Volunteered for All), which the RBF funded. Father Pantin told me it was very rare for a donor to do such a thing – and just recently, he told me he has never forgotten it. For me, the day was both a direct window into the impact of one of our grants and an inspiring reminder of the quality of the people whose efforts we were supporting; for Father Pantin, I think, my presence was an important signal of the Fund's confidence and interest in his work.

Experiences such as this are not only personally rewarding, but a credit to the RBF's and the Rockefeller family's philanthropic traditions.

knowledge in ways that respected local insights and perspectives, and who viewed their role as providing *transitional* help – just until they were no longer needed or could be replaced by local people.

But in keeping with the Fund's – and my own – interest in enabling, empowering, and inspiring local people to solve their own problems, more than half of our grants went directly to indigenous NGOs.

Taking reasonable risks

When the Caribbean program was approved, the board and officers of the Fund encouraged me to be opportunistic and experimental in implementing the program, including by identifying local groups and leaders on the islands that the Fund might support. It was not the first time (and certainly not the last) that I was struck by a quality that had emerged as one of the hallmarks of the RBF's philanthropic style: the willingness to take reasonable risks.

What did this willingness mean in practice for my work? Our grantmaking in the Caribbean was not necessarily more risky than our grantmaking in other regions – although we did face some unexpected and distinctive difficulties in the Caribbean. Strangely enough, one of the primary obstacles to change in the Caribbean was the smallness of the places where we mainly worked (which was also a factor in the islands' vulnerability in a region prone to natural disasters). In the size of their landmass and populations, these islands were like counties in the US; and just as in some counties, political leaders on the islands had been able to hold on to power – often since colonial times – through various patronage schemes. In the 1970s and 1980s this smallness, together with high levels of poverty and unemployment, meant that the pool of people who had university or even high-school-level educations was small; many aspiring young people were emigrating to the US, UK, or Canada – and those who wanted to stay and challenge the policies of established leaders or play leadership roles themselves sometimes faced stiff opposition. We also found that some local people were skeptical about American philanthropy, since the only Americans they had seen were well-to-do vacationers. In addition, it was sometimes difficult for the RBF to persuade other funders to join us in Caribbean projects. 'You can't be serious,' said a few of our foundation colleagues. 'You should be working in a place like Africa, where there are *real* problems.'

But looking back on the Caribbean program, I am reminded of why the ability to tolerate some risk – and to manage it carefully and creatively – is such a critical dimension of effective philanthropy.

Funding local self-help initiatives, the IRS-approved way

By its very nature, grantmaking in developing countries requires a certain tolerance for risk (I'm not referring here to the risk of political instability or even military conflict, although those risks are very real in some places). As I discovered in Africa and to some extent in Latin America, NGOs in developing countries do not always have the kind of staff capacity and organizational stability that US foundations tend to look for in potential grantees. But a more fundamental challenge is that few foreign organizations have been able to obtain legal status as 'public charities' and therefore most do not automatically qualify to receive direct grant support, under the IRS (Internal Revenue Service) regulations that govern the activities of American private foundations. In the Caribbean, where most of the islands were at the beginning of their nationhood, community groups were springing up everywhere with little attention to legal frameworks.

In my trips to the islands, I became acquainted with many creative, energetic, and proactive local groups that had good ideas and impressive work plans. These candidates for RBF support were not recognized legally as public charities – they would not even show up on the radar screens of big donors – but they were already working hard to improve people's lives and build a better future for their countries.

Fortunately, the IRS has laid out some options for funders that want to support such local initiatives and are willing to follow some additional procedures in order to do so. One option is for the foundation to determine that the local organization is the 'equivalent of a US public charity.' The second, somewhat more demanding option is for the foundation itself to exercise what is called 'expenditure responsibility,' to ensure that grant funds are used for charitable purposes. A brief overview of these options is provided in the box overleaf.

Some international grantmakers prefer to avoid this extra work, and instead channel all of their funding through developing country governments and various intermediary organizations. It is true that the IRS requirements are strict; but the RBF's willingness to comply with them actually freed us to play a direct role in strengthening local action for eco-development on a number of Caribbean islands.

To cite just one example, the RBF made an expenditure responsibility grant to a newly formed organization of local schoolteachers and community development workers on the island of St Vincent, called the Organization for Rural Development (ORD). ORD was created to generate jobs, improve agricultural practices, and raise nutrition standards in rural areas. With modest start-up funding from the RBF, this group was able to extend the reach of its nascent agricultural extension programs,

Grants to non-US organizations

To make an equivalency determination (i.e. to show that a non-US organization is the equivalent of a US public charity), the foundation must obtain and translate into English the founding documents of the organization, including documentation of the legal restrictions on private-benefit, non-charitable activities as well as on lobbying and participation in political campaigns; a detailed description of the purposes of the organization and its past activities; and detailed financial records. This information must be accompanied by an affidavit attesting to the equivalence, signed by an officer of the applicant organization. (Foundations do not need to prove equivalence for religious, medical, or educational organizations.)

Most of the work associated with an equivalency determination takes place before the grant is made. If equivalency cannot be demonstrated, an American private foundation may choose to exercise *expenditure responsibility* – that is, to take responsibility itself for ensuring that grant funds are used for charitable purposes. In this case, the foundation must do more work along the way. After a pre-grant inquiry to ascertain that the grantee is capable of fulfilling the charitable purposes of the grant, the foundation and the grant recipient must conclude a grant agreement that commits the grantee to spend the money only for specified charitable purposes; to maintain the grant funds in a separate account for charitable purposes; and to report in detail on how the funds have been spent. The foundation must monitor the grantee's compliance with this agreement.

Should a foundation fail to fulfill its obligations under either of these IRS provisions, that foundation could be penalized and might lose its own charitable status.

meeting a critical need that was not being addressed by government or private agencies. ORD also facilitated other self-help development efforts – for example, by helping villages to experiment with growing high-lysine corn and wing beans, both of which are efficient sources of nutrients and proteins that are important for human health.

As ORD gained strength and met new challenges effectively (the St Vincent government even asked ORD to help with disaster relief after the devastating eruption of the La Soufrière volcano in 1978), the RBF renewed its funding, which totaled $120,000 over six years. Our last, multi-year grant to ORD was for building staff capacity, especially in management techniques, business practices, community development, and agronomy. Long past the time when the RBF ceased to make grants in the Caribbean, ORD continued its work and was widely recognized as an important model for promoting rural development in the region. ORD inspired an entire generation of Vincentians to appreciate how they might grow more of their own food and reduce their dependence on imports. Some ORD projects are still going strong today; the organization's founder, Jethro Greene, is still engaged in public service on St Vincent, and some of the young people who staffed ORD in the later 1970s have matured to become respected community leaders and educators. This is an excellent example of how the RBF's support of community groups helped to cultivate local self-help initiatives and contributed to lasting change.

Nor is ORD an isolated instance. Most often, the risks we took in funding local groups paid off – partly because we had to check out the groups pretty thoroughly in order to meet the IRS criteria, and partly, I think, because we combined our willingness to offer early start-up assistance with a focus on organizational capacity-building. While the projects we funded tended to be modest in scale, they provided important training and employment opportunities that changed people's lives, and they demonstrated fresh, promising approaches to farming, fishing, and forestry. In the new, small countries of the region, such opportunities and demonstrations made a real difference, as did the passion and energy of the local leaders whom we helped to empower.

Going out on a limb ... with a safety net

Although not always utilized by foundations, the IRS-defined procedures described above are familiar options for international grantmakers. But on one occasion during my work in the Caribbean, I persuaded the RBF to deploy a highly unusual grantmaking strategy in order to reduce the risks associated with what I believed might be a good 'bet.' Here was a case in which I wanted to be bold and show that the Fund was responsive to the ideas of emerging local leaders; but I also knew that the officers of the Fund (and I) would be going out on quite a limb, and we would need a safety net of sorts.

In my travels to the region, I had met a group of well-educated Caribbean activists – seven young men from various locations – who were in the process of establishing an organization called Action for Caribbean Transformation (ACT) that would help low-income people in rural areas of the islands improve their own economic and social situations. Some members of the group were motivated by a desire to right historical injustices, but as they described their vision, it seemed to me that ACT's primary mission would be to provide technical assistance, education, and training for eco-development, and to promote improvements in the production and marketing of foodstuffs. This group of highly qualified individuals and their ideas impressed me, as did the multidisciplinary and multinational nature of their proposed collaboration.

In 1976, when ACT was still just a very promising vision, the group asked me if the RBF would step up and make an early commitment that might encourage other funders to look seriously at the organization's potential. While foundations do sometimes approve small 'planning grants' to help with the development of a project idea, this amounted to a rather different proposal. We were being asked to promise support to an organization before it had even been properly incorporated as an NGO – and before its work plan, key staff, and budgetary assumptions could be assessed.

I immediately wondered if the RBF might make a conditional commitment: if ACT was successfully incorporated by the end of 1977– and if its program plan and organizational structure were clearly laid out, credible, and consistent with the RBF's priorities – then the RBF would release a start-up grant payment of $40,000. When I proposed this strategy to the executive committee of the RBF board, they approved it, and a conditional grant was made.

In early 1977 I met with the group in Trinidad to learn how they were progressing. To my dismay, they had not developed any specific work plans for the early years, or drafted a budget with indications of where the money might come from. Even more troubling was the fact that the group's draft articles of incorporation included references to taking direct political action and influencing legislation – activities that would make it impossible for the RBF to demonstrate ACT's equivalency to a public charity. I could have urged the group to define a set of clearly charitable activities, to be conducted under the aegis of an existing NGO; in that case, I might have recommended to our board that the RBF fund those activities with an expenditure responsibility grant to the established organization. But I knew that even this would be a hard sell for me at home, given the explicitly political nature of the group's intentions and the founders' general reluctance or inability to comply with the requirements that the RBF (and I) were obligated to meet. So in the end I made it clear that our conditional grant could not be paid without changes in the draft articles and more detailed information about how the organization would operate.

As the year went on, ACT never presented revised incorporation papers or program and budgetary materials. Apparently, the group could not get its 'act' together. At the end of 1977 our grant simply lapsed, unpaid.

Throughout my career, I continued to believe that it was part of my job to provide informal advice, whenever possible, to emerging leaders who wanted to create new projects and organizations that might advance the RBF's goals. But in this special case, where we had a high-risk opportunity to help launch a unique new organization, I am grateful that I had the option of offering a conditional grant – and grateful for the RBF's recognition that there are many different kinds of tools in the grantmaker's toolkit.

Tolerating disappointment – and riding out bumpy starts

The decade during which we were active in the Caribbean was also an era of pioneering research and experimentation in renewable energy technologies and the use of scientific aquaculture to address the depletion of fish stocks from overfishing.

In the Turks and Caicos Islands (which is still an overseas territory of the United Kingdom), the RBF had an opportunity to help demonstrate how such sustainable resource-utilization practices could help to conserve an existing ecosystem and create jobs. With a small population of under 10,000, these islands had considerable arable land lying fallow; yet food imports were growing each year. Tourism was emerging as a source of income; but development was taking place without sound planning.

I first traveled to Turks and Caicos to visit the vacation home of a foundation colleague – Charles (Chuck) Webster, president of a family foundation – who shared my interest in conservation in the Caribbean. He introduced me to Chuck Hesse, an American marine biologist and engineer who had settled in Turks and Caicos with his then wife, Kathy Orr (an artist and writer), with the intention of making seminal contributions to sustainable resource use in the Caribbean. It was a serendipitous meeting, during which I learned that the couple had started a non-profit organization called the Foundation for PRIDE (Protection of Reefs and Islands from Degradation and Exploitation), which was conducting experimental programs in wind and solar energy, and the mariculture of conch and spiny lobster.*

A special dinner guest

Meeting Chuck Webster was serendipitous for me in more than one way. As I spent more time with him, I learned that he was also chair of the Garden Committee at The Cloisters, a branch of the Metropolitan Museum of Art located in northern Manhattan. One day in 1984 Chuck called and invited me to dinner at his home on Long Island. It turned out he had invited only one other person to dinner that evening, the head gardener at The Cloisters, Susan Taylor Leach. Susan arrived in her red pick-up truck and afterwards offered me a ride back to the office. Less than two years later, she became Susan Moody; the wedding was held in the garden of Chuck Webster's Long Island home.

I was excited to recommend RBF support for some of these endeavors, which were quite entrepreneurial and even daring (especially the mariculture program). Through successive multi-year grants, the RBF ended up providing a total of $186,000 to PRIDE.

---

* Mariculture is a specialized branch of aquaculture involving the cultivation of marine organisms for food and other products in the open ocean, in an enclosed section of the ocean, or in tanks, ponds, or raceways which are filled with seawater. Mariculture has expanded rapidly since the 1980s and produced important economic, nutritional, and other benefits – although it has also become the subject of some controversy regarding its social and environmental impacts.

Unfortunately, PRIDE's work on renewable energy did not take hold. After PRIDE set up successful model wind and solar projects in Turks and Caicos and elsewhere, Chuck put together a major renewable energy initiative for which he sought funding from a number of venture capitalists. He lined up several deals (totaling about $400,000), but a couple of investors had to pull out at the last minute, and everything fell through. Chuck was crestfallen and exhausted; he decided to focus all of his energies on mariculture.

While PRIDE's renewable energy projects achieved less than we hoped, PRIDE's mariculture initiatives were more productive than we expected. PRIDE built a conch farm in Turks and Caicos that was a state-of-the-art facility. With start-up funding from the RBF and complementary support from other donors, the Turks and Caicos Conch Farm became a leader in the mariculture field. In this case, Chuck succeeded in attracting investors for a for-profit affiliate, called Trade Winds Industries (TWI). By the 1990s TWI was shipping juvenile conch fillets – dubbed 'ocean escargot' – and other products around the world, to specialty restaurants and the aquarium trade. TWI has never sold products within the Caribbean region, in order to avoid competing with local fishermen. The Conch Farm itself has become an eco-tourism attraction.

In addition to our support for PRIDE, I encouraged the RBF to help launch a Turks and Caicos Development Trust that would underpin and promote sustainable development-related activities in the protectorate – including training, education, resource management initiatives, agricultural programs, small-business development, and youth assistance programs. We made grants totaling $90,000 to the Trust between 1982 and 1987.

The Trust got off to a difficult start because of tensions between the local members of the board and the first director. Then the search for a local director failed to turn up anyone suitable. At this critical juncture, Jessica Brown, a young American who had been an intern at PRIDE, was invited to take the reins. She knew the islands and their people quite well by then, and she had an intuitive sense of how to invite interest and cooperation in the mission of the trust.

During her two years as director of the Trust, from 1983 to 1985, Jessica launched important new programs; put the Trust on a more stable financial footing; forged working partnerships with local organizations and youth centers; and gained widespread recognition and respect for the

Trust. Three years after the Trust was founded, Jessica was able to turn the director's baton over to Dalton Jones, a young farmer and agricultural officer from North Caicos, who built upon the active outreach programs that Jessica had started. Then, in the 1990s, the government of Turks and Caicos established the Turks and Caicos National Trust. With broader backing and financial support, the National Trust was able to absorb the entire program and staff of the Development Trust and continue some of its programming. As this experience illustrates, when funders take the risk of supporting new enterprises, they may need to allow time for organizational adjustments and reconfigurations – including, perhaps, changes in leadership – before deciding whether or not a given program is living up to its potential.

Of course, knowing when to 'let go' is also important; most experienced program officers can name a handful of grant relationships that probably should have been terminated earlier than they were, so that scarce dollars could be dedicated to other projects. But looking back on my career, those are the exceptions rather than the rule. I can think of far more instances in which innovative projects that we chose to support – after careful vetting and due consideration – got off to a bumpy start but went on to make a significant impact.

The road not taken

When a foundation decides to commit itself to a particular grantmaking strategy, that typically means *not* pursuing some other strategy. Most foundations do not have the luxury of investing in all of the approaches that might be taken to solving a given problem; my colleagues and I frequently had to remind ourselves that the RBF 'can't do everything' and that we should not spread our grant budgets too thinly. There are also strong arguments to be made for building on the progress made and lessons learned from one's past grantmaking.

In the Caribbean we chose to make ECNAMP a centerpiece of our grantmaking because we believed in the innovative ideas and the grassroots focus that animated Kenton Miller's work in Latin America and were highly relevant to eco-development challenges in the Caribbean. We also knew that in addition to working effectively with local NGOs and community groups, Kenton Miller and Allen Putney had a real ability to identify and help individuals in local, provincial, and national government circles – as

well as in local universities and high schools, parks, and protected areas –
who were interested in eco-development and understood the importance
of land-use planning. We chose to dedicate as much of our remaining
budget as possible to the direct support of indigenous organizations and
emerging leaders, because we wanted to take every chance we could to
empower local people and communities that were already working to solve
their own problems – and because we were acutely aware that many other
donors were either not willing or not able to search out such opportunities.
With hindsight, though, I am very aware that I could have recommended a
rather different path for our grantmaking.

As I mentioned at the beginning of this chapter, Laurance S
Rockefeller – who was chair of the RBF board when I began focusing
on the Caribbean in the 1970s – had a strong interest in advancing the
wise use of resources in the region. Laurance and his advisers had a
close working relationship with Dr Edward Towle, an American scientist
and historian who had moved to the Caribbean with his wife Judith in the
late 1960s. Ed Towle was one of a handful of environmental leaders at
the time who were confronting the complexities of modern development.
In 1972 Ed and Judith founded the Island Resources Foundation (IRF), a
non-profit organization which aimed to protect and enhance the development options of small island systems through research, planning, and providing assistance to self-help efforts. It was Ed who encouraged Laurance
to provide start-up funding for the Caribbean Conservation Association
(CCA). The CCA, which initially was housed at the IRF in the US Virgin
Islands, went on to dominate the conservation landscape in the Caribbean
in the 1970s and 1980s.

I met Ed and Judith during my early program-planning visits to the
islands. I could see that the IRF would be a valuable resource for everyone
who worked on environmental issues in the Caribbean. The IRF clearly
played a unique role in the region, with its emphasis on science-based
problem-solving, technical assistance, proactive analysis of needs, information services, and educational outreach. Because Laurance had supported the Towles in several other endeavors, I could undoubtedly have
built a Caribbean program around the IRF. But I chose not to. I chose to
build on experiences, concepts, relationships, and commitments from my
work in other parts of the developing world, as well as on my own analysis
of needs and opportunities for RBF grantmaking.

While the Fund ended up channeling some support to the IRF between 1977 and 1980 (which they employed very effectively), there came a point when other program priorities and budget constraints prevented me from recommending further funding. While I stayed in touch with the Towles during the late 1970s and early 1980s and had cordial relations with them, they must have felt (as did I) a certain distance between us; because of their earlier relationship with Laurance, I suspect they were puzzled by it.

Edward and Judith Towle, founders of the Island Resources Foundation, dedicated to helping the people of small tropical islands plan for sustainable development while protecting the environmental qualities and unique human cultures and institutions that evolve in island settings. (photo Bruce Potter, taken in the offices of the Island Resources Foundation, 2004)

It is true that I saw more potential through ECNAMP to work with a broad cross-section of people, especially local people at the beginning of their careers. It seemed to me that the IRF was more embedded in traditional scientific and academic networks, often involving a significant number of expatriates. I suspect it is also true that – based on my growing experience as a grantmaker – I was trying to establish a separate pathway from the one Laurance Rockefeller had mapped out in the Caribbean!

Happily, Allen Putney came to know the Towles over the years and turned to the IRF for scientific research and analysis related to some of ECNAMP's projects. In 1985 the RBF and the World Wildlife Fund–US

(WWF–US) commissioned the IRF to conduct a comprehensive evaluation of ECNAMP; the report was exceptionally thorough and insightful. In
addition, in 1986, with modest support from the RBF and the WWF–US,
the IRF launched an analysis of the role of the private sector (for-profit and
non-profit) in the wise management of natural resources in the Caribbean.

Going the extra mile

In 1999, long after the RBF had closed out its Caribbean grantmaking
program, Laurance Rockefeller – who was by then 89 years old – asked
me to become involved again in the region, on a special project. He was
planning a transfer of his last land holding in the Caribbean: Sandy Cay, a
14-acre island with no permanent structures, where he had created a managed 'garden' wilderness area that was open to anyone (as long as they
did not light fires, harm the vegetation, or leave trash behind). Laurance
wanted the island to be a protected area for the use and enjoyment of the
public forever. He asked me to join his close associates, Clayton (Wes)
Frye and Ellen Pomeroy, in pondering his options. When the time came
for us to identify consultants who could help us do our due diligence, I
recommended the Island Resources Foundation, which was still under the
leadership of Ed and Judith Towle. They did a superb job of helping us to
assess broad contextual issues and to review the possible recipients of
Sandy Cay – including international NGOs and a number of local institutions in the British Virgin Islands (BVI).

We all eventually concluded that the most appropriate recipient
would be the BVI National Parks Trust, but the Towles recommended that
we address some institutional capacity-building challenges and legal
framework issues before making a final decision. Laurance was willing to
provide additional funding for this purpose, and after a number of years – in
2008 – Sandy Cay was officially transferred to the National Parks Trust.
The ceremony was moving and impressive; I only wish that Laurance, who
died in 2004 at the age of 94, had been able to attend.

I am grateful to have had the opportunity for periodic one-on-one
conversations with Laurance in those last years before his death, remi-
niscing about everything under the sun. His handling of the Sandy Cay
project was in the best Rockefeller family tradition of going the extra mile to
increase the chances that a project will succeed for the long term.

Our small grants led to a large multi-year grant from USAID and support from other donors for a decade-long program to provide technical assistance and training to environmental NGOs in the region. Insights from this project helped prepare me to think about capacity-building for the NGO sector in Central and Eastern Europe, my next geographical area of responsibility.

In telling this story of the 'road not taken,' I have naturally asked myself if I would make the same choices again, given the opportunity. The answer is that I probably still would have recommended that we support ECNAMP, because of the needs we identified in the Eastern Caribbean and the opportunity to build on RBF-supported work in Latin America. I would not back away from that judgment and recommendation. At the same time, with the benefit of hindsight, I would have reached out much earlier to the IRF and taken more advantage of Ed's proven expertise and Judith's organizational and writing skills. I can see that the RBF's Caribbean program could have benefited considerably if I had worked more closely with the IRF in the early and mid-1980s.

Closing reflections

The RBF's work in the Caribbean illustrated many features of the Fund's philanthropic style that have been highlighted already, such as flexibility, the willingness to act quickly, and a non-bureaucratic approach to the grantmaking process. People in the US and the Caribbean who were acquainted with the philanthropic and foreign-aid sectors regularly commented on how productive the RBF's style was – and how unusual, especially for its time. My own tendency to bring a 'personal touch' to my work and my interest in mentoring emerging local leaders were also viewed as important contributions. I received even more feedback on the importance of this quality from Caribbean partners than I did from people in Africa or Latin America, perhaps because people on the islands were more comfortable expressing themselves in English, and more familiar with Americans generally.

Our work in the Caribbean also strengthened my commitment to another tenet of RBF grantmaking – that organizational capacity-building and leadership development should be part of a foundation's agenda in the developing world (and elsewhere as well). Foundations understandably want to dedicate grant funds to problem-solving, so capacity-building needs often go unmet. But in order for problem-solving work to be sustain-able, there must be skilled and creative people – and effective organiza-tions – available to do it. Making and monitoring an initial project grant to an organization is a way of learning about its strengths and weaknesses, and establishing mutual trust. I felt that if the RBF was willing to consider renewed or multi-year support for an organization, we should also consider whether we could help with building the capacity of the organization and its staff. In addition to incorporating support for capacity-building into our direct grants to NGOs, the RBF also funded organizations that provided skill-building opportunities, including through workshops and training, for local people working on a variety of issues (ECNAMP and the IRF are good examples of organizations that offered such opportunities).

Just as the prospects for sustainable change are enhanced when funders support both project work and capacity-building, the impact of foundation grantmaking can be enhanced by working simultaneously at the grassroots level and at the policy level. In retrospect, I do not think we did enough to fund advocacy and research on business strategies and gov-ernment policies that would have an impact on the environment. Perhaps we would not have been able to make progress on both levels at that time – and perhaps this would have exceeded the limits of our budget and my own capacities. But it is a strategy for change that I was able to incorporate much more effectively into our later work in Central and Eastern Europe.

'Staying the course' – remaining involved for long enough to make a difference – also enhances the prospects for sustainable change, and it has always been an important feature of RBF grantmaking. The RBF has typically remained involved in places and regions for long periods to address tough challenges as effectively as possible. Internationally, that has meant being willing to stay active in a given region for more than a dec-ade and sometimes close to two. But other factors and considerations do sometimes intervene. Our Caribbean program had only been under way for about four years when the RBF board formed a committee to propose new program goals for the Fund; the committee was made up primarily of the 'cousins' serving on the RBF board (children of founding brothers and their sister), plus a couple of non-family trustees. This effort – the first major program review to be led by the brothers' children – was part of the intergenerational shift that had begun to take place within Rockefeller family philanthropy at the time, and it is treated at some length in the next chapter. The point is, I knew by early 1982 that our grantmaking in the Caribbean – and in the developing world generally – would most likely be phased out in the coming years.

Two strategies for managing the leaving of a place – or an issue area, for that matter – are worth mentioning in the Caribbean context. One is the development of an 'exit strategy,' a plan for gradually withdrawing support over a number of years, and for tying off support in a way that leaves an organization as well positioned as possible to sustain itself and grow after the RBF leaves the scene (final support for capacity-building might be appropriate in some cases, for example). In the Caribbean, where many of the islands still faced significant problems of environmental degradation and economic stagnation that continue to stymie their development to this day, I pushed hard for a gradual exit from the region. Ultimately, I was able to make grants in the Caribbean through 1986, some of which were to be paid out through 1988, so the program was not as truncated as it might have been. In a recent communication (2013), Allen Putney mentioned that the RBF's gradual exit was a key factor in allowing ECNAMP ultimately to survive without the Fund's support – and in enabling the establishment of CANARI as an independent NGO that eventually became entirely locally run. I was grateful that the Fund's board and officers shared my sense of the importance of a sound exit strategy. In my view, having such a strategy is imperative for any responsible grantmaking organization.

The second strategy for managing the closure of a program is not in any sense obligatory, but I have found it to be an extraordinarily rewarding and productive option. That is for program officers who care about a region or issue area to find 'non-grant' ways of contributing and remaining involved – with approval from the foundation's senior officers, if time is to be taken from work. In the mid-1980s, for example, I helped to start a foundation, the Jamaican Agricultural Development Foundation (JADF), and was a member of its governing board in the early years. The brainchild of Greg Vaut, who worked at Land O'Lakes (a Minnesota-based dairy cooperative), the JADF contracted with USAID in the 1980s for the shipment of surplus American cheese and butter to Jamaica, where those commodities were then in short supply. The JADF sold the commodities to a processor for retailing to the local population, and the proceeds from those sales went to the foundation's endowment and enabled it to make grants related to agricultural improvement in Jamaica. The JADF is still going strong – and

I turned to Greg Vaut a few years later, when I wanted to help start up an agricultural program in Poland.

I also joined and served for 20 years on the board of a small US foundation, called the Mukti Fund, which had been established in the early 1980s by a law school classmate of mine, Michael Dively. Small though the grants from Mukti were (totaling less than $100,000 a year), they helped to strengthen civil society and foster grassroots action for conservation and eco-development on St Kitts and Nevis. In many respects, these grants carried the RBF's priorities forward – at least in one country – for many years after we closed out our Caribbean program.

Summarizing these 'extracurricular' involvements brings home to me, and perhaps to readers as well, how much I was doing in the 1970s and first half of the 1980s – juggling several overlapping grant programs and devoting a significant share of my own time and expertise to projects in some of the many places I cared deeply about. The truth is, overextension was becoming a challenge for me. When I reviewed the Towles' excellent evaluation of ECNAMP in preparation for writing this chapter, I felt acutely that I should have done more probing and asked some of the very good questions that Ed and Judith raised. I simply did not have the time. For the remainder of my career, I would struggle to balance my desire always to do more, with the desire to nurture important efforts that were already under way. I would also struggle to balance a stimulating, demanding professional life with the needs of my family.

Part Two

CHAPTER SIX

Setting the Stage
1980 to early 2000s

Now, at a time when the leadership of the Fund will soon pass to the next generation, the Planning Committee has reaffirmed the broad goals set forth by the founders of the Fund and is suggesting new strategies for the 1980s. Their recommendations are appropriate to changing times, while still adhering to the long-accepted traditions.

David Rockefeller (then chair of the RBF) and David Rockefeller, Jr (who became chair in 1987), from the preface to the Planning Committee report, released 30 June 1983

In 1980 I was 41 years old and had been working at the RBF for about a dozen years. Quite simply, I loved my job. The philanthropic style of the RBF and the Rockefeller family had proved to be wonderfully compatible with my instincts and convictions. I had been encouraged to embrace new opportunities and responsibilities that expanded my horizons and taught me invaluable lessons. In fact, I felt that my 'generation' of program officers at the Fund had begun to put its own stamp on the RBF's grantmaking approach and strategies. I derived daily inspiration and energy from the realization that my colleagues and I were making a difference on issues that affected the lives of ordinary people – by supporting projects that helped individuals and communities to help themselves; by nurturing new leaders, at all levels of society; by fostering partnerships based on mutual trust and respect; and by advancing promising new strategies for creating a more just and sustainable world.

The next two decades, 1980–2000, would represent the peak of my career, the period during which I felt I was at my most creative, effective, and productive. This was a time of dramatic change in the world; 'grantmaking in the thick of history' is a theme that runs through the next three chapters. It was also a time of transition at the RBF, where a new generation

of Rockefeller family members took the lead in grappling with the implications of those shifting global dynamics for the Fund's programming.

It was a time of professional challenge as well. All of the RBF's
program officers entered this period with severely reduced grantmaking
budgets as a result of the Creel Committee process of the late 1970s.
Then, in 1983, a broad new program framework for the Fund was adopted,
the product of a strategic planning process led by trustees from the 'cousins' generation'. This program framework reflected a clear and compelling
vision, but deliberately left unanswered many questions about how and
where the new thrust should be implemented. I realized that the grantmaking programs in Africa and Latin America for which I was responsible,
still young though they were, would have to be phased out in light of the
new framework, as would the program we had recently launched in the
Caribbean. But at the same time, I had a chance to develop a new grantmaking agenda, for a different region of the world that would advance the
RBF's new strategies. When unexpected opportunities opened up for us
in Central and Eastern Europe (CEE), I came to believe that we could play
an important and timely role in that transforming region.

International context

The 1980s and 1990s were decades of rapid change in many arenas –
technological, social, economic, and geopolitical. Increasingly, national
boundaries were irrelevant to the spread of ideas and ideologies, products and capital, environmental stress and armed conflict. The fundamental interconnectedness of the world and its peoples (and the interconnectedness of the problems that threaten our well-being and that of the planet)
became more evident than ever.

Of course, not all of the decades' trends and developments were
directly relevant to the RBF's international grantmaking program, as it was
framed during those years – although the broad themes of interconnectedness and change would profoundly inform the new program framework.
Perhaps the most crucial developments of the period, from the standpoint
of shaping the Fund's work, took place in the context of East–West relations. And those developments were stunning.

At the start of the 1980s the Soviet Union appeared to be gaining
ground in the Cold War, with show-piece industrial projects, space expe-
ditions, and a growing nuclear arsenal. But by mid-decade it became clear

that beneath the apparent achievements lay rampant corruption and failing economies, as well as deep restlessness in the Eastern bloc countries.* Even before Mikhail Gorbachev came to power in the Soviet Union, with his policies of *glasnost* (openness) and *perestroika* (restructuring), the communist government of Poland was being challenged by the Solidarity movement, spearheaded by shipyard workers in Gdańsk under the leadership of Lech Wałęsa. In Hungary reformers within the communist party were gaining some sympathy and traction; environmentalists protesting against construction of the Nagymaros Dam on the Danube River were leveling criticism at the political system that generated such top-down, short-sighted industrial projects.

To be sure, martial law was imposed in Poland from late 1981 to mid-1983, partly in an effort to squash the Solidarity movement; and throughout the decade, rigid leaders in Czechoslovakia and East Germany refused to budge. Yet cracks kept appearing within the mosaic of communist states, culminating in the historic events of 1989 – the fall of the Berlin Wall and Czechoslovakia's Velvet Revolution – and ultimately in the break-up of the Soviet Union (into the Russian Federation and other independent republics) in 1991. The long Cold War was over and the Iron Curtain was down!

The decade that followed the end of the Cold War saw the gradual and sometimes uneven introduction of democratic practices and free-market principles in the formerly communist countries of Central and Eastern Europe. These societies in transition faced thrilling but daunting challenges in the areas of governance and civic engagement, economic development, and environmental sustainability.

The map of Europe was altered in other ways as well after the Cold War ended. The bloody Yugoslav Wars (1991–5) tore the old Yugoslavia apart shortly after oppressive communist control was lifted. Slovenia, Croatia, and Macedonia declared independence in 1992 and eventually received international recognition. However, an inter-ethnic war continued in Bosnia and Herzegovina until the Dayton Peace Accords of 1995 (negotiated with US, European, and Russian leadership) stopped the bullets and established the Federation of Bosnia and Herzegovina and the Republika Srpska. Serbia (including Kosovo) and Montenegro formed the Federal

* Albania, Bulgaria, Czechoslovakia, East Germany, Hungary, Romania, and Poland.

Republic of Yugoslavia (FRY) in 1992. Serbian military repression led to the Kosovo War of 1996–9, which was ended through action by NATO forces, leaving the question of Kosovo's future status unresolved. While the RBF did not become active in the Balkans until 2000, as described in chapter 10, our observation of events there in the 1990s informed the Fund's decision to consider developing a grantmaking program in the Balkans that would address important needs and take advantage of our experience in Central and Eastern Europe.

A new program framework: One World

By the early 1980s the board and senior staff of the RBF realized that it was time for the Fund to take a fresh look at its grantmaking program. Several factors contributed to this awareness.

The RBF had just emerged from a tumultuous period, the 1970s, during which the staff feared for a time that the Fund might be spent out of existence. Staff and board alike entered the new decade with a sense of relief at the compromise by which less than half of the Fund's endowment was expended – through the Creel Committee grants – and the rest preserved for grantmaking in perpetuity. But we also knew we needed to recalibrate our expectations, at least for the foreseeable future, in light of the Fund's diminished resources. In fact, by the end of 1980 we had already made some necessary adjustments to the scope of our grantmaking programs and their staffing.

By early 1979 three of the brothers and their sister, Abby Mauzé, had passed away. Most of the two dozen children of the brothers and their sister had reached adulthood, and some were already in their 40s and 50s. As the new decade opened, five cousins were elected to the RBF board, making a majority of the nine family members then serving as trustees (Laurance and David, the surviving brothers, and the widows of JDR 3rd and Nelson were also on the board). Over time, many family members from this 'Fourth Generation' – and now, some of their children – would become active trustees, bringing fresh thinking and energy to the Fund's work. Four of the board chairs who served during my tenure were from the cousins' generation: David Rockefeller, Jr, Abby O'Neill, Steven Rockefeller, and Richard Rockefeller (who died tragically as this book went to publication, in a crash of his small plane). All brought discernment and dedication to their roles, as well as active engagement and total

commitment. Clearly, the Fund's leadership had passed to a new generation of Rockefellers, who naturally wanted to put their own stamp on the
RBF's goals and strategies.

RBF board meeting in June 2003 at the Fund's Pocantico Center, when Steven C Rockefeller
was board chair. Among the board members present were five chairs from the Fourth
Generation: Richard Rockefeller (sixth from left), Valerie Wayne (seventh from left), Steven
Rockefeller (eighth from left), Abby O'Neill (fifth from right), and David Rockefeller, Jr (third from
right). (photo: Jerry Thompson)

Finally, we all sensed that, going forward, we would be operating
in a rapidly changing global context. While neither the staff nor the board
could predict what would happen in the world during the coming decades
– and while we recognized that rapid change was hardly unique to our times
– we did appreciate that as a foundation with an international perspective,
we needed to figure out how to address a growing list of complex global
problems with very finite resources.

At this juncture, the RBF created a Planning Committee, chaired
by a cousin, David Rockefeller, Jr, to examine considerations and options
for the Fund going forward. The committee included three other cousins
– Abby O'Neill (daughter of Abby Mauzé), Laurance (Larry) Rockefeller
(son of Laurance, one of the founding brothers), and Jeremy P Waletzky
(then husband of Laurance's daughter, Lucy) – along with two younger
non-family members of the board: Gerald Edelman (a Nobel Prize-winning
biologist affiliated with Rockefeller University) and Peter Goldmark, Jr (an
environmentalist and journalist who then headed the Port Authority of
New York and New Jersey and later became president of the Rockefeller
Foundation).

During an 18-month process that involved the entire board and staff as well as outside advisers, the Planning Committee developed a set of recommendations that represented a fresh vision for the future but also incorporated the core values and concerns that had animated the RBF's work for 40 years. The underlying theme of the Committee's recommendations was to be 'interdependence' – an assertion that was music to my ears! While that term was not then a regular part of my lexicon, the concept certainly was one in which I had believed since my own young adulthood. My belief had only been strengthened during my tenure at the Fund and my interaction with key members of the Rockefeller family, who saw themselves as active citizens of a city (New York), a nation (the United States), and the world.

To quote the Planning Committee report:

> The basic theme of the recommended program – interdependence – presupposes a global outlook and, hence, internationally oriented activity. Such grants are not new to the Fund, although they will now assume a larger proportion of total annual grant funds than before. We expect that United States problems and United States grantees will receive considerable attention [the Fund's longstanding commitment to New York City was also maintained], but within the context of global concerns, not simply national ones.

The Planning Committee explained, in broad terms, what this theme implied for the RBF, and offered a formulation that all of us were now invited to flesh out:

> We have noted as one of the fundamental trends of our period the convergence of national and international frames of reference, and believe this must be the point of departure for an independent foundation which wishes to address and affect the major problems of the end of the twentieth century.
>
> There are many ways in which a grantmaking foundation can respond to this unique challenge. With limited funds to address unlimited problems, we recognize the need to avoid overstating expectations and to bring discipline and imagination to the task of giving our programs the appropriate scale, context, and level of generality.

> With this reality in mind we recommend that the principal part of the
> Fund's program be organized around a global theme – 'One World' with
> two major components: Resources and Security.

While I did not know at the time how this new vision would play out for
me, I felt reaffirmed in what I had been trying to do for the past 15 years.
Input from the program staff received close attention from the Planning
Committee (an approach that was typical of the RBF's management style),
and I was proud that my own submission to the Committee – a memorandum dated 1 July 1982 – proved to be so consistent with the Committee's
analysis. In the conclusion of my memorandum, I wrote:

> In today's world, age-old problems of hunger and poverty and peace persist
> while dramatic new problems of survivability reach center stage. However,
> advances in science and technology, along with prospects for shared
> responsibilities and imaginative analyses, offer a basis for making progress
> with these difficult challenges.
>
> In the process of exploring possible roles for the RBF in responding to
> these problems, the Fund might find guidance both externally, in the reality
> of interdependence – which calls for a global perspective – and in the need
> to leverage limited resources through careful consideration of what other
> agencies are doing; and internally, in the potential for impact provided by
> (1) the tradition of international leadership of the Rockefeller family, (2) the
> Fund's reputation for innovation, and (3) the record of the Fund's programs.
>
> The Fund has valuable experiences in its national and international pro-
> grams that provide a springboard for future action. Four areas that seem
> especially promising for future exploration, and in which an open trustee–
> staff dialogue could lead to fresh thinking, are: (1) leadership and shared
> responsibilities in a changing world, (2) sustainable development, (3)
> opportunity and justice, and (4) philanthropic initiative and cooperation.

Phasing out and phasing in

In the wake of the Creel Committee grants and the 1980 restructuring
of my program to accommodate a smaller budget, I was already talking
to grantees in Africa and Latin America – and shortly thereafter, in the
Caribbean – about the need for a 'phase-down' of the Fund's support. I
was not yet talking about a phase-out. But by late 1982, with the Planning

Committee process more than halfway completed, the handwriting was on the wall. The Committee was aiming for continuity and evolution, rather than dramatic change (indeed, the RBF has avoided the radical shifts of direction that often accompany foundation leadership changes). That said, I could see that a continuation of the Fund's work to promote development in poor countries was not what the Planning Committee had in mind.

I began to think hard about how to exit these programs responsibly, after more than a decade of grantmaking in most instances, and I talked about the situation with our grantees, in a spirit of openness and mutual trust. In retrospect, I should have spent even more time than I did discussing the phase-out with grantees and brainstorming with them about how best to handle it – a lesson I was able to apply some 20 years later, when it became necessary to phase out our CEE-related grantmaking.

Fortunately, it proved easier than I had feared to maintain a meaningful level of activity in the developing country programs. Since so many of the developing country grants were related to sustainable resource use, I was able to make the case that they were not incompatible with the 'Resources' category of the new One World agenda. My success in making that case stands as further evidence of the RBF's flexible and non-bureaucratic style and its commitment to 'staying the course.' In any event, I did not have to rush to close down those programs. We remained engaged in Africa and Latin America into the second half of the 1980s and in the Caribbean for a little longer, even as I became deeply involved in designing and implementing a new international grantmaking program.

It was serendipity as well as close analysis that led me to recommend Central and Eastern Europe (and initially, the Soviet Union) as a new focus for our international work. In late November 1981, at a meeting hosted by David Rockefeller for the President of the General Assembly of the United Nations, David was approached by Bohdan Lewandowski, then Under Secretary General of the United Nations. Lewandowski asked David if the Rockefeller family might be able to help the Polish people at a time when the Jaruzelski government, faced with threats from Moscow as the Solidarity movement gained strength, was forced to take action to control the situation. When President Jaruzelski's measures provoked public protests and economic stress, the police cracked down on the populace. This was the kind of humanitarian crisis that the Rockefeller family has typically tried to help address, and I was tasked with figuring out how the Fund

might be helpful. Ultimately, I recommended as a first step the establishment of a program that would enable Polish scholars and writers who were
living abroad to remain there safely.

As I learned more about Poland and its neighboring countries, I
began to realize this was a region where the RBF could use its limited
resources to address important resource management and security problems, while building new bridges between East and West. Relatively few
American or Western European foundations were active then in CEE countries or the Soviet Republics (ethnically based administrative units that
were subordinated to the government of the Soviet Union). To the extent
that funders focused on the Soviet Union, the emphasis was primarily on
superpower relations and nuclear worries. Concern about environmental
problems in the region was just beginning to appear on the agendas of
private and government donors. The door was still wide open for a US
foundation like the RBF to make a meaningful contribution to East–West
relations and to address issues inside CEE countries and the Soviet Union
that often had much wider impacts.

In late 1983, with the full backing of then RBF president Bill Dietel,
I recommended the establishment of a CEE/Soviet Union initiative under
the new One World program. Given our limited funds, I suggested that we

Overview of my budgets in the 1980s and 1990s
**Africa, Latin America, the Caribbean, and international
cooperation (phase-out process)**
The total budget for this purpose was reduced to $1.2 million in 1980 and
remained at this level until the end of 1982. In 1983 the budget began to
drop by $200,000 a year – down to $400,000 in 1986. This was the last
year of developing country/international cooperation grantmaking, with
final payouts in 1987 and 1988 at the annual rate of $300,000.

**New One World program: Central and Eastern Europe
and former Soviet Union**
Budgeting for this new programming began in 1983 at $200,000 and
increased to $600,000 in 1984, to $1 million by 1988, and to $1.6 mil-
lion by 1994. It remained at $2 million between 1996 and 2000, with a
phase-down and phase-out process continuing until final grants were
paid in 2004.

take an opportunistic approach in the beginning, with special attention to Poland, Hungary, and what was then Czechoslovakia – the northern tier CEE countries – and that efforts be made to determine if appropriate Soviet Union-related grantmaking might be possible as well. My proposal was approved by the board, and a dynamic, evolving new program was launched.

Initially, in the 1980s, we seized opportunities to address both the 'resources' and the 'security' dimensions of the One World program in selected CEE countries and (through support of broader work on East–West relations) the Soviet Union. In the 1990s, eager to respond to the momentous political developments of 1989, we refined the program to focus on promoting sustainable resource use and the rebirth of civil society in Central and Eastern Europe (specifically in Poland, Czech Republic, Slovakia, and Hungary), where communist regimes had destroyed efforts to create or recreate the democratic civil societies that several CEE countries – especially Czechoslovakia – had known after the First World War.

The evolution of the Fund's CEE program is traced in the next three chapters – from those early years of opportunistic grantmaking, when we pursued a diverse range of strategies; through the tremendous burst of optimism and energy that followed the fall of the Berlin Wall; to the second half of the 1990s, a period of recalibration as we saw local environmental groups being outmaneuvered by well-financed, politically savvy developers and business interests, and attempted to respond to the capacity needs of the nascent NGO sector in the region.

Back in the 1980s and 1990s, such means of communication were still essential! Here I am in Budapest, Hungary. (photo: Susan Moody)

Closing reflections

Looking back on this productive and immensely satisfying phase of my career, I realize how fortunate I was to work for an organization that enjoyed extraordinary staff and board leadership. The dedicated Rockefeller family members and other knowledgeable individuals who served on the RBF board provided consistently sound guidance and governance – and they were interested in my work and eager to learn about it. In fact, in 1991, the RBF board and senior staff came to CEE on a 'trustee trip,' which brought them into direct contact with some of the individuals and organizations we were supporting, as well as with a broader cross-section of people living in the region.

Three remarkable presidents – Dana Creel, who was director from 1951 to 1969 and then president until his retirement in 1975; Bill Dietel, who served from 1975 until his retirement in 1987; and Colin Campbell,

A new chapter in my personal life

The 1980s was a transitional decade for me personally, bookmarked by my divorce from Katie at the outset and my father's death at the end of the decade. My two sons, Scott and John, were teenagers, becoming young adults; I was living in a small apartment on the Upper West Side of New York City, and they stayed in the family home with their mother in Larchmont, about 30 minutes north of NYC on a commuter train. So we were not far apart geographically – but I regretted deeply not being able to spend as much time with them as I had imagined I would when they were young. It was not good for them or me, as I look back. I treasure memories of summer vacations with the boys at my parents' cottage on Lake Michigan, a trip to Europe (including Prague and Moscow) with John during his senior year in high school, and Scott's surprise week with Susan and me in Europe after his graduation from college and during my sabbatical there. As I write this book so many years later, I realize how proud I am of both of my sons.

And it was in the middle of the 1980s that I met and married Susan Taylor Leach, my wife now for more than 27 years and the mother of our daughter Megan. Two remarkable women! Both have helped to shape my thinking over the years, including about how to live in a way that respects, preserves, and protects the environment. Both have brought a great deal of joy to the new chapter of my life that began in that transitional decade.

who led the Fund from 1988 until he left in 2000 to become president of the Colonial Williamsburg Foundation – contributed to the positive atmosphere which sustained and propelled me through those two decades.* Bill and Colin were both experienced leaders of staffs and organizations; each in his different way nurtured, encouraged, and sometimes cajoled me. Russell Phillips was a wise and thoughtful executive vice president, who also served ably as interim RBF president between Bill's departure and Colin's arrival. The board chairs who followed the brothers Laurance and David – David, Jr, Abby O'Neill, Steven Rockefeller, and Richard Rockefeller – were visionary yet practical. RBF staff had regular contact with these family members, as well as with the other committed trustees. Without such exceptional leadership, I am not sure I would have been able to manage the converging challenges and opportunities that are described in this overview and in the following chapters.

During this period, I suppose I became a happy 'workaholic.' I loved my work and had lots of energy. But senior staff at the Fund recognized that I was working long hours month after month, and had been doing so as long as anyone could recall. I was content – but it's true that I wasn't always realistic about taking on additional challenges, and I was always inclined to think I could 'do it all.' When Russell Phillips suggested that we catch up over lunch, in the late summer of 1986, I assumed we were going to review various program and budget considerations. Instead, Russell told me that Bill Dietel and he were concerned that I was going to burn out; they urged me to take a block of time off – and they offered a one-year paid sabbatical overseas.

Once I got over worrying that this was the RBF's gracious way of letting me go, Susan and I planned a year in Europe filled with time to explore, observe, read, and engage with local people. I also chose to devote part of the time to developing a better understanding of the Central and Eastern European countries. We rented apartments in Warsaw, Kraków, and Budapest, and traveled widely in Poland, Czechoslovakia, Hungary, Bulgaria, and the regions that would become Croatia, Montenegro, Kosovo, and Serbia. Susan received a work reassignment from the Metropolitan Museum of Art to study medieval plants and gardens in Western, Central,

---

* The influence of Stephen Heintz, who became president of the RBF in 2000, was felt primarily during the years covered in the third part of this book.

and Eastern Europe for The Cloisters. During the course of my sabbatical year, she met with botanists, monks, seed growers, herb specialists, and garden librarians and was introduced to their collections. Wherever we went, from villages to high mountain meadows, our walks would slow to a crawl when Susan spotted a familiar medieval plant growing in the wild and halted to take its picture! Susan returned to New York filled with fresh ideas and plants for the Museum's gardens – many of which thrive to this day. I returned with insights and experiences that I would draw on for the next 20 years of my professional life.

I will always be grateful to Bill and Russell and the board for knowing me better, perhaps, than I knew myself, and for giving me time to recharge my batteries at a critical point in my career.

From left to right: John, Megan, and Scott Moody in the 1990s, in our apartment in New York City.

With my wife Susan, a decade ago, in front of the waterfall at the Simon Pearce glass-blowing facility, showroom, and restaurant on the Ottauquechee River in Vermont.

Finland

Norway

Sweden

Estonian
SSR

Latvian
SSR

Russian SFSR
(Soviet Federative
Socialist Republic)

Lithuanian
SSR

Denmark

Netherlands

Byelorussian SSR

Belgium

United
Kingdom

German
Democratic
Republic

People's Republic
of Poland

Ireland

Federal
Republic of
Germany

Czechoslovak
Socialist Republic

Ukrainian SSR

France

Austria

People's
Republic of
Hungary

People's
Republic
of Romania

Moldavian
SSR

Federal People's
Republic of
Yugoslavia

Italy

Switzerland

People's Republic
of Bulgaria

Georgia

Spain

Turkey

People's
Republic of
Albania

Portugal

Greece

Cyprus

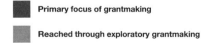 Primary focus of grantmaking

Reached through exploratory grantmaking

SSR   Soviet Socialist Republic

CHAPTER SEVEN

The Convergence of Opportunity and Strategy
Central and Eastern Europe, 1980s

Moral resistance, though seemingly hopeless against systems
that are based on political and military force, functions like
a grain of sand in the cogwheels of a vast but vulnerable
machine. The idea of a civil society – even one that avoids
overtly political activities in favor of education, the exchange of
information and opinion, or the protection of the basic interests
of particular groups – has enormous anti-totalitarian potential.

Bronisław Geremek, from a speech delivered in 1991 at a conference,
The Idea of a Civil Society, hosted by the National Humanities Center[*]

In the latter half of the 19th century, when John D Rockefeller began to accumulate unprecedented wealth, he also started to receive letters – ultimately,
baskets full each day – from individuals asking for financial assistance.
Given his strong Baptist commitment to charitable giving, Rockefeller tried
to review and assess all of those letters, sending money when he deemed
it appropriate. Eventually, though, he was overwhelmed by the thousands
of requests. With the help of his associate and adviser Frederick Gates,
he began to look for more systematic and lasting ways to contribute to the
betterment of society. Their search led ultimately to the establishment of a
philanthropic foundation – the Rockefeller Foundation – that would focus
on root causes and lasting solutions to pervasive problems.

But over the years, even as organized philanthropy became an
increasingly important channel for Rockefeller giving, members of the

[*] Geremek, who died in 2008, was an influential participant in the 'Round Table Talks' in
1989 between Solidarity and the communist authorities that paved the non-violent way to a
free and democratic Poland. A social historian, Geremek was widely respected in Poland
and throughout Europe and served as Poland's Minister of Foreign Affairs between 1997
and 2000.

family continued to respond to humanitarian crises and to individual appeals that they believed offered opportunities to make a positive impact on their communities, the nation, or the world. When Polish diplomat Bohdan Lewandowski took David Rockefeller aside for a private conversation in November 1981, he certainly was aware of the family's past humanitarian efforts. Lewandowski would have known, as well, of David's deep personal interest in international affairs and strong opposition to communism. By this time Poland's Solidarity trade union movement was making good progress in opening space for debate. But the Polish government, led by General Wojciech Jaruzelski, feared a Soviet invasion of the sort that had taken place in Czechoslovakia after the Prague Spring of 1968, and was considering establishing martial law to head it off; such an action would suppress Solidarity. Lewandowski was worried about the consequences for Polish citizens if martial law was to go into effect, and asked if David and his colleagues at the RBF might take an interest in the plight of Polish citizens.

Neither David (who was then chairing the RBF board) nor the RBF had played any philanthropic role in Poland, but David believed we should consider this request carefully to determine if we could help. David turned to RBF president Bill Dietel, who turned to me. I began to investigate the possibilities. Our response to the Lewandowski request ultimately led to our creating the first independent foundation to be established in Poland and probably in the entire region since the Second World War – and pointed the way toward what would become a multi-decade program of grantmaking in Central and Eastern Europe and later in the Western Balkans.

Early efforts lead to further RBF involvement

Shortly after I began my analysis, President Jaruzelski instituted martial law, on 13 December 1981. The official government position was that martial law was necessary to forestall a Soviet occupation, but in fact many Solidarity leaders were interned, as were others who had voiced criticism of the regime's policies or legitimacy. I learned that steps to help the Polish people were already being taken by the Catholic Church, Polish diaspora groups in various countries, and other non-governmental, governmental, and international agencies. But, on the basis of my consultations with a range of experts, including Poles and others in the US, I learned about one need and opportunity that was not being addressed and that had special

With Bohdan Lewandowski, former UN Undersecretary General, in front of the Ghetto Heroes Monument in Warsaw, Poland, in the mid-1990s. (photo: Barbara Liberska)

long-term appeal: the plight of Polish writers, academics, and students who were then visiting or studying in the West. Many of these individuals were losing their stipends and being summoned home, where they faced persecution or incarceration.

To address these challenges, the RBF took the lead in organizing a 'stranded scholars' program, which was administered by the International Research and Exchanges Board (IREX). We spearheaded a fundraising effort that provided over $500,000 from several sources – including the Ford Foundation and Chase Manhattan Bank – to more than a hundred scholars stranded in nine countries, allowing them to continue their work and residencies abroad, with their families, until martial law was lifted in mid-1983.

Even as I threw myself into this project, in 1982 and early 1983, I remained very involved in my existing grantmaking programs in the developing world – which would gradually be phased out over the coming years, as explained in the previous chapter. And like all of my colleagues, I was following and occasionally contributing to the work of the RBF's trustee Planning Committee, which had been tasked with developing a new vision for the future of the RBF at a time when the leadership of the Fund was passing to a new generation. The committee's official recommendations had not yet been polished or approved; the board would not actually endorse what was eventually called the One World program until the summer of 1983. But already it seemed likely that the committee would reaffirm the Fund's longstanding interests in resource management and international relations/security, framed within a global context of increasingly complex problems that would require for their solution the building of new bridges between East and West.

My research on Poland and nearby countries led me to believe that this was a region where the RBF could implement such a new vision while also pursuing some of the proven strategies that had guided our work in the developing world – like empowering local people to face their challenges more effectively and building trust through collaborative, practical efforts in areas of concern to the Fund. Many CEE countries and Soviet Republics had strong conservation ethics before the communists took power and began the wholesale exploitation and destruction of the region's natural resources (a trend with negative implications not only for CEE but for Europe as a whole). Some CEE countries also had a tradition of philanthropic activity and civic engagement. Furthermore, these countries were often considered to be a kind of 'transmission belt' between the East and the West. CEE scholars and writers were more able to teach or study in the West than their Soviet counterparts, who might be allowed to travel to a Central or Eastern European country but not to the West. When travelers from CEE returned from the West, they shared what they learned not only with their own colleagues, but also with visiting academics from neighboring countries, including the Soviet Republics. Only a small number of donors, including the Ford Foundation and, later, George Soros, were funding opportunities for this kind of East–West (and East–East) contact in the early 1980s.

All this notwithstanding, those were very tense and dramatic times in Poland. After the imposition of martial law, there were shortages of many essential items; the lines at food shops were blocks long, and concerns were growing about food availability in urban areas. There were daily riots in Warsaw and the police were using tear gas and water cannons routinely to disperse the crowds. Diplomatic relations between the United

States and Poland had been suspended and the US ambassador with-drawn. It was against this backdrop of promise and hardship that Bill Dietel encouraged me to follow my train of thought, and to investigate some of the options for further RBF involvement in Poland.

Among those with whom I consulted in these early days were a colleague at the Rockefeller Foundation (RF), Dr Edward Deagle, director of the International Relations Division there, and his postdoctorate intern from Poland, Dr Marcin Sar. Ed, Marcin, and I quickly recognized the potential for synergy and the advantages of our two foundations working together. Patricia (Trix) Smalley, then philanthropic adviser to David Rockefeller – who by then had retired as Chase CEO and board chair but was just as active as ever from Room 5600, Rockefeller Plaza – agreed to roll up her sleeves, too. While the joint payroll arrangement that allowed me to be employed both by the RBF and by individual members of the Rockefeller family had been terminated some years earlier, I had continued to collaborate periodically and enjoyably with David and Trix (who died prematurely in 2011) on special projects that were related to the RBF's priorities, so ours was a very comfortable partnership.

Ed, Trix, and I – with considerable help from Marcin – organized sev-eral RF/RBF-sponsored meetings to learn from a cross-section of people with experience in East–West relations, Central and Eastern Europe, and specific topics of interest to both foundations, such as agriculture and the environment. We asked the Rockefeller Foundation's senior agricultural-ist, Dr Norman Borlaug (a Nobel Laureate and considered by many to be the father of the Green Revolution), to take an inspection trip to Poland; a longer trip was arranged for Dr Borlaug and a small team of experienced practitioners and experts some months later. The team's report indicated that the agricultural sector in Poland presented urgent needs and special opportunities. In contrast to the situation in other countries behind the Iron Curtain, Poland's communist authorities never successfully collectivized the agricultural sector. Even in the early 1980s, private farmers continued to work 75 per cent of the arable land and provide nearly 80 per cent of the farm produce in the country – this despite pricing, marketing, and land tenure schemes that discriminated against private farmers, and the gov-ernment's efforts to prevent them from securing such basic supplies as farm machinery, spare parts, fertilizers, seeds, and pesticides, as well as up-to-date know-how.

We began to ask ourselves how we might help to revitalize the agricultural sector in Poland – which had once provided substantial surpluses for export – while also promoting East–West dialogue and modeling an approach to self-help that could enhance public confidence and improve the prospects for change in Poland and elsewhere behind the Iron Curtain. We formed a steering committee and together began to sort through some of the legal, political, and practical issues that would arise if we were to take this course. The committee was chaired by Dr Leon Irish, an international lawyer and a former law school classmate of mine, and directed by Dr J B Penn, a seasoned agricultural expert who had been part of Dr Borlaug's assessment team.

Creating a new institution

The steering committee realized that in order to empower and support Poland's private farmers, we would need to create a new institution that was independent of the government; that could earn the trust and respect of farmers themselves; and that had the courage and muscle to push back against communist leaders who might try to block any steps taken toward market-oriented principles and practices. In 1984, with strong support from Bill Dietel, we initiated what would turn out to be four years of complex and often frustrating negotiations with officials of the communist government about the legal framework and charter of the institution that would become known as the Foundation for the Development of Polish Agriculture (FDPA).

While Ed and Marcin left our team in 1984 (when the RF's grant-making priorities changed and Marcin's postdoctorate came to an end), Trix and I, together with Lee Irish and J B Penn, stayed the course – with David Rockefeller an occasional but active participant in the process. David spent many hours staying up to speed on matters relating to the project, and met several times with Polish leaders (including President Jaruzelski) to advance it. He visited Poland to launch the foundation; then, a decade later, he and I traveled to Poland again to assess the progress being made. His personal involvement was noted and deeply appreciated by colleagues on the ground in Poland.

Our negotiations with the Polish government produced some important results that not only would help the FDPA function effectively,

'Western Fund to Aid Polish Farmers'

From an article by Kathleen Teltsch, published in the *New York Times*, 21 February 1988; illustrated by a photograph of David Rockefeller and Polish president Wojciech Jaruzelski in Warsaw:

> With help from David Rockefeller and encouragement from the Polish authorities, a foundation has been set up in Poland to stimulate the lagging agriculture and food industries.
>
> It is believed to be the first enterprise of its kind: a foundation in an Eastern bloc country using private, Western start-up money for an economic venture whose profits will go for philanthropic activities benefiting private farmers . . .
>
> 'To me this is what philanthropy is all about,' Mr Rockefeller said, before he and Dr Borlaug flew to Warsaw this weekend for the foundation's inauguration . . . 'It is my hope that this foundation will serve the farmers and people of Poland, increase dialogue and continue to improve Polish–American relations and serve as a model for the creation of similar institutions in socialist countries throughout the world.'

but also would provide a model for other entities in the region that sought to engage in philanthropic or international transactions.

– The steering committee was instrumental in the creation of a legal provision that was then unique in Central and Eastern Europe, permitting the establishment of foundations that defined philanthropy broadly as 'socially beneficial action.' This law enabled foundations to engage in revenue-producing commercial activities, so long as the surpluses, profits, and income are invested exclusively in the philanthropic purposes for which the foundation was established.

– Our negotiated agreement gave the FDPA both actual and perceived independence from Polish government authorities, by ensuring that 60 per cent of the governing council seats would be held by non-Polish nationals. The Polish government would have the authority to veto but not to nominate candidates for the remaining 40 per cent of the seats.

– The steering committee negotiated for the FDPA a ten-year period free from income and sales tax, in order to buffer it from the bureaucratic and political vagaries of communist rule (which we assumed would continue for the foreseeable future).

The FDPA held its inaugural meeting in February 1988, well before the historic changes that took place throughout Central and Eastern Europe in the autumn of 1989. Its original governing council had the 'muscle' we thought the FDPA would need to operate in a hostile political environment. The council consisted of 40 members, including members of our steering committee plus respected individuals from Western Europe, North America, and Poland. After Poland elected a democratic government in August 1989, a streamlined governing board was created. The new, smaller governing board consisted of some people from the former governing council and some entirely new members, with special attention paid to identifying non-US individuals whose presence on the board would make the point that this was not an American-run show. I remained on the governing board for about a dozen years, as Polish nationals, over time, replaced the original steering committee members on the board.

Foundation for the Development of Polish Agriculture: programs and operations

The FDPA hit the ground running, with some big initial successes. Today, more than 25 years later, the foundation is going strong. But there were stumbles and struggles in the interim, both with respect to management (staff leadership in the 1990s was uneven, and the FDPA did not succeed in finding a suitable Polish candidate for CEO until 1998, a decade after the foundation began) and with respect to programming.

1988-90

The FDPA's initial focus was on providing concrete and practical assistance to Poland's farmers and agricultural sector, while also building the FDPA's own capital base. A ham export project, for example, initiated with the help of a $2.4 million line of credit from an Austrian bank, distributed more than 6,000 tons of feed to some 5,000 private farmers in 1988 and 1989, which helped farmers raise more hogs, export more ham, and respond to domestic demands for meat. This project generated hundreds of thousands of dollars in revenues for the foundation that were used (for example) to bring international scientists together to help address the late-blight threat to potato production in Poland and elsewhere, and to establish a program of seminars that gave hundreds of farmers access to new agricultural technology. In 1989 the FDPA secured a contract to manage a European Community aid package worth $60 million, putting farm inputs (pesticides, fertilizers, and seeds) in the hands of private farmers and producing more than $2 million in net revenues for the FDPA. Unlike earlier Western food donations to Poland, which benefited urban consumers but neglected the needs of farmers, this program directed substantial assistance to Poland's agriculture sector. Among the several contractors involved in this program, the FDPA had the best track record for efficiency and scope of distribution.

1990s

This was a challenging decade for the FDPA. Some of the investments that it undertook with surpluses from earlier revenue-producing projects proved to be unwise and poorly implemented. At one point, net losses from what was called the Demonstration Investment Program nearly wiped out the FDPA's capital base. In addition, the dramatic market oriented reforms and government transitions that followed the end of communist rule in Poland produced upheavals in the agricultural sector and food economy. The closure and downsizing of state and cooperative farms led to increased unemployment in rural areas.

Fortunately, one of the strategies that the FDPA had begun to deploy to stimulate business and job creation in rural areas – micro-lending – began to make significant contributions to the foundation's financial stability. In 1991 the FDPA launched a program called Women in Rural Enterprise Development, which disbursed more than 600 loans (together with entrepreneurial training and advisory services) and created nearly 2,000 jobs in its first seven years. This was the forerunner of a major micro lending program that has grown significantly since then and helped to put the FDPA back on a sound financial footing.

Other innovative programs were also launched in the 1990s, but unfortunately the FDPA's financial struggles meant that it was not able to follow up on all of them – including promising pilot projects that focused on promoting small-scale rural tourism and sustainable farming practices. These projects, dear to the hearts of some governing-board members (including myself and Bill Dietel, who retired from the FDPA board in 1992), proved to be difficult to fund and so did not receive the staff attention they would have required to take hold. I have been pleased to note that the FDPA has moved sustainability concerns to the foreground of its work in more recent years.

1998–2012

By the late 1990s it was becoming increasingly clear that agriculture and the food economy alone could not support economic development and improved living standards in rural areas. More attention was needed to non-farm employment generation, and to the bigger picture of sustainable rural development.

Based on lessons learned during the early 1990s, the FDPA restructured and enlarged its micro-lending program for rural small businesses. Interest rates and repayment schedules were adjusted to ensure that the lending program covered its own costs and produced small surpluses for the capital fund; these changes encouraged more international agencies to contribute to the micro-loan fund. Since 1999 the FDPA has attracted more than $20 million (about PLN 60 million) from the World Bank and other sources to build a micro-loan fund that amounts to $30 million today. There has been a fourfold increase in the number of active loans (from 250 to 1,000), with a loan default rate of less than 2 per cent. Through more than 2,200 loans, FDPA has helped to create about 3,800 new jobs in rural areas of Poland. The FDPA is now consistently among the top ten micro-lending institutions active in Poland today, according to the Polish Association of Lending Funds.

Also in the past 15 years, the FDPA has begun to act as a policy think-tank, producing biennial reports on rural development that cover economic, social, demographic, environmental, and political considerations. As one of the most influential NGOs in the region, the FDPA recently has become a leader in creating and coordinating various regional networks that encourage the exchange of knowledge and experience among non-governmental and governmental agencies that focus on rural development challenges (including challenges associated with accession of CEE countries to the European Union).

The FDPA was a pathbreaking initiative before the Berlin Wall came down; after the historic events of 1989, the FDPA matured (despite difficulties along the way) into an important and increasingly self-sustaining not-for-profit organization. The foundation has been an innovative and bold player in both the rebirth of democratic civil society and the restoration of a market economy in Poland. The FDPA made mistakes, but learned from many of them – thanks to staff and governing-board members who were committed to working through problems and repositioning the foundation when it became necessary.

Long-term engagement and the willingness to take risks

I have told the FDPA story at some length because it illustrates a number of Rockefeller philanthropic traditions that already had shaped and would continue to shape my career at the RBF.

Of special importance to our first decade of involvement in CEE was the Fund's ability to think long-term about its commitment to an issue or region, and to 'stay the course.' I felt from the start that any RBF effort to help improve the lives and prospects of the Polish people would need to be sustained for at least a decade if it was to have meaningful impact. My colleagues and the Fund's trustees were willing to embrace that kind of commitment. In the end, we remained active in Poland for 23 years (1981– 2004), and for almost that long in neighboring Central European countries.

Equally important was the RBF's openness to seizing unforeseen opportunities. In our CEE programming, as in a number of other new program areas over the years, we program officers were encouraged to explore and experiment during the initial phase of program implementa- tion. We realized that as newcomers to a region or issue area, we had our own learning curve to follow. Even in established program areas, the Rockefeller philanthropic tradition left space for opportunistic actions. I believe this tradition of flexibility and responsiveness, backed up by the Fund's tradition of careful due diligence and attention to legal require- ments, made a positive difference in our grantmaking. Sometimes, I admit, this approach ended up putting the cart before the horse; certainly, the proper balance between flexibility and adherence to stated grantmaking goals and strategies is a subject for legitimate debate.

The FDPA story also illustrates the RBF's willingness to take risks – and to tolerate stumbles and course corrections along the way. We did not have a roadmap to follow in creating the FDPA. Among other consid- erations, our decision to emphasize revenue-producing activities as well as traditional philanthropic programs definitely complicated the FDPA's set-up and its ongoing operations. My colleagues and I on the governing board believed such activities would be essential to the FDPA's long-term financial sustainability, and when FDPA staff proposed some big, risky investments in the early 1990s, a divided steering committee ultimately gave them the green light. The resulting losses nearly undid everyone's hard work. Fortunately, we had an open internal process by means of which the FDPA staff and board could assess what was going wrong and work together to correct course. I am sure there were times during the 1990s when some RBF trustees and staff felt that the FDPA initiative was proving to be too risky; but the predisposition to persevere for the sake of an important project was always there.

Obviously, the story of the FDPA is also the story of a deeply engaged program officer. As previous chapters have shown, the preference for active engagement was both part of my own style and personality, and part of the Rockefeller philanthropic tradition. The role I played in the creation and evolution of the FDPA, however, stands out as one of the most intensive and important involvements I ever had with a grantee organization.

Can a staff member of a donor organization appropriately serve on the governing board of a grantee organization? This is a controversial subject! I struggled with 'conflict of interest' questions throughout my long tenure on the FDPA governing board (and during my service on a few other grantee boards over the years). That tension took various forms. In the early 1990s, when we debated those investment decisions that proved to be so unwise, my role as representative of the largest donor organization made me hesitate to oppose the majority preference, so I did not voice my own reservations as strongly as I should have. But I do believe that there are times when one can wear two hats effectively and accountably – as is common practice for venture capitalists. Given the risks that the RBF was taking and the fact that the FDPA was breaking new ground in many respects, I thought this was one of those occasions on which the benefits outweighed the risks. Of course, I took steps to ensure transparency and recused myself from certain kinds of discussions.

Did the actively engaged FDPA governing board – myself included – spend too much time on this initiative? It is true that deciding when to 'let go' can be difficult for program officers who care deeply about the work of their grantees. On the other hand, I am fairly certain that the FDPA would not have survived the 1990s without our steady commitment, and that would have been a real loss.

Building out a new grantmaking program

The FDPA story unfolded in parallel with my own and the Fund's growing excitement about Central and Eastern Europe as a region where the RBF could usefully pursue both of the One World program goals that were adopted in summer 1983: encouraging sustainable approaches to resource use that blend social, economic, and ecological considerations; and improving the prospects for world peace, including by bringing East and West together in substantive arenas of mutual interest. In late 1983 the RBF board had approved my recommendations for an opportunistic grantmaking initiative focusing on sustainability and security challenges in Poland, Hungary, and what was then Czechoslovakia (the northern tier CEE countries), with an accompanying exploration of whether some Soviet Union-related grantmaking might be possible as well. So even as I became intensely involved in the establishment of the FDPA, I was also deeply engaged in developing this new program area, which rekindled the keen interest I had felt in Europe as a history major at Northwestern University and as a foreign-exchange student in Geneva and Brussels.

As I had discovered through my work in the developing world, I really enjoyed the challenge of helping to shape a new grantmaking program. And while tensions remained high between East and West, the decade of the 1980s also was characterized by great ferment within the USSR and CEE. A generation of leaders was aging, brave citizens were questioning the legitimacy of their non-responsive governments, and new communications technologies had begun to pierce the Iron Curtain. It was a time of fresh thinking, experimentation, and protest throughout the region. The RBF was able to identify quite a few indigenous organizations with missions relevant to our broad One World program goals (key passages from which are excerpted in the box overleaf). This was especially true in the area of sustainable resource use. That said, it was not easy to make grants directly to organizations in the CEE and Soviet Union; there were problems in ensuring that the money would reach the proper bank accounts and be employed by the intended recipients for the desired purposes. So just as in the developing-world context, but for different reasons, we sometimes

One World program guidelines (excerpts)

One World: sustainable resource use

Goal: To encourage more efficient and renewable use of natural, human, and man-made resources, in an approach that blends social, economic, and ecological concerns.

Strategies: Defining and advocating the philosophy of sustainable resource use on a global basis through action research and other projects that employ comprehensive approaches to resources management; implementing the philosophy of sustainable resource use through support of clusters of organizations and projects in forestry, agriculture, fisheries, and bioenergy that are creating more renewable resource practices which are less destructive to land, forest, air, water, and human resources.

One World: global security

Goal: to strengthen arms control, improve international relations, and encourage development, trade, and finance – recognizing that prospects for world peace are threatened not only by competing political philosophies or differing religions and cultural traditions but also by frustration and aggression bred by inequities in sharing of food, energy, goods, and services produced by the world economy.

Relevant strategy: Supporting interrelated activities of public information and education, exchanges, internships and joint work with the Soviet Union and, particularly, Eastern Europe in substantive fields of mutual interest.

turned to intermediary organizations that could receive the funds and work in collaboration with local organizations on the ground.

Overall, during the 1980s, we provided a total of $2.5 million through 25 grants for sustainable resource use-related purposes, and nearly $3 million through 20 grants for security-related purposes. A few examples from each issue area will illustrate the rich opportunities that were opening up during these years.

Sustainable resource use

The communist economic and political system had tragic environmental consequences for the Soviet Union and countries behind the Iron Curtain. Communist ideology encouraged humans to try to conquer nature, upending local practices that typically emphasized conservation and wise use of

Traveling in the region

In 1983 I made my first visit to Central and Eastern Europe and the Soviet Union since I was in college, traveling from Warsaw to Minsk to attend an international conference. Departing from Warsaw Central Station for the 16-hour trip, I shared a sleeper compartment with a young Polish mathematician who spoke fluent Russian, ten words of English, and no French. Yet somehow we talked to each other, cobbling together multi-language sentences and making charade-like gestures. While I did not smoke, I carried packs of Marlboro cigarettes as gifts in those days, and gave him one; in exchange, he shared the apples and sausage sandwiches his mother had packed for his journey.

Late at night, we reached the Soviet border at Brest, where the undercarriage of each train car had to be widened for Soviet-gauge tracks (the gauge had been established in the 19th century by the tsarist government, when the railway was first built). By the time we arrived in Minsk, just before dawn, I knew I was in the Soviet Union. Massive statues of Soviet 'heroes' dominated public squares; much of Minsk felt and looked cold, gray, and tired – although many of the people I met at the conference, including some from the communist-ruled countries of Central and Eastern Europe, were very welcoming, and I never once felt threatened or unsafe.

In total, I made about three dozen valuable journeys to CEE during 23 years of grantmaking, and nearly a half-dozen eye-opening trips to the Soviet Union during the Fund's seven years of grantmaking there.

resources. Communism's planned economies fostered inefficient monopolies and focused only on production quotas, to be achieved by whatever means necessary. In Moldova (then still in the USSR), I visited farming areas where nothing would grow because excessive use of chemical fertilizers and pesticides had ruined thousands of hectares of soil. In the Tatra Mountains, between Czechoslovakia and Poland, I saw huge expanses of evergreen forest that had been killed by acid rain from nearby industrial zones. Critical water sources were so severely polluted that when my wife Susan and I visited Kraków during my sabbatical in 1987, we chose not to drink coffee or tea in restaurants because no amount of boiling could remove all of the contaminants in the city's water, especially the heavy metals. Throughout CEE and the Soviet Union, life expectancy was dropping, in part because of diseases caused by air and water pollution, combined with the deterioration of healthcare services.

During the 1980s the RBF's sustainable resource use grantmaking concentrated on bringing together academics and practitioners from CEE and USSR with their counterparts from the West, to address common environmental concerns. Some of these meetings and workshops paved the way for new forms of collaborative action. Overall, they accelerated thinking and action on sustainable resource use in the CEE region.

For example, RBF support to the University of Minnesota Foundation funded an East/West workshop in Poland in 1989 that focused on how to structure national and municipal efforts at environmental management and pollution control. With historic changes under way in the region, this workshop helped to inspire experiments in using economic mechanisms for environmental protection and encouraged the establishment of independent environmental think-tanks in several CEE countries, a number of which the RBF would later help to launch or support. Multi-year RBF support helped the US National Academy of Sciences launch a series of binational workshops on environmental issues with counterpart academies in CEE. These workshops, involving scientists, politicians, government officials, and environmental practitioners, emphasized strategies (such as organic farming, the subject of a workshop I attended in Czechoslovakia) for addressing air, water, and soil pollution problems that affected all CEE countries and a number of regions in the United States.

While it was not always possible, I tried to participate in at least some of these gatherings, since I learned so much from being part of the dialogue. We funded efforts by the International Network of Resource Information Centers (known then and now as the Balaton Group) to strengthen a network of academics and practitioners that included members of the Soviet Academy of Sciences and the Global Modeling Center in Moscow, as well as Hungarian experts on systems dynamics. The Balaton Group's annual meetings introduced participants from the USSR and CEE countries to new technologies and research methods for promoting sustainable resource use – and introduced me to many talented and committed individuals from the region who were working on sustainable resource use issues.

Hungry for contact with the West

One way that I communicated my observations and insights during the second half of the 1980s was through letters back to the RBF. In a letter I sent to David Rockefeller on 17 September 1987, while on sabbatical in Europe, I reflected on the importance of exchange and bridge-building as part of our strategy:

Dear David,

I am now more convinced than ever that the RBF is in a position to employ relatively modest amounts of funding in its new East–West program for highly constructive work aimed at increasing East–West contacts and improving East–West relations while addressing significant common challenges and hopefully making measurable progress with respect to them. I have encountered Poles and Hungarians, as well as their immediate neighbors west of the USSR, who consider themselves to be Europeans – not Eastern Europeans (a term they do not appreciate) – and who are eager, and I think able, to proceed along many new, constructive pathways with Europeans and North Americans. However, most of these people still do not have access to valuable, international scientific and other journals or required hard currency to participate in important meetings in the West – in short, normal opportunity for regular, fruitful contact with foreign colleagues.

I remember how thrilled people were to have the nine or ten copies of the 1987 *State of the World* report from Worldwatch Institute that I carried with me to Poland, Czechoslovakia, and Hungary, and I am convinced the copies will be widely and usefully circulated. RBF grants to date to the National Academy of Sciences, International Network of Resource Information Centers (Balaton Group), Institute for East–West Security Studies, International Union for Conservation of Nature and Natural Resources (IUCN), and others have already taken a recognizable step forward in this promising process of increasing contacts, but there is a long, usually complicated and often frustrating, way to proceed, and I am surely glad to be able to spend a lengthy time in Europe to gain a better perspective on this matter. My growing network of colleagues and friends all over the continent offers special opportunities for collaborative work in the future . . .

Intimations of change

From a letter I wrote to RBF staff, dated 27 November 1987:

> Greetings to everyone. I spent four full days last week in Moscow, where I met with Soviets of all ages: an academician, a lawyer, a philosopher, a sports writer, several ecologists, computer modelers and other scientists. I had a good talk with our relatively new ambassador Jack Matlock and other members of the US Embassy. What a dynamic time to be living or posted in Moscow. While I didn't see any sunshine like this postcard suggests (and I even jogged in sleet early one morning), I felt a sense of openness that I had not observed in previous visits. It was easier to make appointments and talk substantively. Even formerly sour-faced clerks in hotels and at customs speeded up their work – sometimes with a smile.
>
> As press reports indicate, this is a complicated time, and no one knows for sure how well Gorbachev's *perestroika* and *glasnost* are going to fare in the months ahead in the face of the resistance that exists. Nevertheless, re-examination and admission of past mistakes are now occurring in virtually every conversation (e.g. scandalous pollution). A philosopher friend confessed at dinner that he is rewriting a book comparing the US and USSR that he started several years ago. He has a new burst of confidence and he is ashamed he didn't have more courage when he started . . .

Global security

Even before the changes of 1989, the CEE countries were perceived by security experts to be important in global superpower relations, partly as a 'transmission belt' of information and insight from West to East and back. During the 1980s more and more people behind the Iron Curtain were becoming active in challenging the communist system and seeking contact with the West. Just as in the arena of sustainable resource use, the Fund's global security grantmaking in CEE concentrated on bridging gaps and building confidence at a time of ferment and opportunity.

Support for the Institute for East–West Security Studies (now the EastWest Institute) facilitated pathbreaking programs that brought together mid-career security specialists – the next generation of security leaders – from the USSR, CEE, Western Europe, and North America. Ours was the Institute's first foundation grant, and the RBF went on to make numerous other grants to this critical education, discussion, and policy center. After the historic changes in 1989, the Institute also began to address regional development challenges, while maintaining its interest in East–West relations. The Institute is now a global organization working on important international issues involving a wide range of countries in Europe, Asia, and North America.

Young adults were the focus of an exchange program operated by the American Center for International Leadership (ACIL), then based in Columbus, Indiana, and later in Baltimore, Maryland. Notably, ACIL succeeded in involving young people and local sponsors from towns and rural areas all over the United States (not just coastal cities) in exchange programs with their counterparts from CEE and Soviet countries. RBF support helped to establish this program, and later funded the ACIL-sponsored New Visions Project, undertaken by Jenny Yancey and Dan Siegel, that identified emerging leaders in Central and Eastern Europe – some of whom would play important roles (along with Jenny and Dan themselves) in our grantmaking efforts after the historic changes in 1989.

In addition to funding other exchange programs involving academics, government officials, journalists, and citizen leaders, the RBF supported efforts by the European Cooperation Fund in Brussels, Belgium, to provide translation and publication opportunities to East European writers and to assist the small publishing operations in Western Europe that provide outlets for these writers.

Because the RBF's One World program implied a broad definition of global security – arguing that the prospects for peace could be improved by encouraging equitable development and broader participation in the world economy – we also used our global security budget to help establish Western-style business schools in Hungary, Czechoslovakia, and Poland. This strand of our grantmaking was consistent as well with the brothers' longstanding commitment to opposing communism. The Fund made its first grant for this purpose in 1988 to the University of Pittsburgh, for the creation of the International Management Center (IMC) in Budapest, Hungary. We worked closely in this endeavor with George Soros (founder of the Soros Foundation in Hungary and the Open Society Institute) and Mark Palmer (then the US ambassador to Hungary). The IMC has since become a part of the Central European University in Budapest, and the other business schools we helped to establish in the region also continue to function to this day, in various institutional settings.

The Fund's broad definition of security also allowed us to explore civil society-building and democratization issues while communism was still in the process of imploding in the USSR and CEE. In July 1989 the RBF and the Foundation for Social Innovation in Moscow co-sponsored an international seminar on 'Foundations in a Civil Society: Principles and Core Concepts,' which examined how to create a social and legal environment in which foundations could flourish. The following summer, after the Velvet Revolution in Czechoslovakia, the RBF was a principal sponsor of an international conference in Bratislava on foundations and the voluntary sector. During the 1990s the rebirth of civil society would become a major focus of our grantmaking in CEE.

Closing reflections

I conclude this chapter with a couple of reflections on the big theme of 'grantmaking in the thick of history,' which I have evoked to describe the Fund's work in Central and Eastern Europe during a period that saw the implosion of the Soviet empire, the end of the Cold War, and complex transformations of political and economic life in countries throughout CCE and the former Soviet Union. Grantmaking is never done in an historical vacuum; in the Caribbean and parts of Africa, for example, historic independence movements shaped the context of our grantmaking. But as our programs in CEE took shape, history was unfolding in *real time* – in the very parts of the world where we were becoming active. I think this is a valid distinction, and it raises some important questions. Were our efforts during the 1980s primarily responsive to events, or proactive? Were they primarily opportunistic, or strategic? Was the RBF just a bystander in these years, or can we claim to have had some influence on the course of events?

Responsiveness and proactivity, serendipity and strategy were closely interwoven in the period covered by this chapter.* I am not sure we would have focused on Poland in the early 1980s if Bohdan Lewandowski had not happened to have that conversation with David Rockefeller in 1981. On the other hand, David might not have been quite so responsive

---

* I have chosen to use the word 'responsive' here rather than 'reactive,' which (rightly or wrongly) has come to have negative connotations. In fact, as I hope this book has already illustrated, I think both responsive and proactive strategies belong in the effective grantmaker's toolkit. By the same token, I believe serendipity and opportunity are valuable resources, not to be dismissed by funders seeking to put together meaningful – and strategic – grant programs.

to Lewandowski's appeal if he (David) had not been mindful of the RBF's own strategic review process, which had been prompted in part by a sense that the world was changing in some historic ways – and which seemed likely to open doors for the RBF to work on East–West challenges. I knew from past experience that the Fund's board appreciated the need for an initial period of listening, learning, and experimentation before a coherent, targeted grantmaking program could be formulated – and that staff recommendations based on such explorations would be taken seriously. So once the stranded scholars program was under way, I felt I had the freedom to begin digging deeper into possible additional strategies for addressing the needs of the Polish people under communist rule – even though the RBF's new vision had not yet been articulated.

My recommendation that we try to help Polish farmers was a response to needs identified by people on the ground as well as experts on the region; I thought we had a high-leverage opportunity to improve conditions in rural areas and to encourage private farming in the face of communist pressure for collectivization. Perhaps such a project was not exactly what the RBF Planning Committee had in mind as they formulated a new strategic vision for the Fund. Perhaps the cart got out in front of the horse, as my colleagues and I dedicated time and energy to developing our ideas. But once we began negotiations to create an independent and credible Polish institution, we found ourselves deeply engaged in just the kind of East–West collaboration and trust-building – around an issue of common concern to the participants (and related to one of the RBF's priorities, resource use) – that the One World program strategy ultimately called for.

So I would have to say that responsive and proactive, serendipitous and strategic approaches to grantmaking converged in the work described here. That blend has always, to some extent, been characteristic of the RBF's grantmaking; it could not be otherwise, given the Fund's philanthropic style and traditions. But the description rings true in a heightened way for this program, in this period of historic change.

Did we have any impact whatsoever on history's course? In 1987, during my sabbatical in Europe, a joke about Gorbachev's reform efforts in the Soviet Union was making the rounds in CEE. It went something like this: 'The leaders of Romania, Czechoslovakia, and East Germany have told Gorbachev that, if he continues on the path he is on, they will have to

Among those present at a conference on issues of agriculture and rural life organized by the Foundation for the Development of Polish Agriculture (FDPA) in the 1990s in Poland were governing-board members, including myself (second from right); Jonathan Taylor, longtime board chair (third from right); and Bill Herbster, longtime treasurer (fifth from right).

send in their tanks!' Everyone I met wished Gorbachev well and hoped he would succeed, but most were skeptical about his chances. As aware as I was of the growing frustrations and nascent reform efforts in CEE and the Soviet Union – I had the good fortune (serendipity again?) to live in the region for an extended time during my 1987 sabbatical year – I myself did not anticipate the historic changes that took place in the autumn of 1989. Almost up to the last minute, that joke about Gorbachev's reforms remained painfully funny. The events of 1989 were astonishing and exhilarating, never to be forgotten by the people who lived through them or by people, such as myself, who felt a part of them.

I cannot prove that the programs and activities the RBF supported in CEE countries or the USSR had a role in producing this wonderful outcome. Nonetheless, I believe the cumulative impact of our work added to the momentum for change. RBF support energized and empowered academics, practitioners, students, and others – and contributed, perhaps, to a growing sense of hope that the dreary, oppressive yoke of communist rule might be lifted. Some of our grants helped to jump-start substantial programs at US-based and international organizations that were looking to take advantage of cracks in the Soviet monolith. In my view, many of our

activities during the 1980s helped in one small way or another to acceler-
ate the collapse of communist rule in CEE countries and in the USSR.

One thing is certain. Thanks to our involvement in the region during
the 1980s, we were in a good position to take stock of what we had learned
and go immediately to work in a new era. We had funded some multi-year
projects that now would have new space in which to blossom. We had
helped to create several non-profit institutions that could play important
and ongoing roles in a changing context. Where it was not possible to
establish such institutions, we had supported needs assessments and
planning efforts that would facilitate the creation of new institutions once
conditions changed. And we had become acquainted with courageous
local people who were fighting the communist system in non-violent ways,
including by trying to put in place laws and strategies for managing natural resources wisely. In short, we were already up and running when the
transformative events of 1989 created new challenges and opportunities.

Primary focus of grantmaking

CHAPTER EIGHT

Harnessing Optimism and Creative Energy through Cooperative Action
Central and Eastern Europe, 1990 to 1995

We can now say that 1989 had results that place it beside
1789 as a date in world history. Not only was it the beginning
of a swift and fundamental change of system in the countries
of Central Europe. It was also the end of the Cold War, which
had started in the 1940s over these same countries. This alone
meant that it directly affected many other regions of the world,
such as southern Africa, southeast Asia, and Central America,
whose politics had been deformed by the global competition
between the Soviet Union and the United States, communism
and capitalism, 'East' and 'West'. In fact, it is difficult to find
a country in the world that was untouched by the end of
the Cold War.

Timothy Garton Ash, *The Magic Lantern* (Vintage Books, 1990;
new afterword to 1999 edition)

Euphoria was in the air when I returned to Central and Eastern Europe in
February 1990. Everyone wanted to tell me where they had been and what
they were doing when the historic events of 1989 unfolded in their countries. A surge of hope and energy swept through the region.

How could I not feel that I was in the right place at the right time – and
incredibly lucky to be there? What's more, I had some valuable experience
already under my belt, a network of dedicated colleagues and courageous
grantees, and access to financial resources that could contribute in a modest way to the rebuilding of entire societies. I was working for a foundation
whose trustees and officers (including a new president, Colin Campbell)
had an acute sense of the historical significance of this opportunity and

were determined to provide me with the encouragement and flexibility that I needed to respond to the unique circumstances in which I found myself.

The foundation supported me in another important way as well. Almost before I had admitted it to myself, Colin and the board recognized that we would have to reduce the geographic scope of our program if we were to use our modest resources to maximum effect. After careful

First-hand accounts of the Velvet Revolution

During my first visit to post-communist Czechoslovakia, in February 1990, almost every encounter began with colleagues and friends telling me about their involvement in the events of the previous winter, when the brutal beatings of student activists by the special police, on 17 November, produced the spontaneous outpourings of anger and resistance that became the Velvet Revolution.

My longtime Czech friend Vilik Hubner, then a 28-year-old editor in a scientific publishing firm, and his Slovak wife Tea were a typical 'grey zone' couple (deeply concerned but not politically active), with a seven-month-old son. They heard about the police brutality on Voice of America and Radio Free Europe (the local TV and radio broadcasts had lied, as usual, about what really happened). Vilik and Tea concluded that this time they must do something to express their hatred of the corrupt communist government. The same horror and disgust brought thousands of people to Wenceslas Square on 19 November – the day on which Vaclav Havel and his fellow dissidents formed their democratic movement, Civic Forum. Starting on Monday 20 November and continuing for the entire week, Vilik and untold numbers of his fellow citizens went to work at 8 a.m. and left at 4 p.m. to join the demonstration in Wenceslas Square, even though it was not clear until the 23rd or 24th that the special police would not take additional brutal steps to suppress dissent.

A colleague from the 1980s, Eva Kruzikova, then in her mid-30s, told me she was at the symphony on Friday 24 November. At the end of the performance, someone announced from the stage that the Communist Party Secretary, Miloš Jakeš, had resigned. Eva said she would never forget the instantaneous rejoicing and tearful embraces that filled the concert hall. Yet another Czech friend, Jiří Musil, who was in his early 60s, told me, wistfully, that he wished he was young again and had a long life ahead to help rebuild his country.

deliberation, the RBF decided to phase out the work it had begun in the USSR; within Central and Eastern Europe, we decided to focus our attention on the northern tier countries: Poland, Hungary, and Czechoslovakia, which soon was divided into the Czech Republic and Slovakia. While we made a handful of grants to projects based in or including Romania and the Baltic States during the 1990s (and I would eventually serve as the first chair of the Baltic American Partnership Fund), we felt that the northern tier countries held particular promise for building open democracies with market-oriented economies. These countries had known versions of this kind of society before the Second World War – and we believed they could become models for other countries in the region and the former USSR.

We also reduced the substantive scope of our grantmaking in CEE, to achieve greater impact. Given the environmental mess left behind by the communist regimes and a growing RBF interest in the complex challenge of rebuilding civil society in the northern tier countries, the board decided in 1995 to phase out completely the Fund's security-related grantmaking in the region. This decision also reflected the fact that in some of the arenas where we were active under the security heading – for example, supporting the establishment of Western-style business schools – other public and private funding sources were coming on stream. We would pursue our work in the region under two RBF program headings: Sustainable Resource Use and Non-profit Sector.

There was an additional change made early in the decade. I secured the help of another RBF program officer, Nancy Muirhead, who took the lead in the non-profit sector component of our CEE grantmaking. Nancy had been directing the Fund's South Africa program and had already proved herself as a program officer. Going forward, she would continue her South Africa-related grantmaking and also play the key role in our non-profit sector grantmaking in CEE. I am sure her two areas of responsibility added up to well over 100 per cent, but she managed to do it all somehow. She became a wonderful partner and ally for more than a decade. Also in the early 1990s, the US economy began to improve and the Fund's endowment started to grow again. The CEE program's annual budget increased to $2.4 million and held steady at that level for many years – higher than the budgets for any of the other programs that I directed, before or after.

Despite the availability of these new assets, I could not really regret the narrowing of the Fund's geographic focus or the phasing-out of our security grantmaking in CEE. We had more than enough to work on from 1990 to 1995, as the pages that follow will attest.

RBF trustees visit the region

In the autumn of 1990, Colin Campbell proposed a first-ever overseas trustees' trip to CEE that would give board members a chance to observe conditions there first hand and to meet some of the people whose work we were supporting. Planning and managing this trip was a daunting task, but the experience significantly enhanced trustees' understanding of and support for our grantmaking program in the region.

Of course, there were a few glitches on the trip! For a formal dinner in Budapest at the home of the US ambassador, we had arranged a performance by a group of Roma (Gypsy) musicians, who unexpectedly took the occasion to present a petition to the assembly, expressing their community's interest in contributing to the transformation of post-communist Hungary but describing the long history of injustice and neglect from which the Roma had suffered. It was an awkward moment for me, since I was as surprised as anyone by the musicians' statement. But the episode was a vivid reminder for the trustees – and perhaps for other guests as well – of some of the difficult societal challenges facing countries in the region.

It was on this trip that Stephen Heintz, who would become president of the RBF in 2001, first met the trustees and senior staff of the Fund. Based in Prague as executive vice president of the EastWest Institute, Stephen hosted a meeting of the Fund's board at the Institute's European Studies Center just outside the city.

This is a chapter about *beginnings* – about the blossoming of long-suppressed civic values and grassroots activities, and the emergence of a new determination on the part of many citizens to help shape decisions that would affect the environmental, economic, and cultural well-being of their communities. In this chapter, a number of projects are introduced whose stories are continued in chapter 9 (in which I focus on the latter half of the 1990s). Despite the occasional awkwardness of this arrangement, I hope it conveys the incredible spirit of creativity, optimism, and revival that we all shared during the first half of the decade.

Building capacity to address environmental problems

Forty years of communist rule left behind widespread environmental dam-age as a result of policies and practices that failed to protect the natural resources and patrimonies of countries in the region. The RBF adopted a two-tier grantmaking strategy to address this challenge. First and fore-most, through a cluster of reinforcing grants, we sought to strengthen the capacity of grassroots groups to address local environmental problems. We supported technical assistance and training, and we contributed to budgets for equipment, salaries, and experimental ventures. When war-ranted, and when sufficient mutual trust had been established, I also rec-ommended grants for unrestricted, multi-year support. These grants were viewed as pure gold by local groups, because they enabled organizations to plan ahead and hire staff, and to focus on the work they thought was most important – not just on projects that one or another funder wanted to support.

The centerpiece of this first grantmaking strategy became the Environmental Partnership for Central Europe, in which the RBF, the German Marshall Fund of the United States, the Charles Stewart Mott Foundation, and other funders from Europe, the United States, and Japan pooled their resources to establish a locally managed program of small grants, technical assistance, and training for NGOs and municipal governments.

The second strand of our grantmaking program focused on creating independent centers for policy analysis in the northern tier countries – six centers in all – to encourage the formulation of policies, laws, and regu-lations at the municipal and national levels that would promote sustain-able development and integrate environmental concerns with economic advancement policies.

Between 1990 and 1995 the RBF made nearly 60 sustainable development-related grants in CEE, totaling approximately $6 million.

The Environmental Partnership for Central Europe
Fast, flexible, and non-bureaucratic

Readers who are familiar with the world of philanthropy will know that foun-dations are hardly immune to the 'not invented here' syndrome; real collab-oration in project development (as distinct from collaborative funding) is relatively rare. One of the things I am proudest of in my career is that I have been able to facilitate and contribute to a number of effective, creative donor partnerships. The Environmental Partnership for Central Europe was an example of such donor partnership. And in fact it had its origins in a partnership between two foundation program officers.

Group photo taken during an annual meeting in the 1990s, in CEE, of the foundations that constituted the Environmental Partnership for Central Europe (now called the Environmental Partnership Association). This group includes staff and board members from the foundations in the Partnership as well as from the foreign funding organizations. These annual gatherings were valuable not only for analyzing progress being made and challenges faced, but also in building mutual trust.

During the 1980s I had come to know and respect Marianne Ginsburg, then the Program Officer for Environment (including emerging Central and Eastern European countries) at the German Marshall Fund of the United States (GMF). We got into the habit of comparing notes periodically, as a matter of course. By 1989, and certainly after the fall of the Iron Curtain, our conversations began to focus on the numerous inquiries we both were receiving from small groups scattered all over Central and Eastern Europe that were looking for small amounts of money to support their efforts to address environmental problems in their communities. The RBF was not structured to respond to these requests; neither we nor the GMF had a presence on the ground in the region, which made it impossible for us to evaluate the merits of foreign-language proposals from remote towns and communities. But we knew that the few funding sources which did exist for such self-help efforts were highly bureaucratic and typically quite slow.

Marianne and I wondered whether there might be a way to create fast, flexible, and non-bureaucratic funding sources *in the region*, led and staffed by local people. Frank Loy, then GMF president, was thinking along similar lines, as were colleagues at the Charles Stewart Mott Foundation. Local organizations could re-grant pooled funds from US and other donors in more creative and responsive ways than foreign donors often could manage. The availability of such grants could encourage civic engagement, and the development of such local grantmaking capacity could help to rebuild philanthropic traditions in the northern tier countries.

To determine if this idea had merit, we asked our respective foundations to commission situation analyses in Poland, Czechoslovakia, and Hungary. The analyses confirmed that small amounts of funding were critically needed to motivate and engage communities and to provide technical assistance and training for community self-help efforts in the environmental field. These reports laid the groundwork for what would become a consortium of four regional programs, called the Environmental Partnership for Central Europe.

By 1994 all four Partnership offices – in Poland, the Czech Republic, Slovakia (after Czechoslovakia split into two countries), and Hungary – were all under local leadership.

Funding and early activities of the Partnership

On the basis of those situation analyses and the momentum they created, Marianne and I persuaded our bosses that the GMF and the RBF should become core funders of the Partnership – a commitment that we expected would extend over many years. Early in the start-up process, the Charles Stewart Mott Foundation (Mott) of Flint, Michigan, with its own outreach into CEE, joined us as a core funder; on the Mott staff, Jon Blyth was the counterpart to Marianne and myself. As core funders, our foundations were prepared to provide multi-year general support grants (which would be renewed on the basis of strong performance) for at least the first six years and probably considerably longer. While we did not want to create a relationship of dependency, we knew that it would take time to ensure the sustainability of the Partnership offices. The Sasakawa Peace Foundation, in Japan, also became a core funder for several years, but had to withdraw when financial reverses significantly reduced its endowment. Ultimately, the RBF and the GMF supported the Partnership for 14 years, and Mott continued making grants to and for its activities well beyond that point.

In addition to providing financial support, the core funders contributed considerable staff time. Marianne, Jon, and I assisted informally with training and coaching the Partnership staffs, through periodic one-on-one meetings. We also provided input to more formal capacity-building opportunities, such as study tours in the US for Partnership staff and board members. These were organized with the help of a regional coordinator, based in Poland in the first instance and later in Prague, whose role we funded until the Partnership offices became independent foundations under the laws of their own countries; and of a staff person from the GMF office in Washington, DC, who worked part-time on institutional development challenges facing the Partnership offices. We all wanted to help the local Partnership staffs become as responsive and productive as possible in their grantmaking. They, in turn, would work to build the capacity of the grassroots organizations that their offices would be funding.

Colleagues of the GMF, Mott, and the RBF in these three (soon to be four) countries helped us select local people to staff the proposal review committees at each country office; those people in turn helped us identify candidates to manage the Partnership programs. Marianne and I participated in the job interviews. In all cases, we were able to appoint local professionals, with backgrounds in the sciences and years of experience as environmental activists: Zsuzsa Foltányi (as early as 1991) in Budapest, Hungary; Miroslav (Mirek) Kundrata in Brno, Moravia, in the Czech Republic (succeeding Prague-based short-term directors – first an American, then a local Czech); Juraj Mesík in Banská Bystrica, in Slovakia; and Rafal Serafin in Kraków, Poland (after an important start-up phase in Wrocław, led by Polish-American Krystyna Wolniakowski, who later became a regional coordinator of the Partnership).

Initially, donors to the Partnership made their grants to the GMF, which managed the project and provided a legal framework for it until the Partnership offices had established themselves as foundations (a process that was completed by 1997). As a publicly supported charity, the GMF could receive grants from other US foundations without the need for those donors to exercise 'expenditure responsibility' (see pages 105–6 for an explanation of this legal requirement). Public and private donors from other countries also could contribute easily to the GMF for the Partnership.

The core funders also helped the Partnership foundations think about their own fundraising and make connections with potential donors. We encouraged training for fundraising locally, and on numerous occasions we made direct contact with other donors to stimulate interest in the Partnership and the issues its foundations were addressing. This effort paid off. The core funders contributed $450,000 per year to the Partnership at the start, growing to $600,000. But by the end of 1994 the core funders and new funders from three continents had pledged a total of $5 million for the growing programs of the Partnership offices.

In addition, the RBF sometimes stepped in – as did others among the core funders – to fill the need for follow-up support to local organizations that had received initial support from the Partnership. The Partnership's mission and budget did not allow for long-term, continuing funding – and while some money could be found from local sources and revenue-producing activities by the mid-1990s, there was still a big gap that the RBF was prepared to address when possible and when we saw special learning opportunities.

For example, in 1994 the RBF began to support an NGO called Veronica that had been launched with funding from the Czech Partnership. Veronica developed an Eco-counseling Network of community-based environmental NGOs, to advise municipal governments, businesses, and citizens on such challenges as water and energy conservation, refuse disposal, and pollution reduction. Not only did the RBF help Veronica take the next steps in developing the Network, but we also introduced an anonymous donor from Ireland to Veronica. That donor ended up co-funding Veronica with us for several years, until the organization (which continues to operate to this day) made sufficient progress in implementing its own long-term fundraising strategy. In 1995 the RBF made its first grant to the Beneficial to the Public Fund, which was originally supported by the Slovak Partnership to develop a homegrown strategy for the preservation and advancement of the small towns and rural areas of Central Slovakia, at the base of the High Tatra Mountains. This region had lost a major source of jobs and income as a result of the closing and downsizing of state farms and other enterprises, and proposed highway and other infrastructure projects were threatening agricultural lands, forests, and the High Tatra Mountains National Park. Among other accomplishments, this group put together a coalition of mayors, priests, foresters,

agronomists, entrepreneurs, homemakers, students, and others that sty-
mied the national government's bid to host the Winter Olympics in the
ecologically vulnerable region.

By 1995 – the close of the time period covered in this chapter –
the Partnership offices together had made more than 650 grants, totaling
$2.5 million (making the average grant size about $4,000), and they
had organized or co-sponsored over 90 workshops, training events,
fellowships, and expert exchanges. Partnership grants and activities
had helped to advance environmental education efforts, community
planning and advocacy, public participation in local decision-making, and
cooperative ventures between NGOs and local government. Often the
only resource available to grassroots efforts in a particular locality, the
Partnership was already widely recognized as an effective model for
nurturing community-based self-help in CEE.

Award given in recognition of the RBF's role in helping to create and sustain the Environmental
Partnership for Central Europe. Recognition is always appreciated, and the words chosen in
this instance are especially touching.

All of the original Partnership offices, plus offices in Romania
and Bulgaria that joined the network later, are still active today, a decade after the RBF stopped providing grant support in 2004. They are
now part of the Environmental Partnership Association (EPA), which

includes Environmental Partnerships in the Czech Republic (Nadace Partnerství), Slovakia (Nadácia Ekopolis), Hungary (Ökotárs Alapítvány), Poland (Fundusz Partnerstwa), Romania (Fundatia Pentru Parteneriat), and Bulgaria (Fondaciya EkoObshtnost). While there is some variation among the offices with respect to funding sources and fundraising effectiveness, all are reaching out to individuals, corporations, and government sources, and all have benefited from various European Union programs to strengthen communities and address environmental needs. Some have secured support from Nordic and Swiss government agencies, and some derive income from consulting and other services. Several have built substantial endowments.

Partnership: a familiar theme, revisited

I have commented several times in this book on the RBF's interest in collaborating with other funders, and on the centrality of good partnerships – among funders, sometimes, and certainly between funders and the individuals and organizations they support – to good grantmaking.

The good working relationships among representatives of the core funding institutions increased the prospects of success for the Partnership and enhanced the value of the grants that our foundations made to the Partnership. We trusted one another and none of us needed to 'own' this project or the ideas and insights that shaped it. There was no competition to distract us or send us in divergent or duplicative directions. Such good working relationships did not materialize overnight. Marianne, Jon, and I had known each other for years before we began collaborating on the Partnership, so we had some basis for confidence that we could work well together. As planning for the Partnership began, we three quickly realized that we shared an overall vision. We understood that each of us would have to undertake specific tasks to advance this project. We were all willing to advocate for the Partnership with our bosses.

Also critical to the success of the Partnership were the good working relationships and mutual trust that developed between representatives of the core funding institutions and the local leaders of the Partnership offices. We all reinforced one another's efforts – and from the start, the funder representatives treated those local leaders as full partners in this endeavor. In the early years Jon, Marianne, and I met at least once a year with the directors of the Partnership offices to review programs, finances, fundraising, governance, evolving conditions in each country, and plans for the future. These were serious meetings, which evolved over time into annual meetings for all of the donors and some of the partners on the ground in CEE. The presidents of the RBF, the GMF, and Mott (Colin Campbell, Frank Loy, and Bill White, respectively) traveled to CEE several times to participate in these annual meetings, demonstrating by their presence that all of our institutions were 'in it together,' at the highest level.

Marianne, Jon, and I knew that we had to maintain our professional roles and responsibilities in order to evaluate each Partnership program and the consortium of Partnerships. The folks on the ground in CEE knew that they had to report to us, which they usually did in a timely and highly satisfactory fashion. Marianne, Jon, and I had to report to our own bosses in a timely and satisfactory fashion. So while we all enjoyed our collaboration – I remember going on wagon rides together, and dancing at local

How partnership magnifies impact

From 'Forging Partnerships Among Diverse Interests,' a speech given by Colin Campbell at the Asia Pacific Philanthropy Consortium International Conference on the Non-profit Sector in Asia, held on 11 January 1998 in Bangkok, Thailand:

> Partnerships – and especially partnerships among diverse interests – possess the valuable quality of enlarging the community of actors who are working for the greater public good. Through partnerships, we can mobilize the strengths of other factions and sectors on behalf of the things we care about. In that sense, partnerships embody and help to advance the values of a strong civil society.
>
> The real trick is to make certain that the language of partnership is matched by its reality . . . What makes an organization or institution desirable as a partner are the strengths it brings to the partnership – its human or financial resources, contacts, connections, credibility, expertise, history, and past experiences. When strength is defined this broadly, it becomes clear that the partner who happens to have the money is not the only strong one; all parties to a partnership are in need of something another party provides. By focusing on strengths and pooling them, a partnership can extend the benefits of its members' resources, amplify their impact, and dignify and empower all parties involved.

clubs – there was a business-like quality to these partnerships as well. Above all, we felt that, together, we were building something that was needed and that could really help to advance sustainable development and civic engagement in CEE.

Independent environmental think-tanks

The second strand of our sustainable resource use grantmaking in CEE involved the creation of independent environmental think-tanks. Very little independent policy analysis went on in the communist-led countries of CEE, only in Hungary and Poland, in the late 1980s, did communist governments begin to tolerate some independent policy centers. In the absence of independent think-tanks and policy centers to provide alternative perspectives, sources of information, and forums for debate, major decisions about economic development reflected only politically acceptable views, and environmental considerations typically were not even on the table.

In 1988 the University of Minnesota's Hubert Humphrey Institute of Public Affairs undertook a comparative study of environmental protection strategies in several market and planned economies to see which strategies might be most useful for application in countries that are in transition, including those in CEE. In 1989, with RBF support, the Humphrey Institute conducted a workshop in Poland to consider how mechanisms for environmental protection in market economies might be adapted to the evolving context of CEE. When conversation at the workshop turned to the critical role of independent policy centers, several participants expressed their interest in helping to establish such centers in their countries. After the workshop, they moved quickly to launch conversations about this possibility with environmentalists, academics, and public-sector representatives from various CEE countries.

I attended that workshop in Poland, and it opened my eyes more fully to the need for independent think-tanks and policy centers if the CEE countries were to make significant changes in public understanding, government policy decisions, and business practices. The workshop also opened my eyes to the role that the RBF might play in helping credible experts begin to establish such centers in the region. I already knew and respected a number of those experts, and it wasn't long before I was meeting and receiving funding requests from other academics and government

advisers, some of whom I judged to have the experience, vision, and credibility among their peers that would be required to pull off the creation of a
new institution.

I did not anticipate then that my efforts in this area would turn out
to be the second-largest commitment of my time and RBF funding during
the years I worked in CEE. Ultimately, between 1990 and 1995 the RBF
became involved in the establishment of six policy centers focused on
sustainable development issues – one in Poland, two in the Czech Republic,
and three in Hungary – plus a region-wide 'bankwatch' initiative (which
analyzed the environmental impact of projects funded by international
financial institutions such as the World Bank and the European Bank for
Reconstruction and Development). Later in the decade, we helped to fund
the establishment of a policy center in Slovakia. Each effort was unique,
since the country contexts differed and the founders' visions varied. I was
actively engaged in the creation of three of these institutions: the Institute
for Sustainable Development in Warsaw, the Institute for Environmental
Policy in Prague, and the Environmental Management and Law Association
in Budapest.

As was the case in creating the Partnership programs, the RBF
did not sign up alone to finance any of these initiatives. Some of our colleagues in creating the Partnership (including the GMF and Mott) also
joined us in funding the policy centers (as did the Ford Foundation), and
we often helped the new think-tanks to secure other foundation support. I
was prepared to have the RBF take the lead or to let some other funder be
'the first one in,' depending on what was best for the initiative – and, sometimes, depending on foundation grant approval calendars. As it turned out,
in most instances the RBF's involvement extended beyond that of other
funders, reflecting the Fund's tradition of staying the course. I have since
been told by many of the leaders in this effort that the RBF's extra attention and ongoing commitment were often critical to the development and
sustainability of these new institutions.

The eagerness and confidence with which environmental leaders
around the region began to plan for the creation of think-tanks was not necessarily matched by any immediate impact on policy-making. It was difficult for these new organizations to expand their funding base beyond a few
foundations; attracting support from government agencies and the business sector was particularly difficult, since the think-tanks often criticized

prevailing policies and practices. And some of these institutions suffered the kinds of growing pains that many new organizations endure. The first half of the 1990s saw the creation of a remarkable number of promising centers for policy analysis in the region – amounting almost to the creation of a new sector – and I was thrilled to be part of that process. But in general, the full impact of these efforts would not be felt until later in the decade and beyond.

Institute for Sustainable Development, Warsaw, Poland

Andrzej Kassenberg, a geographer by training, was the co-founder and longtime president of the Institute for Sustainable Development in Warsaw, Poland. In a phone conversation in the autumn of 2012, Andrzej reminded me that he and his co-founders – Krzysztof Kamieniecki (also a geographer) and Zbigniew Bochniarz (an environmental economist) – had begun dreaming about establishing an independent environmental think-tank in Poland in the early 1980s, but knew it would be impossible to do at the time. When the communist government in Poland allowed the Polish Ecological Club (PEC) to be legally recognized as a non-governmental, non-profit organization in 1985, and after PEC had been active for several years under that provision, Kassenberg began to feel a little hope that someday the three of them might realize their dream.

The Institute for Sustainable Development in Warsaw was established in 1990 as the first independent policy center in CEE devoted to linking environmental concerns with economic development. From the start, the small Institute staff reached out to activist NGOs in Poland to devise cooperative strategies for addressing industrial development, pollution, transportation, community revitalization, and rural development issues. Over time, while maintaining the respect of civil society, the Institute began to communicate with local and national government, with businesses, and with international financial institutions in order to try to 'reason through' environmental disputes. As of 1995, these efforts had not yet led to many policy decisions in favor of sustainability. But progress had been made in raising public awareness and improving government and business understanding of alternative approaches to development, and more substantial impacts were felt in subsequent years.

Andrzej Kassenberg, a founder and longtime president of the Institute for Sustainable Development in Warsaw, Poland, celebrating his 40th birthday in May 1988 at my New York City apartment.

Institute for Environmental Policy, Prague, Czechoslovakia
Institute of Sociology, Prague

In 1990 Czechoslovakia was one of the most polluted countries in Europe. Despite the seriousness of this problem, the political, economic, and social reforms under way in the early 1990s did not give adequate attention to environmental principles and practices or to concepts of sustainable development.

The Institute for Environmental Policy, in Prague, was established in 1992 – the first independent policy research organization in Czechoslovakia to concentrate on sustainable development challenges. With a mission similar to the institute in Warsaw, the Prague institute also was emerging by 1995 as a credible, energetic, and practical think-tank that reached out to all sectors of society through its policy analyses, publications, training, and public education activities.

The RBF also provided start-up support for the Institute of Sociology in Prague. This research-oriented center focused on the social and regional impact of environmental pollution, the renewal of old industrial regions and historic city centers, and the stimulation of voluntary civic activities in environmental protection. I viewed RBF support here as complementary to our support of the Institute for Environmental Policy, involving as it did a different network of academics, including sociologists and statisticians.

East European Environmental Research Foundation, Budapest, Hungary
Center for Environmental Studies Foundation, Budapest
Environmental Management and Law Association, Budapest

In the early 1990s RBF support helped to launch or sustain several independent policy centers in Budapest. The East European Environmental Research Foundation ultimately did not thrive, due to a combination of management and organizational challenges.

The Center for Environmental Studies Foundation is an interesting case. It had been launched in 1993 with project support from other donors, including the Hungarian government. But the lack of general budgetary support meant that the Center had to struggle to carry out its ongoing work and build an organization. Marianne Ginsburg of the GMF and I felt that some modest unrestricted funding might give the Center and its excellent staff the boost they needed. While early differences in strategy and style among board and staff members limited the Center's effectiveness, our unrestricted support helped the Center position itself for progress in the second half of the decade.

The Environmental Management and Law Association (EMLA) was established in 1992 by Hungarian professionals in law, management, economics, and journalism who believed that a professional membership organization could advance environmentally sound economic development. EMLA and its affiliated foundation for environmental education focused on three tasks: policy analysis, with special attention to legal issues; professional training on environmental law enforcement and other educational opportunities for students of environmental management, law, and science; and preparation of a database of environmental laws and regulations that would help NGOs and others seek legal remedies for environmental abuses. EMLA started out with only a small grant from a US-based family foundation, and the staff consisted of volunteers who maintained their 'day' jobs. By 1995 EMLA had become the region's first public-interest environmental law firm, an important legal services provider to environmental groups and municipalities interested in using laws and regulations to protect the environment. Since then, EMLA has undertaken 40 to 50 public-interest legal cases a year and become a leading player in numerous regional and international environmental networks. Sándor Fülöp, EMLA's effective director, became the first Ombudsman for Future

Generations in Hungary. When the separate ombudsman positions were folded into one, Sándor returned to EMLA as board chair.

CEE Bankwatch Network

Through a grant to the Polish Ecological Club, the RBF helped a group of environmental activists establish a CEE-wide network to monitor and press for more sustainable investments by international and multilateral financial institutions. When bankwatch advocacy cranked up fully in the latter half of the decade, our early support of projects like this network really paid off, as some of the millions of dollars spent by the international financial institutions in CEE began to be invested in more environmentally friendly ways.

All of the think-tanks described above, except the East European Environmental Foundation in Budapest, are still active today. The Institute for Sustainable Development in Warsaw and the Environmental Management and Law Association in Budapest are perhaps the strongest.

Non-profit sector grantmaking: strengthening the sinews of a democratic society

Throughout the 1980s, as the RBF worked on sustainable development and security issues in CEE and the USSR, trying to help local people take whatever small steps they could to challenge communist-era policies, I was very aware that we were also working to open up space for civic discourse and engagement. One of my heroes from the 1980s was Bronisław Geremek, a courageous intellectual who became Foreign Minister in the early 1990s in Poland. Reflecting on the transformations that took place in 1989, Geremek noted:

> The civil society we were forming in the midst of our struggle against communism would prove a strong buttress upon which a future democratic order could be built after the collapse of authoritarian power . . . The destruction of communism and the recovery of freedom are necessary but not sufficient conditions for the birth of democracy. Democracies are built only over time, through the forming and functioning of democratic institutions . . . The process is one of gradual maturation, both of democracy itself and of people in the ways of democracy . . . In the end, a robust civil society offers the best prospects for overcoming the divergence of state and society and bringing

citizens into active engagement with public life. Only under such conditions can democracy be made secure.*

After the fall of the Iron Curtain, scores of civic groups emerged across the region, and people were beginning to look to civil society to help address some of the challenges facing the countries of Central and Eastern Europe. If these new NGOs were to take on serious assignments, they would need more than volunteers. But very little money was available to help civic groups and NGOs get started, and few of the people organizing such groups had any experience in operating and managing non-profit organizations. I felt there was an important role to be played by a foundation like the RBF, which understood the importance of a robust civil society for a healthy democracy. Among the Rockefeller brothers, JDR 3rd had been a vocal proponent of supporting what he called the 'third sector' – and in fact the RBF had been making grants for many years, through its Non-profit Sector Program, to strengthen the NGO sector in the United States. I was excited and gratified when, in 1990, the board formally extended the scope of the Fund's Non-profit Sector Program to include CEE.

Frankly, I would have loved to do the legwork to build a non-profit sector program in the region. But that simply was not feasible, given my involvement then in implementing the growing Sustainable Resource Use Program in CEE and (at the time) a security program as well. As I mentioned at the beginning of this chapter, Nancy Muirhead's ability to take the lead on the CEE non-profit sector grantmaking was a godsend. While I personally knew or came to know over time almost all of the leaders of the organizations and programs that Nancy recommended for funding, she deserves most of the credit for identifying, assessing, and making the case for support of those organizations, and for managing the grant relationships. We communicated regularly and I reviewed Nancy's work informally – but my oversight of Nancy reflected the RBF's style of management, from which I myself had benefited: select good people, then get out of the way.

Some of the groundwork for our non-profit sector grantmaking in CEE was also aided by a report commissioned by Colin Campbell, the

* From 'The Idea of a Civil Society' (National Humanities Center, 1992), report of a symposium held in November 1991 at the National Humanities Center, Research Triangle Park, North Carolina.

Fund's president, who had a deep interest in the challenge of civil society-building. In 1991 Colin asked social entrepreneurs Jenny Yancey and Dan Siegel to undertake an analysis of realities and challenges facing civil society organizations in the post-communist countries of CEE. Jenny and Dan had done an excellent job on a project for the RBF in 1988/9 (a scan of emerging leaders who were challenging the communist governments in CEE), and their new report was equally valuable. In *The Rebirth of Civil Society: The Development of the Non-profit Sector in East Central Europe and the Role of Western Assistance*, published in 1992, Dan and Jenny identified four essential ingredients for the development of a vibrant non-profit sector in the region: a supportive legal and fiscal framework;

Developing a new civic and political culture

From Yancey and Siegel, *The Rebirth of Civil Society* (1992):

In the late 1970s and early 1980s . . . independent organizations, initiatives, and movements [began to] repopulate the almost barren political and social landscape [of Eastern and Central Europe], and helped to spark the dramatic citizen revolutions of 1989.

The events of 1989 provided the public space to build and expand civic structures. Over the past three years, Central Europeans have utilized the insight, courage, and imagination that prompted their liberation to create new forms of associations and foundations. The advance of nonprofit initiatives, however, has been hindered by several parallel developments.

First, much of the energy, resources, and hopes of these societies – and of Western donors – has been focused on creating market economies and formal systems of democratic governance. The major emphasis of the political transition has been at the national or macro-level: in establishing or revitalizing the rule of law, political parties and parliamentary practices. Less attention has been devoted to building and supporting grassroots, citizen-based initiatives . . .

The next few years represent a critical window of opportunity . . . Entrenched laws, processes, and institutions may soon be developed that do not encourage or nurture civic initiatives. The citizenry, in short, needs to build up the sinews of a democratic society by creating and using the tools which can facilitate the development of a new political culture and insure that the rulers serve the ruled.

trained staff working in the sector; wide availability of relevant information; and effective networking among indigenous NGOs to heighten impact.

This report, with its strong conceptual framework and many specific recommendations, was also published in the languages of the northern tier countries. Local civic, academic, government, and other leaders received the report warmly and were eager to address the opportunities and challenges it identified. While the RBF could not contribute equally on all fronts, we certainly kept these big needs and specific recommendations in mind as we pursued our non-profit sector grantmaking in the region.

Between 1990 and 1995 the RBF made about 35 non profit sector/CEE grants totaling nearly $3 million. Some highlights are provided below. To be sure, almost every grant we made to help local people solve environmental problems also contributed to the strengthening of civil society, as did some of the 30 security-related grants (totaling about $5 million) that the Fund made in the first half of the decade, before that program was phased out. So the distinctions among these categories are somewhat artificial, and the disparity between the total amounts spent on sustainable resource use grants (about $6 million from 1990 to 1995) and on non-profit sector grants is overstated.

Training and technical assistance

The RBF helped to build the capacity of staff in the non-profit sector by funding training and technical assistance programs and by supporting exemplary philanthropic organizations that could serve as models for other initiatives.

- Dr Lester Salamon, director of the Institute for Policy Studies at Johns Hopkins University, was well known worldwide and to RBF staff for his work helping people to understand the principles and practices of a self-reliant, effective voluntary sector. With RBF support from 1992 to 1996, Salamon's team provided in-country training and six-week internships and study programs in the US for over 500 non-profit leaders from CEE and the former Soviet Union.
- In 1992 and 1993 Jenny Yancey and Dan Siegel, in collaboration with key non-profit leaders, organized the Civil Society Development Programs (CSDP) in Hungary and Poland to train a cohort of trainers who in turn would provide a range of services

to all types of civic groups and NGOs. In these train-the-trainer programs, participants learned about all aspects of launching, managing, and sustaining an NGO, through workshops, internships with US and Western European foundations and NGOs, and ongoing interregional networking.

– The RBF supported several philanthropic organizations whose interests did not necessarily coincide with the Fund's program areas, because those organizations helped to incubate other foundations and train NGO staff. In this category I would put our funding for the Hungarian Foundation for Self-Reliance, which helped to incubate the Hungarian office of the Environmental Partnership for Central Europe and now focuses on the needs of the Roma; and the Polish Children and Youth Foundation in Warsaw, which not only addressed the urgent needs of children and youth, but also conducted training sessions for NGOs in many fields, encouraged networking and collaborating among NGOs and local governments, and coordinated the work of a group of lawyers preparing a draft non-profit law.

Facilitating information-sharing and strengthening enabling environments

The new civil society groups in CEE needed access to information, advice, and peer support if they were to thrive. The RBF made numerous grants designed to help create an enabling environment for NGOs in the region.

– In 1993 and 1994 the RBF helped to establish the Information Center for Foundations in Prague and the Nonprofit Information and Training Center in Budapest; we were also among the early funders of the Slovak Academic Information Agency (SAIA) in Bratislava. All of these organizations provided information-sharing, networking opportunities, advisory services, and other forms of support for civil society groups in their countries. The RBF had the longest relationship with SAIA, which played an important role advocating for the young non-profit sector when a hostile post-communist government took charge in Slovakia in the middle of the decade.

- In 1990, with early support from the Fund, the Foundation for a
  Civil Society (FCS) – which was originally called the Charter
  77 Foundation–New York, after a famous underground petition
  circulated by Czech reformers in 1977 – was created to serve
  as a clearing-house of information for American individuals
  and organizations seeking to assist in the democratization and
  economic transformation of Czechoslovakia. Under the dynamic
  leadership of Wendy Luers and with continued RBF funding, the
  FCS became an effective catalyst and facilitator for projects not
  only in the Czech Republic and Slovakia but also in other countries
  struggling with basic transformations. While the RBF's total
  contribution to the FCS (which amounted to more than $600,000

Getting to know local colleagues

All work and no play makes Jack a dull boy! Fortunately, I have not suffered the proverbial Jack's fate. I was brought up to work hard, and along the way – actually quite early – I began to play as well, whenever the opportunity came along. As it happened, many of the people I worked with, whether grantees or colleagues in other organizations, shared the same philosophy, regardless of nationality, ethnicity, age, or gender.

Social activities were a regular part of the annual meetings of the network of Environmental Partnerships in Poland, Czech Republic, Slovakia, and Hungary (and in later years, Romania and Bulgaria). At the end of a day of discussion and deliberation, we might have a picnic in a rural setting, with hay-rides and sports events. Or we might continue our conversations over dinner in a favorite restaurant, followed by a dance party. My stays in Central and Eastern Europe included many other enjoyments as well, some of them planned and some spontaneous: evenings at the symphony or opera or listening to jazz in Warsaw and Prague; visiting night-spots in Kraków; mushroom-picking in the Czech Republic; floating in the thermal baths of Budapest; walking, jogging, hiking in all of the countries where I worked, plus bicycling in some.

Among the most memorable occasions were dinners and picnics in the private homes of local colleagues. These informal, off-the-job activities helped me to get to know our grantees and other partners in meaningful ways that enabled us to work more effectively together.

over 10 years) was modest in comparison to some of the grants and contracts that eventually were secured from other donors, our support got the foundation off to a strong start and helped to give the FCS the flexibility it needed to become a creative, dynamic force in rebuilding Czech and Slovak civil society.

Closing reflections

The period from 1990 through 1995 was like none other in my career. Whoever said that grantmaking has to be hands-off, or that the only role of funders is to disburse the dollars that make it possible for others to take action? I felt I was in the thick of things, to an extent that had not been possible for me in the developing world. I had worked in the region for seven years and lived there during my sabbatical year. I was a seasoned and confident program officer, with an unprecedented opportunity to be a (small) part of history. It was an exhilarating and inspiring experience. Frankly, I cannot believe how much Nancy and I got done and how many new institutions and programs the RBF helped to usher into existence. We could not have managed without our hardworking interns, program assistants, and administrative assistants, as well as the Fund's supportive management and board, who trusted us and gave us the flexibility we needed to be responsive to emerging needs and opportunities for impact in a quickly changing environment.

The successful partnerships we enjoyed during these years, both with other funders and with leaders in the region, confirmed once again my belief in the importance of collaboration and my appreciation for the RBF's commitment to collaborative strategies. Most of the Fund's major involvements in CEE were collaborative (which is perhaps not a surprise, since the RBF was one of the smallest donors working in the region, and had a long track record of effective partnerships). Of course, finding good partners is more than serendipity and luck. I made a point of looking for allies who had appropriate knowledge and experience, credibility among their peers, passion for their work, good management skills (or instincts), and their 'egos in place.' Taking such criteria seriously when evaluating project leadership is one key to effective grantmaking. So is being willing to give proven, trusted partners on the ground the flexibility they need by offering multi-year, unrestricted grant support – when possible and appropriate.

Looking back on this period, I can see that I devoted considerably more attention to some projects – such as helping with the establishment of the Environmental Partnership foundations – than to others. Certainly, my desire and inclination to be an engaged grantmaker, combined with the reality that there are only so many hours in a day, added up to an inability to give 'equal time' to each project. Sadly, I simply did not have enough time to spend on the ground with all of the excellent people I met who had highly promising ideas. I suspect that many of my foundation colleagues would have voiced the same regret, as they tried to maintain a large number of ongoing grant relationships while also evaluating a constant flow of new inquiries.

But it is also true that some project leaders had ideas and styles of operation that caught my attention and captured more time than I expected. The leadership team at the Institute for Sustainable Development in Warsaw, for example, was very creative in designing initiatives that all sectors of society could value and usually embrace. In what was then Czechoslovakia, I was intrigued by the Institute for Environmental Policy's emphasis on the use of media, which was not a typical strategy at the time. I became more involved in advising and serving as a sounding board for the founders and leaders of these two think-tanks than I did for some of the other policy centers. In Hungary I spent more time helping the Environmental Management and Law Association (EMLA) than some other applicants and grantees – even though the RBF was not one of EMLA's lead funders. I was impressed with the project leaders and their plans. Having once practiced law and provided pro bono legal assistance myself, I appreciated the careful attention that EMLA was giving to legal issues – and I had a personal understanding of the potential significance of what this passionate team of young professionals was cooking up. Perhaps I saw a little of myself as a young lawyer wanting to use the law to solve problems and make the world a better place.

I was not a consultant; I was a program officer of a foundation. I tried to balance my deep engagement in some projects with an even-handed approach to all of our grantees, and an openness to unsolicited proposals. I am not sure I always achieved a good balance. But as readers will have grasped by now, there is a certain enthusiasm inside me that bursts out when I feel I can make a special contribution in particular cases.

Though the term was not in vogue then, I practiced a kind of 'venture philanthropy,' characterized by a high level of involvement with grant recipients; a willingness to experiment and try new approaches; and a focus on capacity-building for sustainability. I did not, however, embrace the impatience that sometimes affects venture philanthropy, the readiness to shift funds away from organizations or strategies that do not 'pay off' quickly; any tendency in that direction would have been offset by the lessons in patience I had learned from past efforts to support new ideas and new organizations (as highlighted at various points in this book) and by the RBF's commitment to staying the course. Such a version of venture philanthropy – engaged, eager to encourage innovation, but willing to go step by step with young organizations as they mature – was well suited, I believe, to those unique years in Central and Eastern Europe, when optimism and creative energy were in the very air we all breathed.

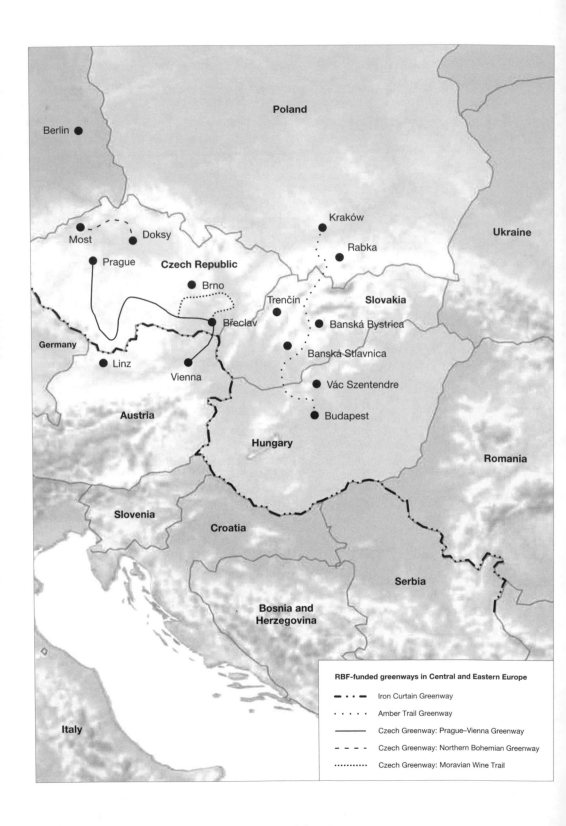

Poland

Berlin ●

Ukraine

Kraków ●

Most ● ● Doksy

Rabka ●

Prague ●   Czech Republic

Brno ●

Trenčín ●   Slovakia

Břeclav ●   Banská Bystrica ●

Germany

Banská Stlavnica ●

Linz ●

Vienna ●

Vác Szentendre ●

Austria

Budapest ●

Hungary

Romania

Slovenia

Croatia

Serbia

Bosnia and
Herzegovina

Italy

RBF-funded greenways in Central and Eastern Europe

▬ · · ▬   Iron Curtain Greenway

· · · · ·   Amber Trail Greenway

─────   Czech Greenway: Prague–Vienna Greenway

─ ─ ─ ─   Czech Greenway: Northern Bohemian Greenway

············   Czech Greenway: Moravian Wine Trail

CHAPTER NINE

Taking Stock and Refining Strategies
Central and Eastern Europe, 1996 to 2004

It takes six months to build a market economy, six years to build a parliamentary democracy, and sixty years to build a civil society.

Ralf Dahrendorf, *Reflections on the Revolution in Europe* (Times Books, 1990)

During the first half of the 1990s, growing numbers of non-profit organizations and community groups in Central and Eastern Europe (CEE), along with many municipalities and some national government agencies and business organizations, brought considerable creativity and energy to bear on the environmental, economic, and governance challenges facing their transforming societies. At mid-decade, these groups (including many supported by the RBF) could point to overall increases in civic engagement and recognizable reductions in pollution in many places, as well as other indications of progress in creating more open and democratic societies. An emerging network of independent think-tanks (also supported in part by the RBF) was working to stimulate debate about alternative policy strategies for creating healthy communities and nations. Legal and fiscal frameworks for the non-profit sector, while not satisfactory, had become more navigable in most countries of the region. Indicators of overall economic development were statistically impressive, especially in Poland and the Czech Republic, and accession to the European Union seemed likely within the foreseeable future for at least the northern tier countries (Poland, Hungary, the Czech Republic, and Slovakia).

But by 1996 public frustration was growing over the uneven distribution of economic benefits, which had not reached rural areas or improved the lot of many working-class people. Consumerism was taking hold, as citizens in the region were encouraged to purchase goods and services in ever greater quantities. Systemic economic changes had forced many people to work harder than ever, and jobs were increasingly difficult to find. These trends began to undermine the public's commitment to balancing economic development with environmental protection for the long-term well-being of the region.

Meanwhile, local environmentalists and preservationists were being outmaneuvered by well-financed, politically savvy developers and corporate interests. The role and value of a strong non-profit sector were still not widely understood or appreciated in the region. Long years of top-down decision-making had left a legacy of dependency and, in some cases, passivity that was slowing the consolidation of democracy. Corruption was still a serious problem, and in many respects the rule of law was taking hold more slowly than had been hoped.

In this complex and rapidly changing context, some of the public and private philanthropic agencies that had been helping to build open societies and promote sustainable development in CEE were beginning to leave the field, either in response to increased domestic demands on their resources, or in order to redirect funds to other regions in transition – such as the Balkans, which were just concluding half a decade of bloody wars, the former Soviet countries, many of which were in free fall, and post-apartheid South Africa.

As of 1996, foreign philanthropic agencies were contributing about $20 million per year to support NGO activity in the four northern tier countries; in the CEE countries to the south and east, the total was probably less than $15 million. By 1998 foundation funding in the northern tier countries had plummeted to well under $15 million per year, while funding for NGOs in the other CEE countries was fluctuating between $15 and $20 million. By the year 2000 the Andrew Mellon Foundation, the Pew Charitable Trusts, and the Joyce Mertz-Gilmore Foundation had phased out their programs in CEE, after having contributed more than $40 million in the 1990s to civil society-related efforts.

It is true that in the late 1990s massive amounts of financial assistance from the European Union had begun to flow into Poland, the Czech Republic, Hungary, and (with some interruptions when the repressive Mečiar government was in power) Slovakia, as those four countries moved toward EU accession in 2004. But this was typically project-funding that could not be used for the type of civil society- and non-profit sector-build-ing that the more flexible grants from private foundations had supported.

The emerging reality at mid-decade was that economic develop-ment and integration into Western Europe had become the driving forces in CEE. While I was encouraged by the energetic efforts and valuable results that had been made possible by the Fund's relatively modest grants program, I began to fear that countries in the region would make many of the same mistakes that had been made by the United States during the previous half-century, when short-sighted, unsustainable land-use, trans-portation, and energy policies had been embraced in the name of eco-nomic expansion. I thought the CEE countries had a chance to learn from our mistakes and to develop in more sustainable ways. But by 1995 and 1996, as foreign investors and business interests moved aggressively into the region, it appeared that much of what had been accomplished in the first part of the decade might be overwhelmed by the velocity of change.

Had we at the RBF been going about our work the wrong way? Should we change our approach going forward? I know that many of my colleagues at other foundations were experiencing the same frustration and doing the same kind of soul-searching that I was.

Taking stock at mid-decade

In the mid-1990s my colleague Nancy and I were asked to prepare a review of our recent grantmaking in CEE – standard practice for all RBF pro-gram officers at roughly three-year intervals. We concluded our review by strongly recommending that the RBF remain active in the region, and we offered a set of objectives and strategies to guide the Fund's CEE grant-making through the end of the decade.

In making our case for remaining active in CEE, Nancy and I argued that the economic, social, and political transformations under way there offered continuing challenges to and unique opportunities for advancing the principles of sustainable resource use. We evoked the RBF's long-standing conviction that no healthy democracy can exist without an active non-profit sector, and reminded trustees that it would take time and sus-tained commitment from foreign funders to rebuild civil society in countries that were just emerging from communist rule. We also pointed out that some of the most distinctive features of the RBF's grantmaking style (and our own style as program officers) had not only proven to be effective but were also deeply appreciated by our NGO partners on the ground. Among the most valued features of our approach were our belief that bottom-up, citizen-led approaches to change are as important as any top-down initiatives; our recognition that tough challenges call for creative, flexible, and proactive grantmaking; and our willingness to offer expertise and active engagement, when appropriate, alongside financial support.

The RBF board decided – enthusiastically – that we should stay the course, with an emphasis on changing conditions in the region and lessons learned since we first began making grants there in the early 1980s. At the June 1996 board meeting, the following objectives for our work were approved: (1) to achieve a greater acceptance of the importance of sustainable resource use; (2) to make solid progress in consolidating democracy and promoting civil society; (3) to contribute to a marked increase in self-sufficiency for promising non-profit organizations; and, in the process, (4) to encourage greater interchange and cooperation between Poland, the Czech Republic, Slovakia, and Hungary – and between those countries and their neighbors to the east and south. Between 1996 and the early 2000s, to advance these goals for the region, the RBF would make about 50 sustainable resource use grants, totaling $5 million, and 34 grants totaling about $2.6 million under the non-profit sector heading. Of course, non-profit sector grants that funded training programs for NGO staffs often benefited groups working on environmental issues; sustainable resource use grants that promoted community revitalization and land stewardship planning also encouraged civic engagement. While Nancy and I had not fully anticipated such a degree of overlap, it played out in some very positive ways on the ground. Whatever confusion this blurring of distinctions may have caused at RBF board meetings, no one attempted to curtail it!

We also explicitly embraced several cross-cutting approaches to our work that we believed would help us to achieve the maximum possible impact. We would be integrative, supporting community revitalization, land stewardship, and transportation planning initiatives with implications not only for the environment, but also for the economy, for heritage preservation, and for the health of civil society. We would seek to build capacity in the non-profit sector, through support for training and technical assistance and by nurturing successful model organizations. And we would foster enabling environments, by helping to build both the public

understanding and the legal and public policy infrastructures that are necessary for the protection and encouragement of NGO and citizen action.
Also with an eye to achieving maximum impact, we determined that we
would work even harder to make connections and to promote synergy and
mutual learning – among RBF-supported organizations in CEE as well as
between those organizations and RBF grantees in the United States and
elsewhere. All of these big, cross-cutting strategies are illustrated in the
pages that follow.

While our 'new' goals and approaches were not fundamentally different from those that guided our work in the first part of the decade, they
were more clearly articulated and designed to frame our work in a more
strategic way.

Supporting integrative approaches to maximize impact
Community revitalization

Even in the early 1990s we had begun to experiment with grantmaking to
support community revitalization projects that used 'visioning' exercises to
help people come together across sectors and disciplines to imagine the
possibilities for their locality and decide on their priorities. From 1996 to
2000, with an explicit commitment to this integrative approach and some
experience to build on, we supported a number of initiatives that empowered local citizens – including youth leaders, entrepreneurs, municipal officials, business people, environmentalists, historic preservationists, health
leaders, and community developers – to devise and pursue strategies for
the revitalization of their towns, cities, neighborhoods, and natural environments. By the end of the decade, thanks in part to the Fund's support of
such bottom-up problem-solving, the notion of local involvement in community improvement and development planning was more widely accepted
by the general public and by municipal officials throughout CEE. Habits of
dependence on central government planning had begun to weaken.*

While our earlier support of community revitalization efforts was
designed primarily to help local communities address environmental
problems, our later funding also explicitly framed community revitalization

---

* Many current reports from Hungary reveal that, under the current right-of-center government,
the pendulum has swung back toward more centralized rule-making, with government
policies and practices usurping, or at least reducing, the roles and opportunities that had
been devolving to localities and their citizens.

as a vehicle for consolidating democracy and building civil society. Our support for Nadace Via (Via Foundation), in the Czech Republic, is a good example. Nadace Via was formerly the Prague office of the New York-based Foundation for a Civil Society (FCS), which turned its two country offices – in the Czech Republic and Slovakia – into indigenous foundations in 1997. Both foundations and their directors became sector leaders in their respective countries and today are recognized throughout Europe for their contributions. We funded Nadace Via for eight years, starting in 1997 (the name 'Via,' which is the Latin word for 'path,' was chosen to evoke the idea of being on a common path toward a vibrant, engaged, and democratic society). Nadace Via provided – and continues to provide – both monetary and capacity-building support for community-based problem-solving throughout the country. Two of our four grants to Nadace Via were categorized as sustainable resource use grants, and two were categorized as non-profit sector grants. Any of these grants could just as easily have been recommended under the other program heading.

As the decade advanced, our efforts to encourage community-based problem-solving benefited from an exceptionally productive collaboration between some of our grantees in the region and a US-based project with longstanding ties to the RBF. Nadace Via figures again in this story of synergy and mutual learning – which also highlights the continued and important role of the local Environmental Partnership foundations.

In 1992 Karel Stránský, director of the South Municipal Center Task Force in Brno, Czechoslovakia, a public–private redevelopment committee, visited the United States on an Eisenhower Fellowship supported by the RBF. During this study tour, Karel learned about the New York-based Project for Public Spaces (PPS), and was impressed by its work to improve the livability of urban areas, promote greater use and enjoyment of downtown areas, and enhance the quality of city life.* Upon his return to Brno, Stránský and some of his colleagues asked the PPS to explore ways in which it (PPS) could help Czech municipalities devise community-driven plans for revitalization. In July 1993, with funding from the Environmental Partnership for Central Europe, senior PPS staff visited a number of towns

---

* The Project for Public Spaces (PPS), which grew out of the Street Life Project conducted in the late 1960s by one of Laurance Rockefeller's advisers, William H (Holly) Whyte, had completed nearly 400 projects in more than 200 cities and towns throughout North America, Europe, and Australia by the time it began helping RBF grantees in CEE in the early 1990s.

and communities that were struggling with the tensions and complexities of urban renewal. In every case, community leaders expressed considerable interest in the PPS's methodology.

In 1994 the RBF began to support efforts by the PPS to implement modest, practical community revitalization projects in the Czech Republic that promoted cross-sectoral cooperation and increased the confidence of local citizens in their ability to achieve concrete results. Two years later, local interest was so strong that responsibility for these programs could be transferred to the Czech Environmental Partnership. With ongoing technical assistance and training from the PPS, the Partnership created a for-profit subsidiary called the 'Partnership for Public Spaces,' which today lives off earnings from its consulting services and returns any surpluses to the Czech Environmental Partnership coffers.

This group photo was taken at a sewage plant in the small village of Hostětín, Czech Republic, which was built with the help of a grant from the Czech Environmental Partnership. Second from the left is Roberta Gratz, author of the RBF-commissioned report, *A Frog, a Wooden House, a Stream and a Trail. Ten Years of Community Revitalization in Central Europe* (2001) Also shown here is David Sampson (the tall man next to Roberta), then executive director of the Hudson River Valley Greenway; Yvonna Gaillyová, executive director of the Veronica Ecological Institute; and (second from right) Miroslav Kundrata, executive director of the Czech Partnership. A typically trans-Atlantic team!

The PPS also helped Nadace Via establish its People and Places program, which eventually was renamed the Center for Rebuilding Communities. Then, in the late 1990s, the Slovak Environmental Partnership adapted these experiences to create a Partnership for Public Spaces–Slovakia program, which focused on revitalizing parks, central squares, riversides, and public markets, as well as on strategies for slowing and reducing car traffic to improve community life and pedestrian safety along roads.

Who will shape the change?

As the end of the 1990s approached, the RBF asked Roberta Gratz, a board member of the Project for Public Spaces and a widely respected urbanist and community leader who had served as an adviser to many community revitalization projects in CEE, to prepare a retrospective of the Fund's grantmaking in the region. In her report, entitled *A Frog, a Wooden House, a Stream and a Trail: Ten Years of Community Revitalization in Central Europe* (2001), Roberta offers valuable general observations, conclusions, and recommendations along with accounts of specific RBF-funded local initiatives. Roberta's report poses the questions that are at the heart of the Fund's work on community revitalization:

> Change is inevitable. Positive change is not. Change can be shaped. The real question and primary challenge is who will shape the change? Will it be foreign retail chains, whose narrow corporate interests have little to do with building healthy communities? . . . Will it be traffic engineers who are more concerned with speedily moving cars and trucks than efficiently, environmentally and cost-effectively moving people and goods? . . . Or, in fact, will the task primarily rest with the people in cities and towns of all sizes whose lives will feel the greatest impact and on whom the future of each country depends?

Land stewardship

The concept of land stewardship represents another opportunity for integrative grantmaking. Land stewardship efforts bring together diverse stakeholders and interest groups to address the objectives of biodiversity conservation, rural economic development, and the maintenance of traditional connections to the land. Like the community revitalization projects we funded, these efforts also strengthen the capacity of local institutions, NGO and government leaders, and individual citizens to address problems facing their communities. Under the heading of land stewardship, the RBF supported training programs on various approaches to rural advancement; the preparation of land-use plans for specific rural regions; micro-loan programs to finance employment generation, small-business development, and agro- and eco-tourism; implementation of strategies for the historic preservation of villages; landscape, natural resource, and biodiversity analysis and preservation; and pilot projects aimed at maintaining rural traditions.

The Fund's support of an effort called A-projekt is a good example of this kind of grantmaking – and once again, it demonstrates how the Environmental Partnership for Central Europe had become part of the 'backbone' of civil society in CEE.

A-projekt was launched in 1995, with RBF support, as a project of the Beneficial to the Public Fund, a 'self-help' NGO in the Liptov region of north-central Slovakia that had been established two years earlier with support from the Slovak Environmental Partnership Foundation. We funded A-projekt's work for six years. In the early days, A-projekt helped residents of the village of Kvačany design and implement a plan for the restoration of historic structures and the improvement of tourist accommodations. As an outgrowth of this on-the-ground effort, A-projekt facilitated the creation of the first rural community foundation in Slovakia, which has since nurtured many public–private and volunteer self-help activities in Kvačany and nearby rural areas. Building on this experience and lessons learned, A-projekt went on to manage regranting and operating programs throughout the Liptov region. All told, in the second half of the 1990s A-projekt assisted in and/or partially financed the development of more than 300 community projects that were implemented by local civic groups. In 2013, after 20 years of activity, A-projekt brought its programming to a halt. By then, many of the 'seeds' it planted had grown into established local NGOs, such as the Liptov Region Community Foundation, the Liptov Regional Development Agency, the Local Action Group of Upper Liptov Region, and the Slovakian Rural Parliament.

Starting around mid-decade, the RBF began to support a particular strategy for land stewardship that we thought was especially promising – the creation of 'greenways,' or green corridors (typically cutting across national borders) along which historic towns would be restored and the surrounding countryside preserved in an employment-generating process that protected traditional cultural and ecological values. Our first such involvement was with Greenways-Zelené Stezky, which in 1992 began to bring communities together in a cooperative effort to develop a green corridor linking Prague with Vienna, through the beautiful valleys and small historic towns of southern Bohemia and southern Moravia. Greenways-Zelené Stezky (the Czech Greenway) was modeled on the Hudson River Valley Greenway in New York, which had been inspired by Laurance Rockefeller – another example of synergy. The RBF began to support Greenways-Zelené Stezky in 1994; by 1996 the Greenway had built a network of 50 participating tourism services along the corridor and was collaborating with local NGOs on projects to safeguard and enhance tourism assets.

Despite some real achievements, an organizational assessment undertaken in 1996 (by the director of the Czech Environmental Partnership) revealed significant weaknesses in the Czech Greenway's governance, management, and financial controls. The Greenway's board asked the Czech Partnership to assume responsibility for the program, as a logical extension of the Partnership's interests in community revitalization, land stewardship, and civil society. In 1997, with the help of a bridging grant from the RBF, the Czech Partnership took on the program. Here again, one of the Partnership foundations demonstrated its strength and maturity. Over the next five years, with continued RBF support and increasing support from other sources, the Partnership strengthened and improved the Czech Greenway program, including by creation of an information database and publication of a newsletter to facilitate coordination among local projects. Under the wing of the Czech Partnership, the Czech Greenway program expanded to become the largest network of greenways in CEE.

In 1998 the RBF took the lead in helping local people in Poland, Slovakia, and Hungary to establish the Amber Trail Greenway – a north–south corridor that was once part of an historic trading route (for amber, among other goods). This greenway extends from Kraków, Poland, through central Slovakia to Budapest, Hungary. The Fund also made an early and crucial commitment to a Central European-wide greenways initiative, the Central European Greenways. This program, officially launched in 2002 by the Czech Environmental Partnership Foundation under the auspices of the Consortium of Environmental Partnerships, was designed to support in various ways the nearly one dozen greenways that existed at that time or were being started in CEE. The RBF made another contribution to the greenway movement in 2001, with early support for creation of the Iron Curtain Greenway.

For a variety of reasons, not all of these greenways have lived up to the visions that inspired them. When I visited the region in 2010, I saw that the Wine Trail Greenway in southern Bohemia was flourishing; local vintners and hoteliers were expanding their facilities and offering new attractions. The Amber Trail Greenway, on the other hand, is not as active as it once was – although many communities and programs along the corridor continue to use the 'brand' for their tourist attractions and economic development strategies. In most cases, though, the greenways have attracted new visitors and new income to local communities, and they have catalyzed new partnerships among the towns on the route, across provincial and national boundaries, and across the NGO, government, and business sectors. Miroslav Kundrata, CEO of the Czech Environmental Partnership, estimates that every RBF grant dollar invested in greenway creation has generated at least $50 in sustainable tourism business in the Czech Republic. Overall, the greenways concept is perceived to be at the core of efforts to preserve the region's cultural heritage and use its natural resources in ways that are both economically productive and ecologically sustainable.

Transportation and energy

In the field of energy, the RBF funded a number of model conservation and efficiency projects at the community level. We also supported monitoring and advocacy efforts to persuade international, multilateral, and other large financial institutions to consider energy efficiency and environmental sustainability in the investments they were making in the region. Since several other funders were focusing on these issues, we decided later in the decade to concentrate primarily on the related challenge of balanced transportation development, a complex issue that was receiving somewhat less attention. In fact, at the time the RBF was virtually the only foreign foundation to venture into this field in a substantial way.

One of the few positive legacies of communism in CEE had been the creation of comprehensive public transportation systems – a relatively seamless network of buses, trams, and railroads. However, after the fall of the Berlin Wall, these systems frayed and services were cut dramatically, while automobile and truck traffic exploded, producing severe air and noise pollution, congestion, and other problems. By the mid-1990s government policies were promoting the rapid development of suburban communities and malls, and favoring highway construction projects over public transportation initiatives.

With the tale of the American streetcar system in mind (see box overleaf), I recommended support for efforts to produce a more even allocation of public funds, so that low-pollution, efficient railroads, trams, subways, and other public transit systems could be maintained and improved, even as some new highways were constructed. In the second half of the decade, RBF support helped NGOs present transportation reform proposals more effectively by facilitating better analysis of the issues and options; promoting stronger coalitions among citizens' groups and municipal governments; and encouraging more sophisticated use of the media.

While serious transportation challenges could be seen in all of the countries of the region, I focused on Hungary and Poland because I identified several excellent groups there to support, and I could only stretch our limited budget so far. In Hungary, the Clean Air Action Group (CAAG), based in Budapest, was our primary grant recipient. Founded in 1988, CAAG had grown by the 1990s into a coalition of more than 50 environmental and community organizations devoted entirely to transportation and energy issues. CAAG orchestrated important achievements through policy analysis, public education, grassroots organizing, and advocacy. The RBF's relatively modest support (amounting to $190,000 over nine years) was critical to this work – and while policy decisions were never completely to the liking of those favoring fully balanced transportation planning, the situation would have been much worse without CAAG's efforts. When I visited CAAG again in 2010, its membership had risen to 130 members and it was playing a more respected role than ever.

In Poland, a much larger country than Hungary, the RBF strategy was different, as no single group such as CAAG existed. We supported the Kraków-based Foundation for the Support of Ecological Initiatives, which was conducting a national campaign for transportation reform;

A cautionary tale

The history of streetcars in the United States offers a cautionary tale about balanced transportation development.

When my father was a child in Battle Creek, Michigan, he could travel by 'inter-urban' streetcars to other communities throughout the state. People living in Michigan's small towns and rural areas could use public transportation to get to bigger cities at a very low cost. I do not know of a single streetcar system in my home state of Michigan today, and the passenger train service is a mere shadow of what formerly existed. In much of the United States, private car ownership and a massive network of highways have taken the place of public transportation.

The elimination of America's streetcar systems was not a natural evolution, an inevitable casualty of progress. In an authoritative documentary entitled *Taken for a Ride* (1990), Canadian film-maker Joseph Klein detailed how the US auto industry, together with the petroleum and tire-manufacturing industries, undertook a sustained, well-financed conspiracy to eliminate streetcars in order to get more people into cars, trucks, and buses – anything that burned gasoline, wore out tires, and required the building of roads. In the 1930s the corporate leaders who took part in this conspiracy created and funded something called National City Lines, which quietly went about purchasing private and municipal streetcar companies across America. Over the next few decades, National City Lines gradually raised fares and reduced service on those streetcar lines, until frustrated passengers were forced to use cars and buses instead. It was easy then for National City Lines to close down streetcar systems, one by one. Unfortunately, few civic groups in the United States were even focused on this issue at the time, much less capable of challenging such an insidious effort or the deep pockets that financed it.

Shortly after the Second World War, when evidence of this scheme was presented in the Federal District Court of Southern California (the venue was later changed to Northern Illinois), the court ruled that an illegal conspiracy had indeed been at work. The defendant corporations were fined a pittance; some paid just one dollar. The court claimed that it was not possible to calculate the damages more accurately.

the Polish Ecological Club, which established a transportation advocacy office in Warsaw; and the European Natural Heritage Fund (based in

Rheinbach/Bonn, Germany), which was conducting a mass-transit initiative in Wrocław in cooperation with local NGOs. While these efforts produced some scattered policy successes, by the time our grant funds had been spent I did not think much progress had been made in mitigating egregious imbalances in the allocation of transportation funds.

Just as in the arenas of community revitalization and land stewardship, we found that NGO leaders working on transportation issues were eager to have the help of more experienced groups, including from the United States. In the mid-1990s we funded visits to CEE by senior staff of the New York-based Institute for Transportation and Development Policy (ITDP) and senior staff of Friends of the Earth France (FOE France). Those trips were the prelude to a decade of engagement in the region, during which the ITDP and FOE France were funded by the RBF to provide technical assistance and training to local groups. At the end of this time, it was clear that the capacity of local NGOs to conduct technically accurate advocacy had been enhanced significantly; some of the NGOs assisted by the ITDP and FOE France were working directly with sympathetic government agencies to provide technical support and to help them secure international financing.

Institutional capacity-building

In an office memo from August 1995, my colleague Nancy Muirhead set the stage for our work on institutional capacity-building in CEE in the second half of the 1990s:

> As the non-profit sector in CEE has expanded and differentiated, a number of NGOs led by charismatic, talented individuals have had significant success, and are growing in both size and sophistication. Many smaller NGOs, however, remain relatively inactive . . . [and] the larger NGOs . . . are now beginning to face a range of challenging organizational and developmental issues. Almost every group that I visited on my recent trip evidenced some of these growing pains. It was almost as if NGOs were hitting a wall that needed to be surmounted before they could reach the next stage of development . . . One of the main problems confronting NGOs is the need to develop the second generation of leadership . . . Serious thought is needed on how to encourage staff and boards to work together . . . Accountability and ethical standards continue to be a matter of concern in the region . . .

Networking and information services also remain a priority. NGOs often still feel isolated, as they do not realize that they are part of a sector.

Even as NGOs in the region faced important organizational challenges, a funding crunch loomed on the horizon as well. The Democracy Network Initiative for Central and Eastern Europe (DemNet), established in 1994 by the US Agency for International Development (USAID), was scheduled to close out at the end of 1997, after allocating a total of $30 million among 11 country programs for technical assistance, training programs, and regranting. In my view, DemNet was one of the best programs USAID ever sponsored. I greatly admired its champion at USAID, Tom Dine, then Assistant Administrator for CEE and Newly Independent States. But to quote a Slovak participant at a conference on 'The Impact and Legacy of the Democracy Network Initiative for CEE,' co-hosted by the RBF in late 1996, DemNet and other USAID-funded democracy projects 'prepared the small child called Slovak democracy to go off into the world much more well prepared than he otherwise would have been. But, the fact is that the child is still much too young to be asked to fend for itself.' His observations about civil society and democracy in Slovakia applied in one degree or another to all of the countries in which the RBF was active.

The end of the USAID DemNet program was one of the reasons (together with the departure of some private foundations from the region) that I proposed the establishment of a Trust for Civil Society in Central and Eastern Europe, at a Ford Foundation-sponsored meeting of CEE donors in 1997. I felt – and I was not alone in feeling – that if the efforts of local groups and their donors were to bear fruit and become sustainable, foreign donors (ideally including USAID) needed to develop some kind of collaborative exit strategy that would soften the blow of their withdrawal from the region and ensure the ongoing availability of strategically placed grants for an additional period of time. The creation of the CEE Trust, which began operations in 2001, is described in chapter 11. But in 1996, knowing that the DemNet money was going to disappear while NGOs in the region were still too young to 'fend for themselves,' the RBF and its private foundation allies redoubled their own efforts to help non-profit organizations put themselves on a more solid footing.

Under Nancy's experienced and thoughtful leadership, our CEE program supported a range of programs to strengthen NGOs and the non-profit sector in the region.

Nancy Muirhead, RBF program officer and my great partner in CEE grantmaking, especially relating to strengthening civil society. (photo: Robert Stone, 2001)

Training and technical assistance

All told, during the last half of the 1990s, the RBF supported at least a dozen organizations that provided various kinds of training and technical assistance to NGOs. By the summer of 1996, for example, the Civil Society Development Programs that we helped Jenny Yancey and Dan Siegel launch in Hungary and Poland during the first half of the decade had reached out to nearly 800 NGOs. In 1996 the programs were transferred to local leadership, and Civil Society Development Foundations were established in both countries. With continued RBF support, these two foundations went on to play a major role in strengthening the non-profit sector in CEE – by providing non-profit leaders with training and consulting assistance; developing information resources and publications to support NGO activity; encouraging links between non-profit groups, local government, and the business community; facilitating networking and mutual learning; supporting cross-border linkages among NGOs; and raising the visibility of non-profit sectors in the region.

While the NGO information exchange centers that the RBF had funded in Prague and Budapest in 1993 and 1994 did not live up to their original promise, partly because it proved difficult for these organizations to sustain themselves financially once foreign funders began to phase out their grantmaking in the region, the Slovak Academic Information Agency did establish a successful Service Center for the Third Sector. In addition to providing training, technical assistance, and networking opportunities for NGOs (at the local, national, and international levels), the Service Center became the administrative home of the Gremium, a membership organization of Slovak NGOs.

The RBF also supported initiatives to promote revenue production by NGOs (e.g. through membership dues, fees for services and product sales, and other options for supplementing grant support). The Non-profit Enterprise and Self-sustainability Team (NESsT, based in San Francisco) was formed in 1997, with seed funding from the RBF, to foster NGO self-financing strategies and to incubate non-profit income-generating projects in emerging democracies, including in CEE. NESsT now operates in ten countries in Europe and Latin America and is a global thought leader on social enterprise development.

Nurturing successful models

In the second half of the decade, the RBF continued its strategy of nurturing the development of local grantmaking institutions that not only provided technical and financial assistance to grassroots NGOs in a variety of fields, but also had the potential to serve as leaders of the non-profit sectors in their own countries.*

Nine such grantmaking institutions benefited from RBF support: two community foundations in Slovakia – the Healthy City Foundation-Community Foundation of Banská Bystrica (central region of Slovakia) and Sami-Sebe ('By Ourselves, For Ourselves' in Slovak) in Pezinok, in the western region not far from Bratislava; two national

* This was in addition to our continued support of the environmental think-tanks that the RBF helped to establish in Warsaw, Prague, and Budapest, which modeled the possibilities for independent policy analysis in the post-communist era.

foundations – the Polish Children and Youth Foundation in Warsaw and the Children of Slovakia Foundation in Bratislava; one foundation concerned with the welfare of the Romani (Gypsy) population – the Hungarian Foundation for Self-Reliance (Autonómia Alapítvány) in Budapest; and the national Environmental Partnership foundations in Poland, the Czech Republic, Slovakia, and Hungary. All grew and matured during the decade and became transparent, accountable institutions with professional staffs and well-defined, well-managed grantmaking programs. While some of these organizations have hit bumps in the road since then, they all still play important and leading roles today.

András Biró, founder and longtime president of the Hungarian Foundation for Self-Reliance (Autonómia Alapítvány), in his apartment in Budapest in the late 1990s. (photo: author)

One of the foundations, the Hungarian Foundation for Self-Reliance (Autonómia Alapítvány), which the RBF funded from its planning and inception in 1989/90 through to the end of the 1990s, was a unique endeavor for its time. Founded with a mission to support the development of the non-profit sector and alleviate poverty, Autonómia soon began to give more and more attention to promoting economic advancement and autonomy for the Romani (Gypsy) community in Hungary, which faced and continues to face widespread discrimination and economic hardship. During the more than ten years of RBF support, Autonómia funded over 500 economic development projects affecting the Roma. The foundation also organized special initiatives, such as a series of trainings for Roma entrepreneurs; an annual Tolerance Prize for journalists whose work focused on the Roma; and the first legal defense bureau for minorities in Hungary.

As a result of these and other projects, Autonómia Alapítvány and its founder and long-serving president András Biró received the Right Livelihood Award (also known as the Alternative Nobel Prize) in 1995 and, subsequently, the Hungarian prime minister's 'For Minorities' Award. By the time the RBF stopped funding Autonómia, its annual budget was close to $1 million, and it was receiving money from the World Bank, the Open Society Institute, and other major donors for various imaginative undertakings.

Fostering enabling environments

As the RBF-commissioned study *The Rebirth of Civil Society* suggested in the early 1990s, progress on consolidating democracy in CEE would depend in part on the cultivation of public understanding of the importance and value of citizen action, and on the creation of legal and public policy frameworks to protect and encourage the development of an independent non-profit sector. Of course, progress on the issues of concern to local NGOs – including sustainability issues – also would depend on fostering public attitudes and government policies that respect the role of citizen action in a democratic society.

In the mid-1990s the RBF ramped up its efforts to address this daunting challenge. For example:

- We funded a number of media-based and other public information initiatives designed to communicate the importance of the work of civil society. RBF support for the Foundation for Public Education in Prague and the Non-profit Foundation in Budapest falls into this category.
- The Civil Society Development Foundations in Poland and Hungary, the Donors Forum in the Czech Republic, and the Slovak Academic Information Agency all undertook RBF-funded efforts to promote appropriate legal and tax frameworks for the establishment and operation of NGOs and non-profit organizations.

- The development of ethical and legal standards for non-profit organizations was the focus of work funded at the Association for the Forum of Non-Governmental Initiatives, in Poland. This initiative built on an earlier RBF-funded effort by InterAction, the alliance of US-based international NGOs, to articulate ethical standards for its member organizations.
- Understanding that decades of forced participation in supposedly voluntary communist organizations had made people wary of the very idea of voluntary action, we began to fund efforts to encourage volunteerism and educate the public about its value. One such effort was the Volunteer Center Association (and its predecessor, the Support Office for the Movement of Self-Help Initiatives), in Poland.
- We funded initiatives to promote philanthropy at the Academy for the Development of Philanthropy, in Poland; the Donors Forum and the Via Foundation, in the Czech Republic; and the Pontis Foundation, in Slovakia.

The problem of corruption

The Fund had largely phased out its security-related grantmaking in CEE by the end of 1995, because the needs and opportunities for sustainable resource use and non-profit sector grantmaking were so compelling. The separate Global Security Program launched by the Fund at about this time certainly could have provided a framework for some useful and complementary grantmaking in CEE. For example, the Global Security Program emphasized the need for 'transparency and inclusive participation' in government and corporate decision-making. This concern was certainly relevant to the functioning of civil society in CEE, where corruption was a growing problem and citizen access to government and corporate information was limited by law and complicated by excessive bureaucracy.

Unfortunately, while we recognized that corruption was emerging as a significant deterrent to democratization, Nancy and I did not have the budget to fund anti-corruption initiatives. If the Fund's grantmaking in CEE had continued into the new century, I believe we would have given priority attention to this challenge. And in the Western Balkans Program that succeeded our engagement in CEE, we were able to devote some resources to promoting transparency and reducing corruption.

A reluctant farewell to the region

By 1999 I had been working on CEE-related challenges since 1981 – almost two decades. I felt that our grantmaking had contributed to some considerable accomplishments in Poland, the Czech Republic, Slovakia, and Hungary. In addition, these four countries were on track to become members of the EU, with all of the financial, economic, and political benefits that their new status would bring. Meanwhile, Nancy and I were preparing for another three-year program review, which happened to coincide with a broader foundation-wide review occasioned by the merger of the Charles E Culpeper Foundation with the RBF, which added over $200 million to the Fund's endowment.*

Given these converging circumstances, I was not surprised to learn from Colin that some RBF trustees were asking whether it was time to close out our long, useful engagement in CEE, and to devote the program's $2 million annual budget to some other purpose. Colin wanted Nancy and me to treat our program review as an opportunity to compare the value of continuing to work in CEE with the value of focusing on some tough challenges in nearby countries, where our experience in CEE could be especially relevant.

Nancy and I were conflicted. On the one hand, it was abundantly clear that the work of promoting sustainable economic development and building strong civil societies in the northern tier countries was not completed. There was little reason to believe that EU funding, while certainly welcome, would replace the kind of grantmaking that the RBF and its foundation allies had been doing.

On the other hand, it looked like the CEE Trust would soon be up and running. And the time was right to address other important challenges – perhaps in Ukraine, which was working hard and uphill to get out from under the thumb of Russia; or as Stephen Heintz, the new RBF president recommended, in the Western Balkans, where bloody wars in the former Yugoslavia were drawing to a close.

* This unusual foundation merger, which was finalized in 2000, came about when the Culpeper Foundation – on whose board Colin Campbell served – was contemplating spending down its endowment because no Culpeper family members remained to carry the effort forward. The Culpeper Foundation's grantmaking interests were not dissimilar from the RBF's current and past concerns, so – with Colin playing a central role – the Culpeper and RBF boards negotiated a plan to fold the Culpeper endowment and some of its program areas into the RBF's. As part of that plan, the RBF board was strengthened by the addition of four Culpeper trustees.

After much thoughtful deliberation by the staff and board, the strategic review committee endorsed a phase-out of the Fund's grantmaking in CEE and the formal establishment of a new program in the Western Balkans, beginning in 2001. At the December 2000 board meeting, the trustees also approved a rare $3 million grant from the Fund's endowment for the CEE Trust. Going forward, I would be the program officer for the Western Balkans, while Nancy would be returning her attention full time to the Fund's South Africa program.

As was the case in the 1980s, when the RBF's developing country programs were closing down and the CEE/USSR program was starting up, the development of a new grantmaking program would overlap with the critical process of responsibly phasing out an existing program. In devising our exit strategy, Nancy and I agreed that a two-year phase-out period would be appropriate for the Fund's Non-profit Sector Program, since the CEE Trust would begin making grants in 2001. A four-year phase-out period was approved for our sustainable resource use grantmaking, given the continuing needs and challenges in this area. Few other foundations, I believe, would have made such a generous commitment of time and money to the phasing-out of a major grantmaking program; even the RBF was not always able to allow for such an extended exit strategy. The Fund's phase-out process in CEE is an example of 'best practice' grantmaking and it contributed significantly to the sustainability of the organizations we had funded in the region.

Most of the 18 RBF-funded organizations that we placed in the non-profit sector category had become leaders in their fields by 2000 and were already playing critical roles in shaping civil society in the region. But like many other indigenous NGOs, these organizations faced ongoing financial and institutional development challenges. Based on individual assessments and face-to-face conversations, we determined what type of tie-off support would do the most to leave each organization on a sound footing. For example, some organizations received contributions to their reserve funds or 'kick-off ' grants for endowment campaigns. We even helped a couple of organizations buy office space, as purchase prices and rents were rising. Our non-profit sector phase-out grants totaled about $2.3 million.

In the Sustainable Resource Use Program area, the RBF's efforts and those of its funding partners (especially Mott and GMF) had enhanced

Exploring opportunities in Russia – again

In the mid-1990s, when I was deeply immersed in my CEE work, I collaborated with two colleagues – Michael Northrop, then and now the director of the Fund's sustainable development grantmaking program, and Peter Riggs, who was then the program officer for Asia – to begin exploring the potential for an RBF grantmaking program in the Russian Far East (RFE). Michael, Peter, and I were struck by the absence of US foundations in the RFE, where local people were trying to address serious environmental and resource management challenges. Colin Campbell, who saw an opportunity to draw together the lessons learned from three different program areas, encouraged us to make a field visit to see for ourselves what was going on and to explore potential partners for some kind of RBF engagement that would draw on Michael's long and wide experience in the environmental field, Peter's Russian language talents and experience in several related fields, and my own experience in CEE.

It turned out to be my only trip to the region, given how overloaded I was with other responsibilities – although Michael, and especially Peter, took the lead in developing an effective program of grantmaking in the RFE that was sustained for ten years. But my ten-day familiarization trip with Michael and Peter was unforgettable. At dusk on our first full day, we were invited into a military vehicle that a local environmental group had transformed into a combined work and recreational vehicle. We rode up the side of a volcano until we reached the rim, where we got out and walked to a camp that had a swimming pool constructed from natural thermal springs. From there we went on to dinner, a musical event, and dancing. Peter played the guitar and sang Russian songs; it was quite a welcome party.

We worked hard in the coming days, and I will never forget some of the local people I met who were bringing remarkable creativity and courage to their difficult work. On 9/11, within hours of the terrorist attacks on the World Trade Center in New York City, the first overseas email I received was from a journalist I had spoken to several times during my trip to the RFE. She wanted to know how Peter, Michael, and I were, and if our families were safe.

the ability of NGOs, grassroots groups, and policy centers to address many environmental and development challenges. But by 2000 what was known as 'sprawl' in the United States had become a major threat to the economic, environmental, and cultural well-being of cities, towns, and rural areas in CEE. Hungary already had more mall capacity per capita than the United States, with nearly 1 million square feet of additional space on the drawing board. Six major shopping centers had recently opened around the edges of Prague, luring shoppers and stores out of the heart of the city. Billions of dollars in pre-accession funding from the European Union was being channeled to highway construction and other large-scale projects rather than smaller, locally inspired solutions.

Again on the basis of individual assessments and consultations with more than 20 grantee organizations, the RBF made final grants totaling $5.7 million to enhance the capacity and sustainability of these institutions, and to focus special attention on anti-sprawl initiatives. The overall goal at the end of four years was to leave behind a critical mass of organizations that could help to spearhead a more formidable indigenous movement for sustainable economic development.

Closing reflections

When I visited CEE in 2005, after the RBF had wrapped up its grantmaking in the region, I was frankly discouraged about the impacts of some of our grantmaking – especially with respect to sustainable development. For example, it seemed to me that our grantmaking to promote balanced transportation planning had not produced many positive results. This was a special concern of mine. During the 1990s I had even started showing Joe Klein's documentary, *Taken for a Ride*, to as many local NGO leaders as possible. I wanted to bring to life how America's auto, tire, and petroleum companies had conspired to shut down the tram system, and how their strategy was connected to the rampant spread of highways and malls and the eventual destruction of urban communities, farmlands, and rural areas. I wanted people in the transforming countries of CEE to be on the lookout for such trends. Based on what I saw in 2005, I gave myself only a passing grade in this 'subject' that I had made both a personal and a professional priority.

Only during more recent visits to CEE did I begin to realize that the RBF's efforts in the transportation field – and elsewhere – had made an impact and were recognized by local people as important contributions to the long process of changing public thinking and promoting alternative approaches to transportation planning. Returning to the region in 2008, 2010, and 2012, I also came to understand some of the less tangible ways in which our approach to grantmaking might have contributed to rebuilding civil society in the region.

Planting the seeds of change

During a visit to Kraków in the autumn of 2012, I met with Olaf Swolkień, former director of the RBF-funded Foundation for the Support of Ecological Initiatives and currently director of another environmental foundation. I was voicing my regrets about the minimal impact of the RBF's grants in the transportation field, when Olaf stopped me mid-sentence. 'Wait, Bill,' he said. 'You're being too critical.' The advocacy efforts that the RBF had funded may not have achieved anywhere near the results we all wished to achieve. But our support, he insisted, helped him and other local leaders energize many people around the country. He expressed particular appreciation for the connection we made between his organization and the Institute for Transportation and Development Policy. 'We didn't have enough muscle to prevent many highway and mall projects,' he acknowledged, 'but with guidance from Walter Hook and his team from ITDP, we became capable of offering real alternative policy choices.'

Olaf assured me that in the years since the RBF left the region, Joe Klein's documentary had been viewed by many groups around Poland. In fact, Olaf himself obtained permission from Klein to produce a Polish version of the film, which is still being used in schools and community centers. And Olaf gently suggested that it was unrealistic to have expected societies that were 'coming out of communism' to avoid the mistakes of history. 'We had to follow the path taken by the US. We had "Hollywood" all over our country from the late 1980s onward.' In their hearts, people wanted those sleek cars and modern homes – even if they knew in their heads that more attention to sustainability would be smarter in the long term.

'The RBF helped plant the seeds for thinking about alternative paths to development,' Olaf said. And he assured me that some of those seeds are bearing fruit. Kraków has a modern tram system, which people love; there are new subway lines in Warsaw; one sees many more bicycle lanes

– and lots of people riding bicycles – all over Poland. Apparently, in a recent speech to parliament, the Polish prime minister even talked about the need to strengthen the national railway system!

Olaf's words were music to my ears, of course. I am still troubled by some of the overall trends. But in my recent visits to the region, and through the process of researching this book, I realized that there are a number of well-established environmental organizations and community groups in the region – many launched with funding from the RBF – that are meeting new needs and reaching out to new generations of leaders and volunteers. The greenway movement endures to this day, with active programs across Europe (including CEE), and public spaces programs are thriving in town centers and markets throughout the region. While progress has been far slower than we all hoped in the heady days after the fall of the Berlin Wall, sustained local efforts, boosted by the RBF and other donors at critical moments, have led to tangible positive results, and people on the ground are better equipped to meet future opportunities and challenges.

The author riding into the Environmental Partnership for Central Europe's annual meeting in 2005 (held in Brno, Czech Republic), to present the Laurance S Rockefeller Award for Environmental Achievement.

Building trust

I have written several times in this book about my belief in the importance of mutual trust between funders and those whose work they support. I know

that this belief was shared by my colleagues at the RBF and at the foundations with which we frequently collaborated. But during my return trips to
CEE in recent years, I have gained a fuller sense of just how different this
approach is from the approach of many government and international funding agencies, and how deeply that difference resonated in the region.

Time after time, friends and former grantees in CEE reminded
me that after the RBF and other US funders left the region, most of the
funding for NGOs and civil society-building came from the European
Union, Western European governments, CEE governments, and international agencies. These donors tend to place so many restrictions and
requirements on their grants that recipients must spend a great deal of
time on reporting, accounting, and administrative details. To be sure, the
amounts of money involved are many times larger than our grants were.
Nonetheless, NGO leaders are often left feeling that their donors care
more about bureaucracy than substance. Of course that is not so, in most
cases; but the distrust-based approach to grantmaking that my friends
described is all too common.

NGO leaders in the region have learned to 'follow the rules' established by today's donors; but they clearly valued and miss the approach that
the RBF and other private foundations had taken in the region. Colleagues
on the ground told me how much they had welcomed the interest that
Nancy and I took in the substance of their work and in their efforts to build
institutional sustainability. Naturally, Nancy and I verified that our trust was
well placed, through face-to-face meetings (usually once a year) and careful review of the annual reporting that RBF grantees are required to submit.
But with less bureaucracy and more trust, it was possible for NGO leaders
to speak candidly about problems and challenges. The development of
mutual trust also enabled the RBF to make a substantial number of general support grants and multi-year pledges, which gave organizations the
flexibility to respond to changing realities and unforeseen opportunities. It
is now almost impossible for NGOs in the region to secure general support grants, funding for capacity-building, or grants for a reserve fund or to
build a capital base for a more sustainable future.

I think our approach enabled us to leave behind not only many strong
local, national, and regional projects, but also stronger non-profit organizations and a stronger non-profit sector. What's more, as I was told repeatedly in recent visits to the region, the approach modeled by the RBF and

some other foundations ended up encouraging many of our colleagues in CEE to work in a similar, trust-based way with their own communities, grantees, and partners.

I now realize that our emphasis on building trust may have had a deeper meaning in the region as well. During more than four decades of communist rule, distrust had become pervasive – between citizens and their government, but also among citizens themselves. Nor did people trust that they could make a difference or even that positive change was possible. Whether in Central and Eastern Europe or here in the United States, democracy cannot thrive under such conditions. Recent conversations with colleagues in the northern tier countries have encouraged me to believe that the RBF's way of working made at least a small contribution to cultivating the basic attitudes of trust on which a healthy civil society depends.

Part Three

Austria

Hungary

Slovenia

Croatia

Romania

Bosnia and Herzegovina

Serbia

Kosovo

Bulgaria

Montenegro

Italy

Macedonia

Albania

Greece

Primary focus of grantmaking

Reached through regional grantmaking

CHAPTER TEN

Last Stop
Western Balkans, 2000 to 2007

Apart from promoting dialogue, especially regarding issues
from the past, helping citizens 'to climb out of the dark hole
of ethno-nationalism' could be done by supporting different
grassroots movements and civil society initiatives by making
them more visible and more influential.

Lucia Vesnić-Alujević, *European Integration of Western Balkans: From
Reconciliation to European Future* (Centre for European Studies, 2012)

I could not have asked for a more satisfying – or challenging – way to close
out my long career at the RBF than by working in the Balkans. I had managed grantmaking programs in African and Caribbean countries shortly
after they became independent, and in Central and Eastern European
countries as they emerged from communist rule, so I knew something
about the challenges of building and rebuilding societies in the wake of
change. But in neither of these settings was the memory of violence so
fresh and horrific as in the Balkans during the first years of the new century.

The RBF began its active engagement there in the wake of the complex, bloody ethnic struggles of the 1990s, shortly after a 1999 NATO
air campaign had halted Serbian military repression in Kosovo. The entire
region had suffered massive economic and societal disruption. Corruption
and organized crime were pervasive.

All that remained of Tito's Yugoslavia (which had once encom-
passed six abutting Western Balkan countries) was Serbia, including
Kosovo, and Montenegro. This small vestige still carried the big name of
the Federal Republic of Yugoslavia (FRY). A United Nations Mission in
Kosovo (UNMIK) was providing governance in that province, which had
formerly been an autonomous political unit of Serbia.

Over the next eight years I was responsible for RBF grantmaking
in the Western Balkans, recommending more than 60 grants that totaled
approximately $6.5 million. During this period the FRY first became a

reformulated country called the 'State Union of Serbia and Montenegro' in 2003; then, in a 2006 referendum, just over 55 per cent of Montenegrins voted for independence from Serbia – a vote that the European Union recognized and Serbia did not challenge. A majority of Kosovars (the Albanian population of the province) also sought independence, having suffered terribly at the hands of Serbia's government and paramilitary forces during the presidency of Serbian nationalist Slobodan Milošević, who was eventually indicted (in 1999) by the UN's International Criminal Tribunal for the Former Yugoslavia for crimes against humanity in Kosovo, and later, for grave breaches of the Geneva Conventions in Croatia and Bosnia and genocide in Bosnia. The Serbian government refused to allow independence for Kosovo, claiming that Kosovo was the ancient cradle of Serbia and its Orthodox faith. A plan for the 'final status' of Kosovo was developed through negotiations led, in 2006 and 2007, by former Finnish president Martti Ahtisaari (appointed to that role by the UN Secretary General), but the Serbs and Albanian Kosovars remained far apart and the Ahtisaari plan was never brought to the UN Security Council for a vote. In 2008 Kosovo declared its independence unilaterally, against the strenuous protests of Serbia and the Kosovar Serb population.*

How could a modest-sized foundation, such as the RBF, make a difference in Serbia, Montenegro, and Kosovo in these tense and still tumultuous times? The three settings were very different – geographically, ethnically, and economically; in Kosovo, there was the special need to prepare for the time when UNMIK oversight would come to an end. But majorities in all three places wanted to build democratic, market-oriented societies that could qualify for eventual membership of the European Union. Economic development was a key concern in all three places, and many citizens and local and national government officials understood the need for wise use of natural resources and the value of heritage preservation. While there were differing degrees of commitment to reducing ethnic tensions, it was clear that progress on this front also would be required if these countries were to become candidates for EU membership. Very

* In 2010 the International Court of Justice in The Hague – which had been asked by the UN General Assembly to rule on the legality of Kosovo's declaration – determined that no international law had been violated. Today, Kosovo's independence is recognized by 99 UN member states (including the United States and most member states of the European Union) and the Republic of China (Taiwan), although many states have refused recognition, most notably China and Russia – and, of course, Serbia.

few private foundations were working in the region at the start of the new century. The international community had undertaken a $2.4 billion 'Stability Pact for South Eastern Europe' in July 1999, to finance a range of programs to promote democracy, economic development, regional cooperation, and peace and security – but the pact was not oriented toward citizen-empowering strategies and projects of the sort that the RBF and other private foundations could support. Another gap seemed to be the lack of funding to build government capacity.

I began my work in the FRY with grantmaking guidelines that focused on basic needs: (1) building democratic capacity, (2) grappling with questions of national identity and challenges of ethnic reconciliation, and (3) developing sustainable communities. In each of these areas, we tried to stretch our modest resources to fund diverse but mutually reinforc-ing programs and projects; we felt that a holistic approach to facilitating change would be more effective than investing in a single strategy. I was able to 'hit the ground running' in the Balkans, partly because of the experi-ence and knowledge of the region that Stephen Heintz, who had become president of the Fund in 2001, brought to the RBF from his time spent in Prague, where he had been working on issues of economic reform, civil society development, and international security throughout Central and Eastern Europe.

The very selective highlights that follow are organized under four cross-cutting headings that emphasize some of the notable grantmaking challenges and opportunities that we faced in the Western Balkans.

Opportunities to adapt models and lessons learned

Stephen's familiarity with the region gave me a head start in the Balkans, but my work in Central and Eastern Europe also provided me with con-tacts and experiences that would be relevant to grantmaking in Serbia, Montenegro, and Kosovo. The grantmaking and training programs that we had helped to launch in Central and Eastern Europe – such as the Environmental Partnership for Central Europe and Nadace Via – proved to be valuable models for the Balkans. In addition, some of the RBF's funding partners in those earlier endeavors had become active in the Western Balkans as well, so we could build together on lessons learned. Longstanding RBF grantees like the Project for Public Spaces also served as important models and sources of inspiration and guidance.

Creating non-bureaucratic, local sources of funding and training

In 2001 the RBF joined the Mott Foundation (where Walter Veirs, a young lawyer in whom I saw a lot of myself, had become a trusted colleague), a Dutch philanthropic agency, and the German Marshall Fund to support the young Balkan Community Initiatives Fund (BCIF), which was dedicated to encouraging and strengthening efforts by citizens' groups and NGOs in Serbia and Montenegro to build strong, harmonious, and integrated communities. Founded under UK law, the BCIF quickly became an indigenous non-profit organization in the FRY, making grants from $300 to $3,000 to local groups for protecting human rights and promoting tolerance, improving ethnic relations, addressing environmental problems, and responding to children's needs. The BCIF also helped build the organizational capacity of local groups, through a range of training and technical assistance efforts. As was the case in the early years of the Environmental Partnership for Central Europe, the RBF and the other primary donors to the BCIF acted as informal advisers to the Fund.

The BCIF has grown and matured over the past decade. From $140,000 in 2003, the BCIF's annual budget has swollen to over $1.5 million, with support provided by a wide range of donors, including local businesses. The BCIF owns office space that it rents to other agencies and has managed to accumulate a reserve fund and begin building an endowment. By 2008 the BCIF had spun off its Montenegro office into an independent foundation, the Fund for Active Citizenship (fAKT). In a short time, fAKT emerged as the leading Montenegrin funder of efforts to strengthen democratic practice, promote sustainable development, and increase capacity in civil society and for civic engagement. From an initial $100,000 grantmaking program, fAKT's budget has grown to $1 million, which includes continued support from the RBF and Mott.

Like the Environmental Partnership foundations, the BCIF takes a holistic and non-bureaucratic approach to its grantmaking. When I spoke recently with former BCIF director Aleksandra (Alex) Vesić, she echoed comments made by the staffs of the Environmental Partnerships, noting that the RBF (and Mott) style of grantmaking became the BCIF's style – responsive and flexible, engaged but not directive, committed to building long-term capacity.

The basic model of the local regranting organization seems to be catching on more widely as well. Alex told me that the European Union is now funding grantmaking organizations in EU-candidate countries. She credited Mott and the RBF with helping to start that trend by supporting indigenous foundations at a time when no other donors saw them as potentially serious actors in the region. Both the BCIF (which recently changed its name to the Trag Foundation) and fAKT have become valuable partners to a variety of donors in the region and are part of a regional network of grantmakers that work together to expand interest in philanthropy and the role of the non-profit sector.

The Green Network of Vojvodina (GNV) took the lead in re-establishing farmers' markets offering fresh local foods in Novi Sad and other parts of the Serbian province of Vojvodina. From left to right: organic farmers from the Vozár Farm – Vladimir Vozár, his mother Zuzana Vozár, and on the far right a worker from the farm. To the right of Zuzana Vozár is Olivera Radovanović, a founder and longtime leader of the GNV.

Adapting proven strategies for revitalizing communities

While on an exploratory visit to Belgrade in 2001, I learned from a Dutch foundation colleague about a new local group, the Green Network of Vojvodina (GNV), based in Novi Sad in the northern Serbian province of Vojvodina. The GNV was founded in 2000 by local academics, farmers, and other community change agents who wanted to revitalize their province by drawing on Vojvodina's pre-First World War history as a 'bread basket' for the Austro-Hungarian empire, where people from different ethnic backgrounds lived and worked together on the land, tilling the rich soil and taking advantage of the good climate conditions.

The RBF began to fund the group, which devised communications and education strategies to encourage young people to remain on or return to the land. The GNV became a major force in the healthy foods movement and in sustainable and organic agriculture in the province. It also played an active role in historic preservation and management of public spaces. More recently, the GNV has been working to link farmers in Vojvodina with their counterparts in Croatia.

While the RBF's unusually flexible approach to grantmaking was important for the GNV in its early years – we were willing to fund equipment purchases, salaries, travel, and other operational needs that most foundations' grants did not cover – our ability to introduce GNV staff to the work and ideas of other groups was equally valuable. In 2004, at a workshop held at the RBF's Pocantico Conference Center, GNV staff learned about the Project for Public Spaces (PPS) and its role in promoting the spread of farmers' markets in the United States. A team from the PPS later went to Novi Sad and helped the GNV create a farmers' market that featured local produce – not the bananas and other imported foodstuffs that were typically available at farmers' markets in the Balkans. At the same RBF workshop, I mentioned the greenways movement in Central Europe. As a result of this conversation, a member of the Czech Greenway staff was invited to visit Novi Sad to discuss the possibility of siting a greenway there. Ultimately, the GNV developed the first greenway in Vojvodina, running from Novi Sad to the Croatian border, which is still a popular corridor for hiking and other forms of green tourism. The RBF also introduced the GNV to the land stewardship work that was being done by the Quebec-Labrador Foundation's Atlantic Center for the Environment. GNV staff began to study the concept and visited stewardship areas in other countries – and eventually, land stewardship became a core principle of the GNV's work.

Pivotal places

Under the revised program architecture that was adopted by the RBF in 2003, the Western Balkans were included in a new category of grant-making called 'pivotal places,' which identified several specific locations on which the RBF would concentrate cross-programmatic attention. RBF president Stephen Heintz borrowed the concept from historian Paul Kennedy, author of *The Pivotal States*. 'Pivotal places' were defined as sub-national areas, nation-states, or cross-border regions which have special importance with regard to the Fund's substantive concerns and whose future will have disproportionate significance for the future of a sur-rounding region, an ecosystem, or the world. The Fund currently works in three pivotal places: New York City, Southern China, and Western Balkans.

Clearly, some of the other places in which I had worked over the years were also 'pivotal,' although that category had not yet been articu-lated by the Fund – think of Central and Eastern Europe after the fall of the Berlin Wall, for example. So the new formulation was quite consistent with the Fund's history, while creating new opportunities for responsiveness to place-based needs.

The challenge of reducing inter-ethnic tensions

Conflict resolution was not an overarching theme of the RBF's grantmak-ing when we became active in the Balkans, although promoting peace and security certainly was a well-established interest of the Fund (today, the Fund has a Peacebuilding Program that makes grants in support of inno-vative and collaborative approaches to conflict prevention, management, and transformation). But as our Balkans program guidelines acknowl-edged at the time, it was impossible to work in the region without making at least modest efforts to support some of the courageous individuals and groups trying to grapple with the ethnic tensions that had fed the violence of the 1990s.

Early on, we recognized the power of the arts and media as vehicles for this kind of public education. We made grants to a number of NGOs for cultural outreach and community affairs programming. For example, a grant to Radio Television B92, in Belgrade, helped to fund the develop-ment of a 'Documentation Center of Wars, 1991–1999,' which assembled a library and video archive that was open to the public, and organized many relevant public programs, not only in Belgrade, but also in Novi Sad and other cities throughout Serbia.

We also funded efforts to promote human rights protection and ethnic tolerance outside of the urban centers of Serbia, Montenegro, and Kosovo. I relished the opportunity to travel to all corners of the region to witness the passion, determination, and humility of the leaders of these initiatives. One of the earliest and smallest grants ($6,000 in 2001) that I recommended in the Western Balkans was for a school music program called the Centre for Multicultural Education, in the southern Serbian town of Preševo. The Centre had assembled an orchestra made up of Albanian, Roma, and Serb children. Orchestra rehearsals were one of the few settings in which these children all could participate in the same after-school program – and the orchestra's performances played to a rare multi-ethnic audience of parents and family members. In another southern Serbian town, Vranje, near the Kosovo and Macedonian borders, I met a local couple who had been fighting human rights abuse for 20 years in communities torn by tensions among Serbs, Albanians, and Roma. For several years the RBF supported their organization, the Committee for Human Rights–Vranje, which created a multi-ethnic news service and provided free legal assistance to victims of human rights abuses from all ethnicities.

In Montenegro we supported the Nansen Dialogue Centre (based in Podgorica), which focused on the poorest region of the country, the Montenegrin Sandžak. This was one of a network of Nansen Centres throughout the Balkans, named after Fridtjof Nansen, a Norwegian explorer, scientist, diplomat, humanitarian, and Nobel Peace Prize laureate (in 1922). Employing proven dialogue and conflict resolution techniques, the Centre in Montenegro has earned a reputation as one of the few genuinely 'non-partisan' NGOs in the region. In addition to supporting this effort in the northeastern part of Montenegro, the RBF also funded New Horizons, in the predominantly Albanian town of Ulcinj in southern Montenegro, which worked to promote tolerance among ethnic groups and the protection of human rights, in addition to educating the public about the role of Albanians in Montenegrin society.

In Kosovo we funded an effort to build trust between Kosovar Serbs and Albanians in five regions that were viewed as potential 'hot spots' for conflict (Mitrovica, Goraždevac, Pejë/Peć, Shtërpcë/Štrpce, and Gračanica). The Community Watch Project (CWP) helped Serbs and Albanians work together to improve life and security in their shared communities. Managed by the New York-based East West Management Institute, with leadership from local people (including Haki Abazi, who eventually became my successor at the RBF), the CWP fostered inter-ethnic action to improve local schools and education, employment and infrastructure, and overall safety. We also supported the Kosova Women's Network (KWN), a network of Roma, Bosniak, Turkish, Serb, and Albanian women which provided training, material assistance, and encouragement to women-led efforts that sought to carve out a foothold for women of all ethnicities in Kosovo politics.

While we focused on projects based in Serbia, Montenegro, and Kosovo, we also realized that these countries did not exist in isolation and that efforts to bridge divides between countries would be helpful and necessary as well. We supported some excellent regional efforts, including the Center for Regionalism, established in 1998, which was one of the first and best groups in Serbia to think regionally and to propose practical strategies for restoring linkages and relationships that had been ruptured by the conflicts of the 1990s. To this day, the Center works to promote democratization and improve inter-ethnic relations in Serbia, Montenegro, and Kosovo and to encourage normalization and reconciliation between former combatants in Serbia, Croatia, and Bosnia. With early support from the RBF, the Center's Igman Initiative (a joint venture of NGOs in Serbia, Croatia, and Bosnia) promoted regional cooperation, ethnic tolerance, and non-violent conflict resolution through exchanges and practical projects. One such project was the creation of an Association of Multiethnic Cities of Southeast Europe, in which more than 70 cities were participating by the end of 2007. In 2002, in cooperation with the Mother Theresa Society in Pristina, Kosovo, and the Organization for Security and Cooperation in Europe (OSCE), the Center launched a unique long-term initiative called the Civic Dialogue, which brought together NGO leaders from Serbia and Kosovo in order to normalize their interactions and develop inter-ethnic trust and tolerance. This process helped to restart dialogues on human rights, inter-ethnic cooperation, women's equality, the needs of young people, and other issues.

Fighting organized crime and corruption

It took courage and far-sightedness to address inter-ethnic tensions in Serbia, Montenegro, and Kosovo during the tense aftermath of the violence of the 1990s. This was – and is – true as well for the individuals and groups that began to tackle the grave problem of corruption and organized crime in the region.

In Montenegro, which ratified the UN Convention against Corruption in 2005, the RBF supported one of the most intrepid NGOs working in this field, the Network for the Affirmation of the NGO Sector (MANS). An early initiative of MANS focused on corruption, bribery, and conflicts of interest in land-use and construction projects, empowering citizens in three communities – Podgorica (the capital), Budva (a city in the south), and Žabljak (a town in the north) – to play a 'watchdog' role. Through media and internet-based public education campaigns and the provision of legal and other technical services, citizens were encouraged to report instances of suspected corruption – on a special phone line that preserved their anonymity – and to request information on legislative and judicial procedures. By 2010 considerable progress had been made. Legal and administrative frameworks now do a better job of defining prohibited behavior and clarifying the rights of citizens to complain. Despite threats to the life of MANS's director, the organization has boldly taken on other forms of bribery and corruption.

Special opportunities for youth involvement

During the 1990s young people had been in the forefront of the opposition to nationalist militarism in the Balkans. By the early 2000s many of the young men and women who had spent their childhoods in poverty and their adolescent years in war felt they had no place in the new economic and political systems of their countries. Some had become cynical about the opportunities for a better future that democracy was supposed to provide. Seventy per cent of Serbia's youth had never ventured beyond that country's borders. At the same time, young people often were more willing than their parents to put aside ethnic and nationalistic prejudices, and there was a cohort of emerging young leaders eager to work for democratic reform. As a matter of course, all of the Fund's program officers, in every issue area, were on the lookout for new and emerging leaders. But in the Western Balkans there seemed to be a particular need and opportunity to work with young people. With urging and commitment from my young program assistant at the time, Grant Garrison, we gradually developed a special focus on supporting youth-led organizations as well as initiatives that raised awareness of the need for youth development.

During a relatively early trip to the region (in 2003) with Stephen Heintz and Grant, we were so impressed by a group of young Serbs and Kosovar Albanians in Mitrovica that we quickly made a grant to their organization, the Multi-ethnic Children and Youth Peace Centre (MCYPC). The Centre offered multi-ethnic English language and computer classes, a radio broadcast, and a monthly magazine published in Serbian and Albanian. The Centre received modest support from the Council of Europe, Kosovo Open Society Foundation, local embassies, and relief organizations, but our $10,000 grant helped keep the organization's magazine (called *Future*) in print for several months during a funding gap.

Other small grants to youth-led and youth-focused programs followed. Grant asked for a chance to spend some extended time in the Western Balkans in order to assess grantmaking opportunities in the field of youth engagement and leadership development. He lived and traveled in the region during the spring of 2005, and returned with many ideas and valuable contacts. Grant ended up playing a leading role in developing this strand of grantmaking, which was maintained after he moved on. In fact, youth engagement and leadership development is one approach of the RBF's Western Balkans Program to this day.

Among the organizations to which Grant called our attention was the Youth Initiative for Human Rights (YIHR), with offices in Belgrade and Pristina. The YIHR was founded by a group of young Serbs and Kosovars to incubate local, youth-led human rights NGOs in the countryside, while pressing government leaders for greater human rights protections. We were impressed by the YIHR's effectiveness at both levels, and provided general support for many years to build the organization.

Grant also became well acquainted with a tight-knit group of (mostly young) editors and journalists who had launched the Balkan Investigative Reporting Network (BIRN), in Sarajevo. BIRN trains and helps journalists to produce accurate, analytical investigative reporting on complex political, economic, and social issues. While encouraging local, national, and regional media organizations to play watchdog roles, BIRN has also made its own documentary movies and TV, radio, and online programs to encourage all sectors of society to debate critical issues openly. With ongoing support from the RBF and other donors, BIRN has become a trusted, influential source of information and analysis about key regional transition issues. BIRN Kosovo created a weekly television show, *Jeta në Kosovë* (Life in Kosovo), that gives citizens a chance to confront decision-makers about critical policy choices; the program quickly attracted more than 350,000 weekly viewers. In 2007 I attended one televised open debate in Pristina, Kosovo. I will never forget the well-moderated but challenging exchanges between government leaders and the Serbs and Kosovar Albanians who asked them probing questions.

RBF support helped to build the capacity of the Student Union of Serbia and (through a partnership between longtime RBF grantee, the Institute for Sustainable Development, and Belgrade-based Civic Initiatives) to create coalitions of young Serbs who worked to influence public officials at the local and national levels. We supported the Center for Civil Society Development (Protecta) in Niš, in southern Serbia, which offered computer skills and English language instruction for young people; helped to build the capacity of grassroots youth clubs; assisted young people with employment searches; and, in 2006, became one of the leaders of a major initiative to return to municipal authorities some of the decision-making power that Milošević had usurped. This countrywide coalition of youth groups, human rights organizations, academics, and concerned individuals has achieved important results in recent years.

Helping government officials to address fundamental challenges

In prior years, the RBF had supported efforts to train new political leaders and elected officials in other regions where the Fund was active. We did some of this kind of grantmaking in the Western Balkans as well. For example, we supported the Belgrade Fund for Political Excellence (BFPE), which educated politicians and emerging leaders about democratic values and principles and practical ways to advance desperately needed reforms. Leaders from all over Serbia and Montenegro, representing diverse parties, came together with the help of the BFPE to consider common governance challenges and to benefit from interactive sessions with seasoned political leaders and academics from Europe and North America. Meeting these aspiring political leaders reminded me of how many people were coming up through the ranks of government with a strong commitment to building healthy, democratic societies and nations in the Balkans.

But we also employed a different strategy to enhance the capacity of the national governments of Serbia, Montenegro, and Kosovo. More than at any other period in my career, we devoted considerable attention and a significant share of our budget to initiatives that worked directly with government officials in hopes of improving government programs and policies.

This was partly due to Stephen Heintz's willingness to be bold and his desire to seize the momentum of change before it dissipated. Stephen also had worked in government early in his career (he was Commissioner for Economic Development of the State of Connecticut in his early 30s), and he understood that direct engagement with governments could be an effective strategy. We pursued such an approach in all three of the countries in which we were active – with a different focus in each place.

Serbia: confronting painful issues

In 2000 the FRY was a country in which a preponderance of the population wanted to become more integrated into Europe and its institutions, while a strong minority in Serbia would not even allow wartime masterminds of genocide to be apprehended for trial in the International Criminal Tribunal in The Hague. But the first democratic government in Serbia, led by constitutional law professor Vojislav Koštunica, seemed to be signaling that atrocities and human rights abuses could and would be addressed in this new era. We believed that some key government figures were ready to grapple with inter-ethnic challenges, and we identified several bold new initiatives that we thought were worthy of early support.

Truth and reconciliation

In 2001 and 2002 grants to the New York City-based International Center for Transitional Justice supported an effort by Dr Alex Boraine, the Center's founder and former co-chairman of South Africa's Truth and Reconciliation Commission, to help the FRY's newly formed Truth and Reconciliation Commission (TRC) get off the ground. With a 'green light' from President Koštunica, the Commission looked like it might achieve at least some modest success. Boraine was treated with respect and provided valuable guidance – but soon obstacles arose within the government that

Koštunica either could not or would not surmount. Financial support for the Commission was never approved; commissioners were not paid; efforts to broaden the composition of the Commission failed; and soon the TRC initiative came to a halt.

We had known all along that this initiative was risky. Some of our advisers had cautioned that it was too soon for Serbia to begin the pursuit of 'transitional justice' (the term used to describe judicial and non-judicial measures taken by societies to redress legacies of massive human rights abuse). Some Serbs felt that any effective transitional justice process would have to be regional, given the legacy of atrocities committed by Croats, Serbs, and Albanians. Others believed that it was important to try to begin what would inevitably be a long, complex process. We were probably too optimistic in our assessment of Koštunica's interest – and perhaps his political courage – when it came to dealing with such a politically sensitive issue. While we were disappointed in the outcome, some of the most dedicated commissioners did undertake valuable preliminary research and held early informal discussions; the debate around this effort was important, and the concept of truth and reconciliation made its way into the media and into dinner-table conversations. Later in the decade, a civil society initiative called RECOM was launched to push for a regional commission on truth and reconciliation. It has not yet achieved its aim, but again, the discussions and debate have raised awareness significantly.

Today, while there is no human rights-related ministry in Serbia, there is a human rights office that helps people who have been victims of ethnic prejudice or persecution. A commission on equality also has been established. The thinking of 'old guard' Serbian nationalists is slow to change. But my contacts in Serbia tell me that the situation now is very different from that of ten years ago. People of all backgrounds know that they can file complaints with the human rights ombudsman or bring discrimination issues to the commission – and they are doing so. Since the EU has pushed applicant countries (including Serbia) to focus on human rights protections, there are now pragmatic reasons for trying to improve relations among different groups.

Do today's human rights office and equality commission have some roots in the two initiatives that the RBF supported in the early years of the century? There is no way of knowing for sure, but my contacts on the ground are convinced that our grantmaking helped to keep those issues alive, even though some of our efforts were premature.

Ethnic relations

The RBF provided early support to the United Nations Development Program (UNDP) office in Belgrade for its role in providing technical assistance and training for personnel of the new Ministry on Ethnic and National Communities in the FRY. Milošević had eliminated such a ministry in the 1990s; when he was ousted in 2000, it was re-established, and Rasim Ljajić was appointed as minister (he was then the only Muslim in a leadership position in the federal government). Sadly, the UNDP program made much less progress than we had hoped. The problem was an insufficient 'meeting of minds' between UNDP and ministry officials, with personality conflicts and competing egos at the root of the impasse. While Stephen and I discussed these challenges and I had several separate meetings with key UNDP and ministry leaders (including Ljajić), we were not able to achieve a breakthrough.

Stephen and I remained impressed by Ljajić and his senior associates, and by their promising ideas and initiatives. The ministry opened storefront offices around the country, where people could go with complaints about discrimination or human rights abuses. The ministry also launched an impressive media campaign aimed at encouraging people to think in new ways and to explore possibilities for ethnic cooperation. Human rights legislation drafted and implemented by the ministry was praised by EU authorities.

Like the RBF's support for a truth and reconciliation commission, our involvement in this effort was understood by the staff and board to be at the risky end of the grantmaking spectrum. While considerably less productive than we had hoped, both of these grants nonetheless supported some very early steps in a long, uneven process of dealing with the trauma of the 1990s.

Montenegro: promoting sustainable development

By the time the RBF became active in the region, Montenegro's prime minister, Milo Djukanović, had been in power since the late 1980s; with some breaks and a stint as president, he still serves as prime minister today (2013). As a young and ambitious politician, Djukanović had been a collaborator of Slobodan Milošević, the nationalist president of Serbia (and later of the Federal Republic of Yugoslavia) who was charged with committing crimes against humanity during the Balkan wars; Djukanović ultimately parted ways with Milošević. The prime minister and his family have long been linked in the media with questionable business groups that own valuable properties and companies in Montenegro. At the same time, Djukanović and his allies allowed (and still do allow) some space for civic engagement in Montenegro, including activities that challenge the government. Government and non-governmental leaders have worked side by side to bring Montenegro, an oasis of relative inter-ethnic tranquility in the region, into the European Union as soon as possible. Djukanović is currently serving his fourth non-consecutive term as prime minister.

The national government also continued to endorse the concept of Montenegro as an 'ecological state,' an idea that had been enshrined in a 1992 amendment to the Montenegrin constitution. Montenegro contains truly remarkable and diverse natural resources – mountains, sea-coast, forests, and agricultural lands – within a country the size of Connecticut, inhabited by a population of only around 700,000 people. Economic sanctions imposed on Yugoslavia (which included Montenegro) in the 1990s helped to insulate the country's natural and cultural heritage against development-related degradation. In the early 2000s accelerating interest in tourism and overall economic development, fueled by corruption in government and business, began to pose threats to Montenegro's natural beauty. Stephen and I both judged that the RBF had an opportunity to help the Montenegrin government promote sustainable development, even as we continued our support of environmental NGOs in the country.

Because we had a good working relationship with the UNDP office in Podgorica, which was active in efforts to improve the effectiveness, transparency, and efficiency of the government, we collaborated with the UNDP on some activities and worked directly with the Montenegrin government in other initiatives. We also supported more than a half dozen NGOs with highly committed and productive small staffs – such as Expeditio in Kotor, Natura in Kolašin, and the Network for the Affirmation of the NGO Sector (MANS) in Podgorica – that were doing very creative and often courageous work to advance the concepts of wise use of natural and cultural resources and overall sustainable development.

Some of the leaders of Expeditio, dedicated to encouraging sustainable development in Montenegro and neighboring countries through activities in cultural heritage preservation, sustainable architecture, and urban planning as well as through contributions to the development of civil society. From left to right: Tatjana Rajić, Stevan Kordić, Aleksandra Kapetanović, and Sanja Bojanić. (This photo was taken in summer 2007, near Parest, Montenegro, on the shore of the Bay of Kotor.)

Some of the activities we undertook were designed to bring Montenegrin government and NGO leaders together with counterparts from Costa Rica, the world's most widely appreciated ecological state. In 2001, through the UNDP, we brought Costa Rican experts – including the highly respected former environment minister Dr René Castro-Salazar – to Montenegro to discuss strategies for sustainable development. A couple of years later, we organized a trip to Costa Rica for a Montenegrin delegation led by Prime Minister Djukanović. The delegation met with President Pacheco and other Costa Rican government leaders, and participated in well-organized seminars and field trips put together by the Costa Rican hosts.

We also provided opportunities for leaders of the Montenegrin government to meet with other experts on sustainable development. For example, in April 2004 the RBF held a Pocantico conference at which the prime minister and the heads of key ministries met with Mark Malloch Brown, administrator of the UNDP; Jeffrey Sachs, president of the Earth Institute at Columbia University; and Len Good, president of the Global Environment Fund, all of whom shared valuable experience and observations with the Montenegrin leaders.

In 2005/6 we funded the RBF-supported Institute for Sustainable Development in Warsaw to consult with Montenegrin officials about options for policy reform and about the possibility of creating a think-tank focused on sustainable development. Also in 2005, the RBF funded the development of the Strategic Framework for Sustainable Tourism in Central and Northern Montenegro, which the Montenegrin government formally approved and which was applauded by many NGOs – but not very fully implemented.

The Montenegrin leaders, including the prime minister, were always cordial and interested. But frankly, I felt they were only going through the motions in Costa Rica and at Pocantico. By the end of 2005 it was clear that the Montenegrin government was not prepared to match its rhetorical support for sustainable development with appropriate action. The government urged construction of a huge dam that would flood pristine mountain areas that were key destinations for eco-tourism. Fortunately, massive pressure from civil society groups (partly supported by the RBF and UNDP), local governments, and segments of the business community, as well as from international organizations including UNESCO and the International Union for Conservation of Nature (IUCN), forced the government to withdraw from the project.

As of my retirement in 2007, I felt that our considerable efforts – measured as much in staff time as in financial support – had not produced the results it seemed reasonable to expect in the early 2000s, although some progress in policy matters and overall management of natural resources probably can be traced in part to our engagement.

Kosovo: determining its 'final status'

Many analysts consider Kosovo to be the place where the disintegration of the former Yugoslavia started. Until it declared independence, Kosovo was a small, autonomous, landlocked province in the south of Serbia, but oppressive measures taken by the communist political elite in Belgrade in the 1980s provoked protests and ethnic tensions between the majority Albanian population in Kosovo and Serbs both inside and outside Kosovo. In 1989 Milošević revoked Kosovo's status as an autonomous province and expelled hundreds of thousands of Kosovar Albanians (over 200,000 workers and 100,000 students) from their workplaces and public schools. These measures led to the creation of two parallel governance systems in

Kosovo, one run by Serb authorities and the other by Kosovar Albanians. These two parallel systems were maintained until 1998, when open conflict started between Serb forces and the Kosovo Liberation Army. Although the international community facilitated several attempts at a peaceful resolution, the conflict ended only in 1999, after a 78-day NATO air campaign against Serb military targets. At that point, UN Security Council (UNSC) Resolution 1244 created the United Nations Interim Administration Mission in Kosovo (UNMIK) to govern the province, with the help of an international security force.

When Stephen and I traveled to Kosovo in the early 2000s and met with the leaders of UNMIK and the Kosovo provisional government that had been established and was being overseen by UNMIK, we began to wonder if there might be a role for the RBF in helping local and international leaders make progress toward determining the province's political future – its 'final status.' At the time, Kosovo had a population slightly in excess of 2 million, half of which was under 25 years of age – and more than half of which was living in poverty or near poverty. Albanians constituted nearly 90 per cent of the population, and Serbs made up less than 7 per cent. Most Serbs in Kosovo and many Serbs in Serbia continued to hold that, because Serbia's medieval kingdom was centered in Kosovo, the province must not under any circumstances be separated from the Serbian nation. Violent clashes between Kosovar Albanians and Kosovar Serbs persisted.

When Kosovar Serbs boycotted parliamentary elections in 2004, it became clear that multi-ethnicity – a critical 'standard before status' requirement in UNSC Resolution 1244 – was practically non-existent. Since the stipulated standards had not been met, the final status of Kosovo could not be addressed through the process of negotiations foreseen (and hoped for) in Resolution 1244. Meanwhile, a popular, elderly Albanian leader, Ibrahim Rugova, and his party received the most votes in the 2004 election. Rugova's campaign had focused on independence rather than on the practical concerns of the people of Kosovo (four years after the official end of armed conflict, no Kosovar political party had a plan to relieve unemployment or provide electricity for the cold months). In Serbia the idea of 'decentralization' – the code word for 'partition,' a way of staving off true independence for Kosovo – was gaining traction.

The need for reliable statistics

Obtaining accurate information on the size and distribution of the Serb population in Kosovo was critical in the final-status debate. The RBF understood the need for sound, independent research to inform policy development; indeed, we had supported the creation of a number of think-tanks in Central and Eastern Europe. We knew that the European Stability Initiative (ESI), in Berlin, had produced impressive analyses of developments in the transitional societies of Southeast Europe, with a particular focus on the impacts of international interventions. Between 2004 and 2006 we funded the ESI to transfer some of its highly regarded research methodology to indigenous Kosovar researchers, helping them to collect important economic and social data from the tiny villages and larger towns in Kosovo. In the absence of any census process, this collaboration generated the most reliable statistics available on the Serb population in Kosovo, by extrapolating from primary school enrollment data. With continued RBF support, local researchers went on to establish the Kosovo Stability Initiative (IKS), which enjoyed ongoing guidance from the ESI for several years.

With the UNSC Resolution 1244 process dead in the water, UN Secretary General Kofi Annan launched a new process, in 2005, to develop a plan for achieving Kosovo's final status. He selected Martti Ahtisaari, former president of Finland, to lead the negotiating team, which included representatives from Serbia and Kosovo as well as from the EU and the United States. The US representative was RBF trustee and retired diplomat Frank Wisner. Since 2003 the RBF had been working with NGOs in Kosovo to improve inter-ethnic cooperation and to encourage peaceful debate about the quest for a final status that would be acceptable to Kosovar Albanians and Serbs alike. But we had also cultivated contacts with government leaders, representatives of international and foreign government agencies, and senior UN staff – and now we had a close relationship with one of the negotiators on the Ahtisaari team. We followed the development of the Ahtisaari plan closely, and weighed in on what we saw as a need for more public participation in planning for the future of Kosovo, and for the creation of a detailed strategy for the first 120 days *after* the presumed acceptance of the Ahtisaari plan. While not yet mentioning the word 'independence,' the draft settlement plan included several provisions that were widely interpreted as implying statehood for

Kosovo. For example, the draft settlement would give Kosovo the right to apply for membership in international organizations, create a Kosovo security force, and adopt national symbols.

Then, in April 2007, we hosted a high-level meeting at Pocantico on 'Developing a Strategy for Kosovo's First 120 Days.' Ambassador Wisner and Ambassador Wolfgang Pitritsch (the EU representative at the Ahtisaari talks) chaired the conference. Participants included Kosovo president Fatmir Sejdiu, Kosovo prime minister Agim Çeku, and other Kosovar leaders; US Under Secretary for Political Affairs Nicholas Burns; former US president Bill Clinton (a hero to many in Kosovo because of his role in initiating the 1999 air strikes); former Secretary of State Madeline Albright; former US Ambassador to the UN Richard Holbrooke; former White House Chief of Staff John Podesta; plus representatives from other post-conflict societies, including the former Afghan finance minister Ashraf Ghani and the former chief negotiator for the talks that led to the dismantling of apartheid in South Africa, Roelf Meyer, as well as other international participants. The Foundation for a Civil Society and the East West Management Institute were partners with the RBF in conference preparation and follow-up, and the Charles Stewart Mott Foundation joined the RBF in funding the initiative.

This impressive group drafted and signed a document called the *Pocantico Declaration by the Kosovar Unity Team*, stating that they all were committed to working collaboratively on concrete issues that would have to be addressed during the 120-day transition period. Ultimately, after Kosovo declared its independence unilaterally in 2008, the Ahtisaari plan did become the basis of Kosovo's constitution and was formally adopted by the Kosovar parliament.

Shortly after the Pocantico Kosovo Forum, the RBF – with Stephen and Frank Wisner in the lead – moved boldly to establish a supplementary fund to help Kosovo's leaders and citizens address the urgent next steps identified in the final *Pocantico Declaration*. Through immediate grants to the Foundation for a Civil Society and the East West Management Institute, this fund helped Kosovar leaders communicate realities and risks to the citizens of Kosovo; draft a new constitution and outline a legislative process; and prepare for a donors' conference. In addition, the fund helped civil society actors work to maintain regional stability as international discussions went on and to increase dialogue between Serbs in Serbia and Kosovo and Albanian Kosovars.

While I played an active role in this work, it was Stephen's and Frank's vision and leadership that inspired the Pocantico forum and the creation of the follow-up fund. Here was a case where a proactive foundation was able to make direct, constructive contributions in a complex international situation, the resolution of which would advance important grantmaking goals of the Fund.

Members of the RBF board and staff, on a board trip to the Western Balkans in the summer of 2007. From left to right: myself; Valerie R Wayne, current RBF board chair; Miranda Kaiser, board member; and Robert Parton, now her husband. To the right of the post, Richard Chasin, board member; Haki Abazi, my successor as program director for pivotal place grantmaking in the Western Balkans; Ariadne Papagapitos, then special assistant to RBF president and now director of the RBF's Peacebuilding Program; and Laura R Chasin, former board member.

Closing reflections

Two features of this last phase of my RBF career are worth revisiting here, because they represent aspects of the practice of grantmaking about which I have not said much so far. The first is the role that my young program assistant, Grant Garrison, was encouraged and enabled to play in the development of our program in the Western Balkans. I know that the RBF is not alone among foundations in making internships, fellowships, and other employment opportunities available to young men and women who are considering careers in philanthropy – although the RBF may have demonstrated an unusual degree of flexibility and creativity in defining the scope of their assignments. I would like to see more foundations create such openings, which benefit both the institution and the individuals involved. There are challenges as well, of course. It is not always easy for senior staff to take on the role of mentor in addition to their other responsibilities; the overextended program officer may be tempted to rely on the extra help provided by a young associate, without giving enough attention to the creation of effective learning opportunities. A foundation's administrative budget may not allow for the hiring of young program assistants (indeed, there were years when the RBF was not able to maintain its commitment to this practice). But invariably, the hard work, passion, and fresh perspective of my program assistants amplified my own effectiveness. For their part, these young people gained valuable insights into the issues the RBF was addressing and the way in which the RBF approached its grant-making. Quite a few of the Fund's program assistants have gone on to careers in philanthropy, and I hope and trust that what they learned and observed at the Fund has influenced their own approach to grantmaking. This book aims to make some of those insights available to a broader audience of aspiring and new grantmakers.

The second feature of this phase of my career that I want to revisit is the relatively larger share of time and resources that we invested in working directly with government officials. I have to admit that this approach did not come naturally to me, although I had tried to maintain productive relationships with government officials at all levels, wherever I was working. I would say that the RBF's experience in this arena from 2000 to 2008 was often bumpy and frustrating. But as is true of any high-stakes endeavor, it was the scale of the potential payoff that drove us to take the risk. Lasting social change requires systemic reforms, some of which can only be implemented by governments. For a foundation with access and opportunities to engage with government leaders, both directly and through its grant-making, there are strong reasons to consider pursuing this strategy – in addition to strategies that work through civil society, academia, the media, and other non-governmental sectors, including the business and faith communities. But it is also important to consider the difficulty of counting on government and political leaders for sustained support. Civil society organizations and citizens' groups, while less powerful, are often able to work in many different ways over long periods of time to effect change on the ground as well as to push for policy change.

* * * *

While I turned 65 at the beginning of 2004, I did not think seriously about retirement until late 2006, when I was almost 68 and began to realize that I no longer had quite the same level of energy that I had felt in the previous 40 years. As I looked back on my eight years in the Balkans, I realized how much I needed and would have gained from having more time on the ground. I recommended that my successor be based, or at least spend a significant share of his or her time, in the region – and that an effort be made to find someone with knowledge of one or more of the local languages.

Stephen Heintz agreed. It turned out that Stephen and I visited the Western Balkans together several times in my last year on the job (including for a trustee trip to the region). On one trip, during a five-hour car ride from Pristina, Kosovo, to Podgorica, Montenegro, we talked about the kind of person we wanted to succeed me. As we traveled winding roads over the Dinaric Alps, we shared ideas about what we were looking for: someone who was respected and passionate about the issues we worked on; who understood the value of thinking long-term and increasing the capacity of local partners; who was willing to invest in trust-building. We each offered examples of people we had in mind. Among the individuals I mentioned was a young Kosovar whom I had come to know in his role as director of an RBF-supported project focusing on community engagement in towns in Kosovo. This young man, Haki Abazi, had worked in Afghanistan and other complicated places. He spoke Albanian, Serbian, and English, and he was living in Pristina.

As we meandered over the mountains and considered a few other people, we found our interest growing in Haki. In the summer of 2007 Haki started work at the RBF. He is now based in the US, for family reasons, but travels regularly to the region for in-depth field visits.

The appointment of Haki Abazi as program director for the Fund's pivotal place grantmaking in the Western Balkans fulfilled my hopes in every regard. He has made some changes in the program guidelines, of course, reflecting his own strengths and convictions as well as the inevitable need for adjustment as a program matures. I have watched the evolution of the Fund's work in this region with great interest and enthusiasm.

CHAPTER ELEVEN

Another View of an Engaged Program Officer

I have used the word 'engaged' frequently in this book to refer to my style of grantmaking, which took me well beyond considering grant applications and handling the oversight requirements associated with the distribution of charitable funds. I wanted to build relationships of collaboration and trust with the RBF's grant recipients, and I tried to think long-term about increasing the capacity of individual leaders and the sustainability of non-profit institutions. I was eager to partner with colleagues at other foundations, so that we could all leverage our strengths and resources on behalf of the issues and change strategies on which our foundations were focusing.

This chapter is about a different form of program officer engagement. It highlights how I used my energies and expertise to contribute to progress in arenas where the RBF did not necessarily have an active grantmaking program, but where I could help to advance the Fund's core objectives. I am talking here about involvements, such as service on the boards of relevant organizations and participation in the creation of new funding collaboratives and associations, in which my primary role was not to shape or implement an RBF grantmaking program, but rather to extend the impact of the Fund's grantmaking through my own endeavors. During my tenure at the RBF, I became involved in many such activities, a few of which are described below.

In emphasizing the prominence of such supplementary engage-
ments in my career, I do not mean to suggest that I was unique among my
foundation colleagues, a number of whom undertook similar activities. At
the end of this chapter, I draw on my personal experiences to highlight
some of the implications of embracing this rewarding but demanding interpretation of 'engagement.'

Elsewhere in this book, I have mentioned staff and trustee trips to regions where the Fund
was active. These were opportunities for colleagues to feel more engaged in aspects of the
Fund's work with which they were not directly involved. In 1998 a few members of the RBF
board and staff traveled to British Columbia to meet grantees working to protect the old-growth
rainforests of that region and to provide economic opportunities for First Nations people. This
photo was taken on the steps of a lodge built by the Haisla Nation, Koweesas Lodge, which
is located in Koweesas Bay, adjacent to the Kitlope Watershed (these are all part of Haisla
territory). At the time the Koweesas was not a protected area, but it has subsequently become
so. The construction of the lodge was an assertion of sovereignty over traditional territory that
was threatened with logging. Participants included (front row from left): Priscilla Lewis, then
program officer for Peace and Security; her husband John Alfieri; on the far right, Michael
Northrop, program director, sustainable development, and leader of the trip; Susan Moody, my
wife, on the left in the second row; at the far right in that row, Antonia Grumbach, RBF general
counsel. I am on the left in the third row (with Antonia's husband George Grumbach right
behind me); also in the third row is Bob Oxnam (in the white jacket), then an RBF trustee, and
Vishaka Desai, his wife and then president of the Asia Society.

Creating the Trust for Civil Society in Central and Eastern Europe

By the mid-1990s Colin Campbell (then president of the Fund) and I were already beginning to worry about the prospect of private foundations and USAID phasing out their programs in Central and Eastern Europe (CEE) before sufficient progress had been made in building the capacity and enhancing the sustainability of civil society organizations in the region. Lord Dahrendorf's reminder – 'it takes . . . sixty years to build a civil society' – was very much in my mind. I realized that our own grantmaking program was 15 years old and not likely to be extended much beyond the millennium. At a meeting of CEE donors in 1997, hosted by the Ford Foundation, Tom Dine, USAID's Assistant Administrator for CEE and Newly Independent States, wondered aloud about the possibility of crafting some kind of collaborative exit strategy for USAID and the very few US foundations that were working in the Caucasus and Central Asia, one or two of which were represented in the room. I was intrigued by the idea and proposed the creation of a public–private partnership for coordinated, long-term capacity-building in CEE – a Trust for Civil Society in Central and Eastern Europe that would help to ensure the sustainability of the local initiatives and organizations that we all had been funding. I envisioned a $100 million pooled fund for strategic grantmaking over a 15-year time span. My colleagues expressed considerable interest in the concept, so I began to put some 'meat on the bones' of this idea, drafting and redrafting a comprehensive proposal.

Sadly, the dream of a public–private collaboration was never realized. Tom Dine became president of Radio Free Europe in 1998 and was thus out of the loop; his successor at USAID was not as enthusiastic about the proposal as Tom was. Then, after the presidential election in 2000, Republicans replaced Democrats in leadership positions at USAID, and the new staff (as is usually the case) were not willing to follow up on a proposal that was identified with an earlier administration and a different political ideology. USAID never did become involved in the Trust.

This was a big disappointment. But with the end of the RBF's grantmaking program in sight and the need for ongoing support of civil society-building abundantly clear, I did not want to give up. Together with colleagues from a core group of private foundations, I began to wonder how much money we could raise even if the US government did not join us. We set to work lobbying for commitments from our own foundations.

In 1998 and 1999 the German Marshall Fund, the Charles Stewart Mott Foundation, and the RBF (the same team that had led the way in establishing the Environmental Partnership for Central Europe), together with the Ford Foundation and the Open Society Institute, made pledges worth over $50 million, with Ford and the OSI each pledging $20 million and Mott and the GMF each pledging $5 million. The RBF committed $3 million as part of its exit strategy for the region – a very substantial amount given the size of our endowment, and a real vote of confidence from Colin and the board. Ultimately, with additional support from Atlantic Philanthropies and some European donors, we put together a total of over $60 million – not bad for a small group of foundation program officers!

Between 1998 and 2000 several of us – Debbie Harding from the OSI, Maureen Smyth from Mott, Irena Gross from Ford, Marianne Ginsburg from the GMF, and Nancy Muirhead and myself from the RBF – devoted considerable energy and time to getting the Trust for Civil Society in Central and Eastern Europe (CEE Trust) up and running as a new foundation with a focus on strengthening civil society for the long term in seven countries: Poland, Czech Republic, Slovakia, Hungary, Romania, Bulgaria, and Slovenia. Since the Trust was intended to help meet transitional needs, it would have a lifespan of ten years, which actually stretched to 12 (from 2001 to 2013).

During the first few years, the CEE Trust, headquartered in Warsaw, functioned through partner organizations in the seven countries. These national partners regranted Trust funds to local organizations to advance several objectives: supporting the legal, fiscal, and political frameworks needed for a healthy civil society; strengthening non-profit sectors through institutional capacity-building; and enhancing the financial sustainability of non-profit organizations. The Trust also undertook regional programs to encourage the exchange of knowledge and experience among partner organizations and others. Other regional programs focused on governance of non-profit organizations and such specific issues as healthcare. In my view, we had a good staff and respected partners on the ground in each country.

We also had differing opinions on the board about the evolving challenges facing civil societies in the region and the best ways to address them. After a mid-term review in 2004, the board decided to undertake direct grantmaking instead of working through partner organizations, in order to gain first-hand understanding of local circumstances. The Trust headquarters moved to Sofia, Bulgaria, and a small administrative office remained in Warsaw. Within this new framework, the Trust made grants to major organizations and promising start-ups – including think-tanks and watchdog groups – to advance women's causes, expand human rights protections, improve the availability of healthcare, and promote transparency and openness in government and other public institutions. But while the Trust reinvented itself and expanded its substantive reach over time in an effort to meet some of the additional needs facing young democracies in CEE, it also tried to maintain a focus on building the capacity and enhancing the financial sustainability of non-profit organizations. And throughout, the staff of the Trust took a non-bureaucratic, trust-based approach to grantmaking that was modeled on the practices of the RBF, Mott, and the GMF.

I was an active member of the CEE Trust board from 2001 until my retirement in 2007, during which time my own grantmaking focus shifted to the Western Balkans. Haki Abazi, my successor at the RBF, took my place on the board of the CEE Trust. Then, in 2012, I was asked to return briefly to the board, as the Trust was winding down. It was a welcome opportunity to re-engage in one of the most substantial undertakings of my career.

The Trust was a major initiative in which a number of foundations invested heavily, and a full assessment of its impact should be made at some point. For now, all of the young democracies in CEE are still 'works in progress,' and I think it is too early to say which organizations and programs deserve credit for what kinds of progress – if that ever really is possible. I believe that the Trust played a valuable role overall and that important lessons will be learned from its evolution, including both its accomplishments and its mistakes.

The Baltic American Partnership Fund

In the 18th century, after a long history of subjugation by more powerful Baltic-rim states, the present-day Baltic countries – Estonia, Latvia, and Lithuania – were incorporated into the Russian empire. They achieved brief independence from Bolshevist Russia between the First and Second World Wars, only to be forced to join the Soviet Union in 1940. In 1991 the three countries seceded from the disintegrating Soviet Union, after a massive campaign of civil resistance against communist rule. While each of these countries had its own language and culture, they all were eager to distance themselves from the oppressive communist past and join the community of democratic, market-oriented nations.

Early in the 1990s I considered proposing that the RBF's program in Central and Eastern Europe be expanded to include the Baltic nations. Indeed, during our exploratory grantmaking phase, we made several grants for Baltic initiatives. I saw many needs in the region that the RBF could usefully address within its program guidelines; and arguably, the Baltic countries faced even more challenges than did the CEE countries when it came to building healthy democracies, since they had spent essentially a half-century inside the Soviet Union. Except for USAID and the OSI, very few American foundations were showing any interest in the Baltic nations.

As it turned out, the RBF did not have enough money or staff to do justice to such an extension of its CEE program. Nevertheless, I continued to follow events in the Baltic countries throughout the 1990s. Along the way, while working in Central and Eastern Europe, I met impressive individuals from Estonia, Latvia, and Lithuania who were doing excellent work in the environmental field and in strengthening democracy.

In 1998, out of the blue, I was contacted by the USAID/OSI team that was organizing a ten-year exit strategy from their foundations' decade of involvement in programs to strengthen democracy in the Baltic region. They asked me to join the planning team for that strategy. Shortly thereafter, they asked me to become the first chair of the board of the Baltic American Partnership Fund (BAPF). This Fund would have a pool of $15 million (half from each donor) to divide among the three Baltic countries for next steps in building civil society and helping key institutions become more sustainable. Baltic American Partnership Programs (BAPPs) were established in each of the Baltic countries, with local staffs to manage and regrant the USAID and OSI funds. The BAPPs also assembled local expert councils to advise them on strategic and other issues.

I served a three-year term as board chair and remained an active board member through the entire lifetime of the BAPF – more than a decade. Not only did the BAPF have a great staff and hard-working partner groups on the ground in each of the countries, but we also had a governing board of highly committed and compatible people. This was a public–private partnership that worked very well indeed. Its smaller scale and scope may have been advantages in this regard, as compared to

Bringing international grantmakers together

The opportunities available to me for board service and other forms of non-grant-related 'engagement' naturally became more numerous in the later years of my career, by which time I had built a substantial track record and developed an extensive network of contacts. But one example of this kind of engagement dates from early in my time at the RBF.

In the late 1970s the RBF ranked among the top ten international grantmakers in the United States. That category is defined broadly to include not only grants made to overseas organizations, but also grants to domestic organizations that focus on foreign affairs or global issues as well as grants for international exchange programs. Even so, overall, only five cents on a foundation dollar was being spent for international and foreign purposes at the time. I decided to try to form an association of donors with international interests, since I could see that the world was becoming increasingly interdependent and I thought it was important to encourage and help more foundations to invest more grant money in this area. The group I took the lead in founding, initially called Grantmakers International and later the Committee on International Grantmaking, was eventually folded into the Council on Foundations and became its International Program. The members of the group ranged from the largest foundations to modest-sized family foundations, with some corporate foundation interests in the mix. This undertaking remained a distinct service and education program of the Council on Foundations for more than 20 years.

the ambitious public–private partnership that was initially envisioned for the CEE Trust. Among the BAPF's accomplishments were enabling the passage of legislation that protected the independence of the non-profit sector; establishing a pan-Baltic community philanthropy network; and creating a strong core group of NGOs and civil society leaders through institutional capacity building grants and professional development opportunities.*

The RBF was never asked to make a financial contribution to the BAPF; the request was for my time. Since the RBF was not able to become active in the Baltic region, I thought this was a way to be helpful. Certainly,

---

* The major achievements of the BAPF are outlined in its booklet entitled *The Baltic American Partnership Fund (BAPF): Ten Years of Grantmaking to Strengthen Civil Society in Estonia, Latvia and Lithuania* (2009)

I drew on lessons the RBF was learning in CEE, where similar problems were being addressed. Given how strongly I had come to feel about the need for a sound exit strategy from any long-term grantmaking program, I felt fortunate to have played a very small role in devising a far-sighted plan that would help the Baltic countries get on their feet as democratic societies.

The Mukti Fund

I first met Mike Dively in law school, in the 1960s. We became reacquainted in the early 1980s, when he was serving as a director and then chair of the American Center for International Leadership, which the RBF funded to establish a young adult exchange program with CEE countries and the USSR. By that time I was beginning to realize that with the One World program ramping up, the RBF's grantmaking in the Caribbean would soon begin to wind down. When Mike asked me for my advice on how he might deploy the small grantmaking budget of a new foundation he had established, called the Mukti Fund, I recommended that he focus on an island in the Caribbean where the needs were great and modest amounts of money would go a long way. I knew that Mike had an international outlook, but I also knew he wanted to be actively involved in the work of his foundation; I thought he could more easily travel to the Caribbean than to Nepal, the other place he was considering.

Tom Fox, an undergraduate classmate of Mike's whom he had also consulted, agreed with me (Tom was by then a vice president of the Council on Foundations, having earlier served as director of the Council's International Program). Together, we suggested that Mike look closely at opportunities in St Vincent, Grenada, St Kitts and Nevis, and Montserrat. Mike chose St Kitts and Nevis, on the basis of the impressive individuals he met there during his exploratory trips. Initially, the Mukti Fund was able to give away only $10,000 a year or so, although that grew to $50,000 per year after Mike received an inheritance from his father. There was no paid staff; Mike volunteered his time, and I was one of the early volunteer trustees.

We did not have specific grantmaking priorities at first, so the grants were opportunistic – contributing to a micro-loan fund for small-business development, for example, and helping to establish a multi-year small-grants program for community-based projects. When the endowment grew, we

Mukti Fund board members and grantees/partners in St Kitts and Nevis. Top row, from left: Tom Fox, former Mukti chair; Larry Armony, then general manager of the Brimstone Hill Fortress National Park, a partner organization in St Kitts; myself; Tapley Seaton, former attorney general of the Federation of St Kitts and Nevis; Maurice Widdowson, businessman and chair of the Beautiful Basseterre Committee (a Mukti Fund grantee); Mike Dively, founder and former Mukti chair; and Weston Milliken, Mukti board member. Lower row, second from left, Victor Williams, local businessman and former government planner; Judith Towle, former Mukti chair and vice president of Island Resources Foundation; and Jackie Armony, then president of the St Christopher's Historical Society, a Mukti Fund grantee.

prepared a strategic plan with an overall focus on nation-building through grants aimed at natural and cultural resources protection and sustainable economic development, and with four primary areas of concentration: supporting civil society; supporting public–private sector initiatives; collaborating with government; and catalyzing new ideas. Across all of these categories, Mukti (like the RBF!) was committed to building the capacity of local initiatives and institutions.

Each board member undertook to follow one or more specific issues related to the Mukti strategic plan, and we played an active, hands-on role in the work of the Fund. The trustees covered most of the cost of their trips to St Kitts and Nevis for board meetings and site visits, but Mike (who received no remuneration himself) found creative ways to acknowledge our volunteer service. For example, the Mukti Fund would match trustees' charitable contributions up to $300, even for projects unrelated to Mukti's priorities. More substantially, Mike decided that the Mukti Fund periodically would make what he called Trustee Recognition Grants, each in the amount of $70–85,000. The honored trustee would choose the recipient of the grant, which would be given in her or his name to support work that was broadly consistent with the goals of the Mukti Fund (although not necessarily confined to the Caribbean). I chose the Quebec-Labrador Foundation's Atlantic Center for the Environment, a highly regarded partner of the RBF in the Caribbean and elsewhere, to receive my recognition grant in 2002.

The grant was used to create the William S Moody Fund for International Conservation. This fund, which has been supplemented by subsequent small contributions that I and others have been able to make, is treated as a special sub-fund within the QLF's endowment. Over the years, the income from that sub-fund has been used for fellowships, exchanges, field assignments, workshops, and publications. The

International House, New York

As the accounts of my involvement in the Mukti Fund, the BAPF, and the CEE Trust attest, some of the supplementary activities that I undertook throughout my career became lasting commitments. My involvement in International House, in New York City, was another such commitment.

John D Rockefeller, Jr, and the Cleveland Dodge family had established International House in 1924 as a residency for foreign students in New York City. Over the years, New York's 'I House' emerged as the leader of a network of similar foreign student residencies on four continents. As the RBF's international program officer in the 1970s and 1980s, I had been responsible for evaluating grants to I House, including the Creel Committee grant from the endowment that tied off the Fund's general support for I House (although we subsequently made occasional program-related grants).

In the early 1990s I was invited to join the governing board of I House. For a number of years I served as chair of the programs and resident life committee of the board, working closely with staff to attract speakers from all fields, including visiting foreign ministers, business leaders, musicians, athletes, and writers. A highlight was meeting one of my preference is for projects that address Caribbean conservation and sustainable development issues; but in the absence of appropriate projects in the region, the sub-fund has supported programs in Latin America, CEE, the Western Balkans, and other settings. The annual draw from the Moody Fund is the only income from the QLF endowment that is directed to the general budget of the QLF's international programs, making it very significant as a source of unrestricted funding for that program area. As I have observed several times in this book, such unrestricted income is invaluable in allowing grant recipients the flexibility to pursue new opportunities and to develop projects that respond to emerging needs.

In the July–August 1992 issue of *Foundation News*, an article on page 16 was introduced with the following teaser: 'Using a small Caribbean island nation as a controlled funding experiment seems like a pie-in-the-sky dream, but the tiny Mukti Fund has always been much more than that.' The article, by Daphne White, described how a small group of people with shared goals and interests was making a big difference with a

heroes, Nelson Mandela, when he came to I House in the early 2000s. I served later on other board committees and performed fellowship reviews – but I am now (as of 2013) back on the programs and resident life committee.

My involvement with I House today gives me the same sense of excitement and hope that I felt 20 years ago, when I first joined the board. For anyone who is feeling utterly discouraged about the ills that plague our world, I recommend a dose of contact with the remarkable and inspiring young residents at the nearest International House.

Meeting Nelson Mandela, a hero of mine, at International House, New York, in 2003. (photo: Ken Levinson, used with permission from International House)

very modest amount of money. When the Mukti Fund wrapped up its work in the Caribbean in 2004, after a wonderful two-decade 'run,' we knew we had provided a type of funding that was not available from any other donors: long-term and sustained, with an emphasis on building capacity and strengthening institutions. The trustees and Mike had developed a real esprit de corps; we had fun while doing Mukti's work seriously. My involvement in the Mukti Fund was an enormously satisfying way for me to continue making a contribution in a region that had been of interest to the RBF, and that I had come to care deeply about.

Closing reflections

The type of 'engagement' that I have described in this chapter is part of the philanthropic tradition of the Rockefeller family. Whether it was John D Rockefeller, Jr's three decades of involvement in the creation of Colonial Williamsburg or David Rockefeller's active leadership of the Council on Foreign Relations (or many other examples), the family has long recognized the value of contributing time and effort – sweat equity – as well as dollars toward the achievement of important goals. Although my activities were not comparable in terms of scale or visibility to those of various Rockefeller family members, I was thrilled to be working in a setting where active engagement is encouraged and respected.

This is not to say that tensions never arise as a consequence of such concurrent commitments, which certainly add to the workload of foundation staff. During an annual staff review discussion with Stephen Heintz in 2002 or 2003, we discussed my heavy overall workload, including my concurrent board service and other volunteer roles. We agreed that while most of those involvements complemented my work as a program officer and the RBF's program interests, their cumulative impact could be stretching me too thin. Stephen asked me to step down from the board of one organization whose work was not directly related to the Fund's concerns – the Belgian American Educational Foundation (BAEF), which had given me a fellowship in 1967 for postgraduate study abroad. I left the BAEF board at that point, but returned after my retirement. For me, volunteering on that board and its fellowship selection committee is one way to pay back the Foundation for giving me such an extraordinary opportunity more than 40 years ago. Also, like my involvement in International House, my continuing engagement with the BAEF gives me a chance to become

David Rockefeller (left) with three RBF presidents – Bill Dietel, Stephen Heintz, and Colin Campbell – at the RBF 75th Anniversary Launch event honoring David in November 2012. (photo: Robert Stone)

acquainted with promising young people from outside the United States who are struggling to improve the future prospects of their countries.

I realized that Stephen was right to focus on my workload (although it was difficult for me to let go even of that one board engagement, which I felt was broadly consistent with the RBF's international program themes). Earlier in this book, I observed that I had always felt I could 'do it all' and did not hesitate to take on additional responsibilities. Obviously, 'doing it all' never was really possible; as I also acknowledged earlier, some things got more attention than others when time ran short. But as my career moved on, there were new kinds of time management challenges to be faced as well. At a certain point, I had to admit that I was getting older. I still felt energetic and had not experienced any significant health challenges – those held off until I retired, a common but perverse phenomenon! I still could not wait to get out of bed and go to work in the morning. But I began thinking about pacing myself slightly differently, and about how to adjust to the reality of aging.

There will always be limitations of one kind or another on a grant-maker's ability to be as 'engaged' as he or she might like to be – and there always is more that could be done. I remain absolutely convinced that complementary activities of the sort described in this chapter can enhance the overall impact of grantmaking programs and improve the prospects for achieving foundation goals. Certainly, the rewards for the program officer are satisfying.

CHAPTER TWELVE

Wrapping Up
Principles and practices

This book has been about the work of helping people in their communities around the world to make lasting, positive change. But the book is also my personal story, about how one foundation program officer employed the opportunities available to him in a very favorable workplace. Because this is a personal story, I made clear from the start that I would not attempt to provide formal evaluations of the nearly 1,000 grants – totaling more than $50 million – the RBF made in my program areas over the course of 40 years. That said, throughout the preceding chapters I have offered many informal assessments of the short- and longer-term impacts of highlighted grants and grant clusters. I begin this 'wrapping up' chapter with some overall thoughts about impact, before turning to a summary of the principles and practices that I believe make for greater effectiveness in promoting positive change at the community, national, and regional levels.

Indicators of impact

As described at many points in this book, most of the organizations we funded in Africa, Latin America, the Caribbean, Central and Eastern Europe, and the Western Balkans achieved at least some of their specific, stated goals. Even some of the very small initiatives we supported produced sizable results. Of course, not all of our grants were equally successful – I have included in this book some of my own misjudgments and some of the (relatively few) grant relationships in which we ultimately were disappointed. And, of course, the RBF cannot take full credit for making possible the results of any of the projects or organizations it has funded. Nonetheless, I think it is fair to say that RBF support contributed to the success of hundreds of local self-help projects, encouraged many productive national and regional collaborations, empowered scores of advocacy efforts that achieved significant legal and policy breakthroughs, assisted thousands of individuals by making training and other learning opportunities more widely available, facilitated broader citizen participation in local and national decision-making, and empowered many dedicated citizen leaders and emerging leaders who had a vision for how to improve their communities and nations, and our shared planet.

The process of researching and writing this book also enabled me to identify several overarching indicators that suggest the RBF's grant programs did indeed help, over time, to enlarge local people's understanding of, and ability to address, sustainable development challenges; to protect human rights and promote international understanding; and to strengthen important dimensions of civil society and democratic practice in transforming societies. The Fund's footprint in the regions where I worked is still discernible:

- Over the years, the RBF and I – joined by colleagues at other foundations – devoted a considerable share of our time, effort, and grant monies to the creation of new institutions (including think-tanks and foundations) that we hoped would fill gaps and address unmet needs. The RBF also 'bet' on many newly conceived institutions in their early days, and helped particularly promising institutions to scale up their operations significantly. Research for this book confirmed that most of the institutions with which we were closely involved are alive and well today and doing good work; some others have merged into larger organizations or taken on a different configuration, but continue to make valuable contributions. Many are now being funded by large bilateral and multilateral aid agencies, as well as by their own national governments and local donors (including businesses). In fact, as these organizations grew and looked to new sources of grant income, support from the RBF often was treated as a 'Good Housekeeping Seal of Approval' by other donors.

- Today, many years after the RBF phased out its grantmaking in most of the regions described in this book, the students and 'disciples' of the influential individuals whose projects we supported during my tenure at the RBF are working in different settings and locations around the world, applying lessons learned from earlier projects funded by the RBF. These 'disciples' are now introducing their own students and colleagues to proven strategies for sustainable development and civil society-building. The creation of such cadres is an important outcome of the programs we carried out in diverse regions.
- Courageous and visionary young NGO leaders whose projects or organizations we helped to launch have since mentored a second and third generation of staff. These young people understand the importance of civil society to a healthy democracy, the peaceful resolution of conflict, and environmentally sustainable economic development, and they see futures for themselves in the third sector. Many of the original civil society leaders supported by the Fund have stayed in their countries and are still working in one way or another to strengthen democratic practice, advance sustainable development, and protect human rights.
- Many of the connections and collaborations that the RBF nurtured continue to this day – including among ethnic groups that have a history of mutual distrust. Organizations that were supported by the Fund continue to seek advice from the US and European experts to whom we introduced them, sometimes as long as 30 years ago. Thanks in part to the continued vigor of the NGOs we funded, the habit of civic engagement is still being cultivated in many of the places where we worked.
- It has become evident to me that sustained RBF support and program officer involvement helped to embed new concepts and problem-solving approaches in a wide range of societies – concepts like wildlands management, heritage preservation, land trusts, small-business and entrepreneurial training, community revitalization, visioning and dialogue techniques, greenways, volunteerism and local philanthropy, and the importance of a healthy non-profit/non-governmental sector. Most of these concepts were not original or 'invented' with funding from the

RBF, but they represented real alternatives to established ways of thinking and doing things. Many of these concepts have gained traction and legitimacy over time; even some ideas that were premature when we tried to introduce them have since become more accepted if not necessarily pervasive.

– In my interviews with grantees and colleagues during the past few years, I encountered more heartfelt and specific expressions of appreciation for the RBF approach to grantmaking (and mine) than I ever expected to hear. Of course, no one is inclined to look a gift horse in the mouth; but what struck me most was the clear sense that our *way* of proceeding, and not just the money we provided, made a lasting difference. Frequently, I was told that our approach became a model for the civil society leaders and organizations – local, national, and regional – whose work we funded or with whom we collaborated. In fact, it was Stephen Heintz, current RBF president and my last boss, who encouraged me to write a book that would focus on the 'how' of helping people to create more just, sustainable, and peaceful communities, at whatever scale. Also, as I began work on the book more than five years ago, RBF grantees, colleagues in other foundations, and some academics in the field of philanthropy reinforced the encouragement that Stephen originally provided.

The remainder of this chapter focuses largely on summarizing key elements of that approach, which drew deeply from Rockefeller family traditions and RBF practices as well as from my own convictions and style.

My 'top ten' principles and practices for promoting positive and lasting social change

The principles and practices that are described below certainly are not unique to the RBF's grantmaking style or to my own personal way of working – and after 40 years, it is somewhat difficult to distinguish between the two. But I find (and I am told) that these principles are honored more in theory than in the day-to-day work of grantmaking. I recommend them to established and new grantmakers, and to anyone involved or wishing to become involved in efforts to empower people to improve their lives, build healthier communities, and advocate for more far-sighted national, regional, and global policies.

1 Think long-term

It is difficult for me to imagine working on any of the major issues of our times without a long-term commitment and vision – a vision that includes a sense of history. In my own efforts, I was usually focusing on issues of sustainable development (combining wise use of natural and cultural resources and employment generation) and democratic practice (civic engagement, tolerance, and open societies) in specific places. I viewed these issues as priorities for the well-being of humankind and our planet. The diverse places where we worked revealed special needs and opportunities. I was thrilled to be able to play a modest role in these arenas over a sustained period of time.

Unfortunately, many of the agencies engaged in these and other important issues can only think in terms of short time frames. There are many reasons for this; government-affiliated agencies and their leaders may have only a single 'term' of four to six years in which to design and carry out programs, for example. But allocations of human and financial resources over such an abbreviated time are not likely to produce maximum results. There are usually too many layers of habits and outlooks to be changed, and too much resistance from vested interests; big shifts do not usually happen quickly, and in fact may require a few decades. Ralf Dahrendorf was not far off, in my view, when he said, 'it takes ... sixty years to build a civil society.'

Happily, the Rockefeller family and the RBF were long-term thinkers, and willing to stay engaged over the long term. I was fortunate to be able to present program plans with long time horizons – typically, ten years – even if our multi-year grants were generally limited to three years at a time, with renewal possible when warranted. We could go forward step by step, making progress along the way and leaving enhanced understanding and capacity behind when we closed out a grantmaking program.

2 Assess progress over time

The notion that big challenges call for long-term thinking has implications for evaluation as well as for engagement. Some of the initiatives we supported more than a decade ago have by now achieved more than we could have imagined – the Environmental Partnership for Central Europe comes to mind. Some of the work we funded has had important long-range 'ripple' effects. For example, RBF-supported wildland management programs in Latin America, which were designed by Kenton Miller, inspired related efforts in the Caribbean and elsewhere; now, decades later, students of Kenton Miller are applying his theories and strategies in many locations around the world. In some instances where our efforts – despite being sustained over a relatively long period of time – did not produce the impacts we hoped for by the time the RBF phased out its grantmaking in that area (our work on sustainable transportation in Hungary and Poland in the 1990s, for example), it now appears that those efforts helped to create a foundation for later progress.

All this suggests to me that grant assessments should be undertaken at several points in time, which is rarely done. It would be ideal if at least a selection of grants could be evaluated 10 and even 20 years later, perhaps with some reframing of criteria. I appreciate that being able to point to prompt results is very important in some organizations and settings, and foundation boards are appropriately concerned about accountability and the effectiveness of grant expenditures. But I hope this book provides some compelling illustrations of the value of approaching assessment within a long-term framework, at least where big, enduring challenges are at issue.

3 Learn on the ground, from a cross-section of people

I believe that foundation efforts to contribute to lasting, positive change cannot be based on impressive written proposals and working plans alone. It is critical also to develop a 'feel' for the communities where grant funds will be spent. Lessons learned from working in other settings can be very valuable, of course, but change strategies almost always have to be adapted to suit different contexts, with their different mixes of needs and assets. Again, input from local people is essential. Investing time and attention in getting a sense of what people are thinking and feeling, whether through formal 'visioning' exercises or informal conversation, also demonstrates respect and builds local trust in outside organizations and funders who are trying to be helpful.

When I was going to be in the field, I alerted my colleagues on the ground that I wanted to make contact with a cross-section of local people.

I gave as much attention to their insights as to academic reports written by experts in the capital city or overseas. I tried to understand diverse points of view, and I took to heart what Fred Kent, president of the New York-based Project for Public Spaces, told me more than 30 years ago: 'Perhaps the most insightful person in a neighborhood or community setting is the grandmother who is in the park every afternoon. Don't forget to talk to her, too.' Even in settings where I did not speak the local language, I learned something from observing the interaction between my colleagues or RBF grantees on the ground and the people they were collaborating with or helping.

4 Choose appropriate people to work with and bet on

I learned early in my career that when I did not pick an appropriate person to support or work with, my chances for excellent results were greatly reduced. I also learned that the criteria other funders used did not necessarily suit my needs or grantmaking approach, which was based on building relationships of trust and fostering collaboration and partnership. In my view, a charismatic leader with brilliant ideas was not always the best candidate to bet on, because his or her big ego might make collaboration with other people impossible, limiting the intended impact of a project.

Eventually, I came up with the following rough list of qualities that I considered essential. I looked to collaborate with and support people who possessed these traits:

- 'fire in the belly' for the work they were asking the RBF to support;
- credibility with peers, which helped to ensure that RBF-supported projects were appreciated and facilitated by a larger network of respected individuals;
- their egos 'in place,' so they were able to encourage and share recognition with co-workers;
- persistence – a willingness to devote years to the challenges being faced;
- an understanding of the need to reach out to adversaries, even if such efforts did not always pay off;
- the leadership and management skills and experience needed not only to guide substantive efforts but also to build strong institutions, staffs, and boards.

Needless to say, I occasionally misjudged people and ran into difficulties. Sometimes, I could talk with the project or organization leader about what was worrying me, and improvements did occasionally result. In other instances, I simply had to acknowledge that I had bet on the wrong person. Fortunately, to my knowledge, this only happened a handful of times, a track record I attribute in part to the early and ongoing attention I paid to the criteria listed above.

5 Build relationships of trust

From a young age, I believed in the importance of relationships based on trust. My father was in the life insurance business for 54 years, and I am proud that even years after his death, people still tell me that he was one of the most trusted people in the community. In conversations with my father, I learned that he only became a 'trusted individual' by developing qualities of honesty, fairness, reliability, and common sense – and that those qualities in other people fostered trust in them. I also learned that building relationships based on trust was a step-by-step process and that it takes time.

As I entered the field of philanthropy and matured in my role there, I realized that if I wanted to have a positive impact, I would be much better off in relationships of mutual trust with foundation peers and grantees. In relationships of mutual trust, people feel they are part of a team, and no one wants to let the others down. I also realized that such relationships enabled me to simplify administrative requirements, to take more risks, and to think longer-term. I give my father credit for focusing my attention on this critical concept at a young age, and I am grateful that my RBF colleagues and members of the Rockefeller family shared my sense of the importance of trust.

6 Collaborate with other donors

Foundations always have more funding opportunities than they have funds; the same is undoubtedly true of most individual donors. Collaboration is a way of leveraging finite resources and sharing costs and risks. Larger goals can be pursued in a 'win-win' fashion. Typically, all parties to the collaboration also acquire useful insights and new perspectives. I was usually representing the smallest funding organization in the collaborations in which I took part, and I learned a great deal from working with a mutually reinforcing team of program officers all focusing on the same issues.

Not every collaboration is equally effective, and there are costs – in time and effort – as well as benefits. I have described some of the challenges involved in collaboration between organizations that have very different institutional cultures and bureaucratic frameworks, as when the RBF worked with the FAO, a large UN agency, on wildlands management in Latin America. Fortunately, with a respected and effective program leader in Kenton Miller, this cooperative effort achieved important goals. I also noted that programmatic or staff changes may cause a partner organization to withdraw from a joint venture, as happened when the Rockefeller Foundation became less involved in the RBF's effort to create the first independent foundation in Poland since the Second World War, the Foundation for the Development of Polish Agriculture. USAID's enthusiasm for collaborating with a group of foundations to create the Trust for Civil Society in Central and Eastern Europe was undermined by a transition in the executive branch. Even in these cases, however, the difficulties did not prevent us from achieving very positive results. When collaboration is based on mutual understanding and similar change strategies; when collaboration enjoys the full, engaged support of senior officers at each organization; when all participants are willing to do their share and to share the credit: then the benefits far outweigh the costs.

7 Build capacity while funding problem-solving

Even given the RBF's long-range perspective and willingness to stay involved with an issue or in a region for a decade or more, we always knew that we would be leaving the scene before achieving all of our grantmaking goals, which were typically complex and often multi-generational. While we usually felt that staying engaged longer would be helpful, there inevitably were other priorities and calls on our limited resources. Building the capacity of local people and institutions was thus an integral part of our planning. When the institutions and people we supported were strong enough to go forward on their own, we could feel reasonably comfortable about moving on ourselves.

Not all foundations are willing to combine grantmaking for problem-solving with grantmaking for capacity-building, perhaps because improvements in institutional and staff capacity are not always easy to measure – and because donors are motivated primarily by concern about particular problems. But a focus on capacity-building can greatly enhance the effectiveness and sustained impact of grant programs. Our efforts to build mutual trust paid off here too, since we were able to have honest conversations with grantees about the kind of institution-strengthening help that was needed in each case. We could look together, early on, at the organization's capacity for project management, financial control, strategic planning, or fundraising; at the makeup and professionalism of its board and staff; at the strengths and weaknesses of its governance provisions. These are complex challenges that many non-profit organizations – especially new organizations, in transforming societies – do not have the luxury to address as they struggle to raise money for their essential substantive work.

8 Use all the tools in the grantmaker's toolkit

Consistent with the tendency of funders to focus on problem-solving rather than capacity-building, it is also true that the lion's share of foundation grantmaking is focused on supporting specific projects and programs. Such grants allow the donor to evaluate outcomes against goals identified in the proposal. I certainly recommended a number of these grants over the years. But much of the more than $50 million that was disbursed in my program areas during my tenure was intended for more flexible use. I was comfortable with this approach because of the criteria I had developed for selecting good people to support; the emphasis I placed on listening; the trust I sought to build with grant recipients and potential recipients; and the collaborative relationships I enjoyed with colleagues at other foundations who were working on similar issues.

In addition to project/program grants, the tools in my grantmaking toolkit included unrestricted, core-support grants; multi-year grants; planning grants; capacity-building grants; matching/incentive grants; and grants for reserve funds and endowments. The RBF did not invent any of these tools, but the Fund was fairly unusual in allowing staff to deploy all of them. I heard time and again from appreciative grantees about how few other funders would provide capital or endowment grants; unrestricted, general support grants were perhaps even more difficult to come by. Even modest unrestricted support is highly valued by grant recipients, because of the flexibility it provides; such support, offered over a multi-year period, also allows for forward planning and institution-building. The RBF's willingness to provide general support, plus its interest in capacity-building and its commitment to staying the course, made for a rare and valuable combination.

9 Design intelligent exit strategies

In my experience, exit strategies for the termination of significant grant relationships and grant programs are among the least discussed subjects in grantmaking circles – perhaps because the closing-out of one involvement typically coincides with the initiation of another, and the new opportunities and challenges tend to take center stage. But as I hope I have illustrated in this book, thoughtful exit strategies that are tailored to the situation can make an invaluable contribution to the sustainability of funded projects and organizations, and of the results that have been achieved. Many of the RBF grant recipients to whom I spoke in researching this book mentioned how much they appreciated our attention to the close-out phase of grantmaking, and how critical that had been to their organization's survival and success.

Ideally, exit strategies will be formulated at a point when project or programmatic benchmarks have been reached and institutional capacity has been increased. In such cases, the RBF would try to reinforce the long-term viability of the grantee or grantees through capital grants for endowment (usually on a matching or challenge basis) or for some equivalent purpose, such as the purchase of office space – a valuable asset for an organization, and a way to reduce fixed costs going forward.

Sometimes, however, the RBF had to close out grantmaking programs earlier than might have been desirable, either to address urgent emerging priorities or because of budget cuts. In such cases, the exit strategy can be even more important. A final round of capacity-building grants was appropriate for some organizations; others benefited from close-out grants that helped to create or enlarge revolving reserve funds that could be used (for example) to cover core operating costs while waiting for pledged grants from other donors to be paid out.

In keeping with our collaborative approach, the RBF also participated in the development and implementation of joint exit strategies with other foundations that were closing out or anticipated closing out their programs in a particular location. The Trust for Civil Society in Central and Eastern Europe is a notable example of this kind of bold and unusual initiative.

10 Extend the impact of grantmaking through 'non-grant' engagement

There is a strong Rockefeller family tradition of contributing time and effort – as well as money – to addressing important philanthropic goals. Over the course of my career at the RBF, I found that I could help to advance the Fund's objectives through such non-grant-related endeavors as serving on the boards of key organizations and helping to create new funder collaboratives and associations. As I have acknowledged, these supplementary involvements are not always encouraged and may be actively discouraged in some foundation settings; nor are they without cost. They certainly add to the workload of foundation staff. But I believe this sort of engagement can significantly enhance the impact of any kind of philanthropy, both directly and indirectly, by enriching donors' understanding of relevant substantive issues and organizational challenges. Among other things, service on the boards of non-profit organizations gives those of us on the grantmaking side of the table important insights into the experience of grantseekers.

Final reflections

I noted early in this chapter that the principles and practices summarized here are not unique to me or to the RBF. If asked to do so, my colleagues at the foundations with which the RBF collaborated most frequently would probably come up with similar lists, as would many other people working in the social change field. But while my experiences and vantage point are not unique, I am acutely – and gratefully – aware that they are not typical.

I had the extraordinary good fortune of landing in a setting that encouraged and enabled me to work in a way that felt profoundly 'right' to me. There was an exceptionally good fit between my own outlook and the priorities and strategies of the Rockefeller Brothers Fund. Of course, I had a tremendous amount to learn when I arrived at Rockefeller Center in 1968; I was not a specialist or expert on any of the issues the RBF addressed. But I felt from the start that I was blending what I was learning from my more experienced colleagues with my own instincts and values. I have always believed that people everywhere want to figure out ways to solve their own problems and become self-sufficient. Confident that the Rockefeller family and the RBF shared that general perspective, I plunged eagerly into the work of helping local people build on the strengths of their own cultures and communities and take advantage of lessons from the experiences of other societies.

Throughout my time at the RBF, the staff and trustees (including the Rockefeller brothers themselves and the members of succeeding generations who joined the RBF board over the years) provided encouragement, support, mentoring, balance, fairness, and a rare level of organizational stability. The four presidents under whom I served managed the big leadership and programmatic transitions described in this book skillfully and without undue upheaval. Staff turnover was low, and because we all could imagine having long tenures at the Fund, we were ready to embrace new challenges and changing times. A good and certainly caring atmosphere prevailed as well. When I was showing signs of burnout in the mid-1980s, the RBF proactively proposed a year-long sabbatical, which I had not even imagined asking for. This is only the most striking of many instances of thoughtfulness that I could mention.

Before I came to the RBF, what I was most interested in I did as a volunteer in the evenings and on weekends, participating in various civic groups and activities that focused on the environment, international affairs, and human rights. Once I joined the RBF, I could focus on these priority interests as my 'day job' – and not just any day job. My colleagues at the Fund, the global recognition accorded to Rockefeller philanthropy, and the RBF's own outstanding reputation opened doors for me everywhere. I tried to walk through these doors in the most thoughtful, intelligent, and humble way possible; I never forgot the symbolism of the understated reception room in Rockefeller Center that was my first impression of the RBF. With my innate curiosity about people and my determination to play a role in addressing the big challenges we face in the world, I thrived in this extraordinary place that addressed issues so dear to my heart and that gave me so much scope for creativity and personalization of the work I loved.

I will say it again, one last time: for 40 years, I could not wait to get out of bed in the morning and go to the office! Of course there were frustrations and disappointments, and the approach described in these pages left me overextended at times. But I would not change much, if I had it to do over – and I would leap at the chance. What an incredible privilege and adventure this work has been.

In November 2012, at the Presidential Palace in Warsaw, Poland, I was among a small group of foundation representatives honored by President Bronisław Komorowski with the Knight's Cross, Order of Merit, Republic of Poland, for their sustained support of the people of Poland (and of Central and Eastern Europe generally) in developing civil society and democratic practice after the historic changes in 1989. (photo: Tadeusz Tekacz)

Acknowledgments

I can't imagine anyone writing a book alone. I know in my case it required the help of many people from many backgrounds. While I accept full responsibility for mistakes and omissions, it is clear to me that this book simply would not have seen the light of day without their interest, support, and input. Given the span of years covered here, there is no way I can fully recognize everyone who contributed to my writing and research process; but I have done my best to identify and express my appreciation for as many of these thoughtful individuals as possible. I have also done my best to identify individuals in the photographs that illustrate this book, and – when possible – the photographer. With the passage of time, this has become more difficult, and I apologize for the gaps that remain in the photo captions.

I probably would not have started down the book-writing path at all if it were not for a suggestion from Stephen Heintz, president of the Rockefeller Brothers Fund. In early 2007, when I told him of my intention to retire, Stephen noted that no one at the RBF had ever been able to look back over the Fund's history in a measured yet first-hand way; there was always too much to do in the moment, and staff attention was necessarily focused on looking ahead rather than back. He asked whether I would be interested and prepared to look at my 40-year career and explain what I had done, how, and why – and what might be learned from my experience. Although I would not be able to work on such a project full time even after

I had retired and recognized that it was likely to be a lengthy process (little did I know how lengthy!), I embraced the prospect. From the outset, this book was mine to write, with no interference or influence from the RBF – just lots of help, including very welcome support to defray many of my costs.

Core team

The luckiest break for me, starting in 2008 and continuing through to the completion of the book, was the involvement of Priscilla Lewis in this project. Her RBF career (first as director of communications in the late 1990s and then as program officer for the Peace and Security Program, through 2005) overlapped for a time with my own. Priscilla was prepared to be my editor and project adviser, and she emerged as an invaluable collaborator in the preparation of the book. With sensitivity and professionalism, she helped to clarify the framework of the book and tighten and enliven the prose within it. Most of all, she was a joy to have as my principal colleague. I am grateful to her in more ways than I can articulate.

I am enormously grateful for David Rockefeller's thoughtful preface; it brings back many good memories of the times we worked together on challenging endeavors. I also consider myself extraordinarily fortunate that Bill and Wendy Luers were willing to contribute forewords to this volume. They both were inspirations to me from the moment I met them.

During the preparation of this book, I had numerous occasions to revisit the RBF's offices. The entire RBF staff made me feel at home again, starting with Leona (Lee) Hewitt, operations coordinator, and Harry Bates, operations assistant, who warmly greeted and kidded me at the front desk. I wish to single out Gerry Watson, vice president for finance and administration, who initially led the small team of staff members that was assembled to advise and assist me at key points. Nancy Muirhead, my wonderful grantmaking partner in Central and Eastern Europe and now corporate secretary, succeeded Gerry in this role and saw it through to the completion of the book. Other members of the team were Ben Shute, the former corporate secretary and longtime director of the Fund's Democratic Practice Program (US portfolio), who retired in 2014 after nearly 35 years at the Fund; Hope Lyons, director of grants management; and Robert Stone, another longtime RBF staff member who is now serving as Nancy Muirhead's assistant. Robert has been the Fund's unofficial photographer for many years and provided valuable advice and assistance in gathering illustrative materials for this book. Added later to this loose team were Lisa Gilson, grants management analyst (who helped with the complex task of assembling the grant listings that appear at the end of the book), and Maurice Fuller, the Fund's IT expert. All of these colleagues were generous with their time and ready to address my questions; their interest and support gave me confidence and helped me to overcome a variety of obstacles along the way. Okey Nestor, whose design firm (On Design) handles the Fund's graphic design needs, prepared the maps that help readers understand the geography of my career and the Fund's international grantmaking. Also, Paul Sager, a recent PhD in history and French studies from New York University, helped me through several, quite old factual puzzles.

Getting the institutional history right

Staff members at the Rockefeller Archive Center (RAC) in Sleepy Hollow, NY, where the Fund's archives are housed, welcomed me time after time to this extraordinary center of knowledge and insight into the history of the RBF, the multi-generational story of the Rockefeller family, and the institutions associated with the family (in addition to the RBF, a number of other non-profit institutions also house their archives at the Center). Jack Meyers, president; Jim Smith, vice president; Michele Hiltzik Beckerman, assistant director and head of reference; Mary Ann Quinn, archivist; and Roseanne Variano, facilities coordinator – all took a keen interest in my research and writing. Their help was indispensable. Special thanks are due to Michele for her patient digging to locate critical information that I needed; and to Jack and Jim, who both reviewed my manuscript. With their deep understanding of the family's and the RBF's history, they were able to identify important considerations that had not crossed my mind.

At 30 Rockefeller Plaza, Peter Johnson, Rockefeller family historian, provided valuable insights and advice. Peter remembered people, places, and events that I had not thought of in decades; his editorial advice was also most helpful.

Others who provided generous and thoughtful advice about the history of the institution include Steven Rockefeller, former chair of the RBF board; Bill Dietel, former RBF president; Russell Phillips, former executive vice president and then acting president; and Stephen Heintz. Their probing questions and excellent memories clarified the text and helped me avoid inaccuracies. A number of current RBF staff members also helped me with fact-checking, including Michael Northrop, program director for sustainable development, and Haki Abazi, my successor as director of the Western Balkans Program.

Looking back on my RBF 'family'

I cannot resist taking this opportunity to look back through my 40 years at the Fund and acknowledge some of the people who were part of my daily life, who helped me in fundamental ways and were such a pleasure to work with. I have expressed my considerable gratitude to Jim Hyde, my first boss and mentor, at several points in this book. Here I would like to thank Emily Voorhis, who was Jim's assistant when I arrived in 1968. She went out of her way to help me, the new kid on the block, and continued to provide valuable support and advice (including during a period when she worked directly for me) until she retired after a long career at the RBF. After her retirement, we stayed in touch until her premature death. She was a remarkable asset to the Fund and to its young people getting started.

Also at several points in this book, I have mentioned the important roles that all of the RBF presidents – Dana Creel, Bill Dietel, Colin Campbell, Stephen Heintz – and Russell Phillips, the Fund's longtime executive vice president, played in my career. I would now like to acknowledge William (Bill) McCalpin, who served two tours at RBF: first, as a young program officer for Asia-related grantmaking; then, after some time away from the Fund, as executive vice president. Bill is another example of an outstanding colleague at RBF who became a lifelong friend.

Sadly, I did not keep a list of all the people who worked for me during my four decades at the RBF. Laura Eastman was my administrative assistant in 1969; during which time her sister Linda got married to Paul McCartney of the Beatles. This occasioned a lot of excitement at the office, but our regular work proceeded without a missed beat, so to speak. Subsequent administrative assistants included Libby Shepp, Cynthia Richards, Maureen Baiardi, Wendy Krat, and Anne Seussbrick, who were typical of the committed, hard-working, and thoughtful support staff at the RBF.

I also recall many bright and dedicated interns and program assistants/associates who worked part-time for me. These included Kathleen

Dunlap, who subsequently spent a highly productive period of time at the Foundation for the Development of Polish Agriculture, which the RBF helped to create, Jutka Jokay, Kirkland Newman, Steve Wunker, Mirna Safcak, Kelsang Aukatsang, Sarah Eisinger, Grant Garrison, and Latoya Morris (who is now a member of the human resources team at the RBF, where her fashion sense as well as her skills are still evident). With their excellent educations, lively curiosity, fresh thinking, and endless energy, all of these young people contributed to the RBF generally and to me personally in ways I will never forget.

Colleagues around the world

One of the joys associated with writing this book was the opportunity to reconnect with grantees and other colleagues scattered around the world. I was not sure I would be able to locate key people related to some of the early stories told in this book, but thanks to helpful friends and contacts, serendipity, and pure luck, I was able to find and communicate with many people I worked with over the decades – including in remote African villages. All deserve my thanks for contributing their time and their recollections to this effort. Their comments refreshed my memory, enabled me to correct mistakes, and helped me to understand more fully how the RBF's work was perceived on the ground.

Africa

I would single out for special appreciation three people in Botswana: David Inger, former executive trustee of the Kweneng Rural Development Association; Sandy Grant, insightful local 'historian'; and Clark Logan, a dedicated medical doctor. Through numerous emails, all three helped me clarify so much from so long ago. I also met, in Princeton, NJ, with Janet Love, national director of the Johannesburg-based Legal Resources Centre (LRC). Her insights into the evolution of the LRC during the last 25 years reminded me of how important it is to examine the impact of grants many years later.

Latin America

Colleagues from Latin America were easier to locate than those from Africa, although our grantmaking in both regions occupied more or less the same time span. Some now live in the US, and many are still in contact with others in the networks that formed during those years. I especially wish to thank Susan Miller, widow of Kenton Miller, and Sue and Kenton's daughter, Natasha. Sue reviewed the entire manuscript, with meticulous attention to names, dates, and facts; Sue and Natasha also helped me identify faces in some long-ago photographs. I am also grateful to Marc Dourojeanni and his wife Maria Tereza Jorge Pádua, who worked closely with Kenton – they were able to help me clarify some historical realities and track down some wonderful photographs – and to John Shores, a former student of Kenton's at the University of Michigan and later a colleague of his.

Caribbean

Judith Towle, longtime vice president of the Island Resources Foundation, reviewed the entire manuscript, making many valuable corrections and editorial suggestions. Allen Putney, who led the Eastern Caribbean Natural Area Management Program (ECNAMP), also provided helpful assistance on a number of occasions. I thank Allen too for allowing me to include a photo of him without a shirt – while on a research mission.

Central and Eastern Europe (CEE)

My reflections on our efforts in CEE were assisted by two journeys I was fortunate to make to the region during the time I was writing this book: in 2010, to Czech Republic, Slovakia, and Hungary, with my wife Susan; and in 2012, to Poland, primarily to join representatives of several other US foundations in receiving awards from the Polish government for our efforts to help the Polish people rebuild a democratic society. Before, during, and after these trips, I received substantial help with the manuscript from a range of people in and related to CEE.

Czech Republic In 2010 Mirek Kundrata, director of the Czech Environmental Partnership, Tomas Ruzicka, deputy director, and other staff members helped me understand the work and impact of the Environmental Partnership for Central Europe (EPCE – now known as the EPA, Environmental Partnership Association), and particularly the Czech Partnership, since I had last visited CEE. Mirek also reviewed the manuscript promptly and provided thoughtful answers to many of my questions.

Jiří Bárta, director of the Via Foundation, and his associate Tana Hlavata, were helpful indeed, as were my friends in Prague, Vilik and Tea Hubner.

Poland I am grateful to Krzysztof Mularczyk, former executive director and later board chair of the Foundation for the Development of Polish Agriculture (FDPA), and to two people based in the US who were involved in the creation of the FDPA: Marcin Sar, with the Rockefeller Foundation in the 1980s, and J B Penn, leader of the FDPA negotiating team and later longtime board member. Thanks go as well to Andrzej Kassenberg, principal founder and longtime president of Warsaw's Institute for Sustainable Development; the Institute's co-founders, Krzysztof Kamieniecki and Zbigniew Bochniarz; Krystyna Wolniakowski, first director of the Polish Environmental Partnership; Rafal Serafin, longtime leader of the Polish Partnership; Dominika Zareba, early Amber Trail Greenway leader; Olaf Swolkień, leader of the Foundation for the Support of Ecological Initiatives; and Tomas Terlecki, founder and former director of the CEE Bankwatch Network.

Hungary Special thanks are due to several colleagues who provided valuable observations about my manuscript and/or helped me in other ways with the book: Sándor Fülöp, former executive director of the Environmental Management and Law Association (EMLA) in Budapest and now its board chair (who was especially probing and thoughtful); Miklos Marschall, deputy director of Transparency International, former deputy mayor of Budapest, and former director of CIVICUS; András Biró, founder of the Hungarian Foundation for Self-Reliance; Zsuzsa Foltányi, founding director of the Hungarian Partnership; and Vera Mora, current director of the Hungarian Partnership.

Slovakia I appreciate the help I received from Pavol Demeš, former foreign affairs adviser to the Slovak president and former regional director of the German Marshall Fund of the US, and from Lenka Surotchak, longtime director of the Pontis Foundation. Thanks are due as well to Beata Hirt, director of the Healthy City Community Foundation in Banská Bystrica; to Juraj Mesik, founding director of the Slovak Environmental Partnership; to Peter Medveď, its current leader; and to Livia Haringová, its financial manager.

I cannot leave CEE without a word about my longtime Irish colleague and friend Ray Murphy, a program officer at Tara Consultants, an international grantmaking philanthropy in Ireland, and then a program director at the Charles Stewart Mott Foundation in the US. In the 1990s Ray and I occasionally made field trips in CEE together. We learned a lot from each other and occasionally recommended co-funding projects. Ray died far too young from illness. I am not the only one in the foundation world who still misses him.

Western Balkans

For their patience with my questions as well as their well-considered comments on the draft of chapter 10, I thank Aleksandra (Alex) Vesić, former director of the Balkan Community Initiatives Fund (now the Trag Foundation), and her successor, Mia Vukojević – both in Belgrade; Anica-Maja (Maja) Boljević, director of fAKT (originally a branch of BCIF and now an independent grantmaking foundation), in Podgorica; Olivera Radovanović, founding and continuing director of the Green Network of Vojvodina, in Novi Sad; and Walter Veirs, regional director, Central/ Eastern Europe and Russia, at the Charles Stewart Mott Foundation.

Other contexts

This is a good place to thank a US-based group of people who offered some very insightful questions and comments on the manuscript: Roberta Gratz, award-winning journalist, urban critic, and author of a valuable report about RBF support for community revitalization in CEE; Marianne Ginsburg, former program officer for environment at the German Marshall Fund; Debbie Harding, former vice president of the Open Society Institute; Graham Finney, former president of the Conservation Company; David Sampson, former executive director of the Hudson River Greenway; Loren Finnell, founder and president of the Resource Foundation; Tom Fox, former vice president of the Council on Foundations and director of its international program, and now chair of ELMA Philanthropies Services; and Brent Mitchell, senior vice president of the Quebec-Labrador Foundation, who worked with RBF grantees in CEE and the Western Balkans as well as the Caribbean – who, by the way, suggested 'staying the course' in the title. Thanks again, Brent!

Alliance Publishing Trust (APT)

I do not know how common it is for an author to express appreciation to the publisher in the very book being published. Be that as it may, I could not resist saying a word about the people I have been working with at APT: Caroline Hartnell, editor-in-chief, and Ben Dupré, editor. To you both, I am grateful that you believed in the theme and content of my book, and that it is a good fit for APT. You have been prompt in your responses, creative with your suggestions, and understanding and patient as I have been challenged in the writing process – frequently puzzled and frustrated by technology – and have ended up being slightly delayed. Thank you, Caroline and Ben – you folks have been so kind and supportive throughout this stage of bringing my book to print.

The Moody family

Finally, I want to express my gratitude to my wife Susan and my children – our daughter Megan and my sons Scott and John. I know they bore some extra burdens during all those years when I was traveling overseas on RBF business. I appreciated their flexibility then and do so even more now, in retrospect. They also deserve enduring recognition for their patience with me during the past five plus years of book-writing. I am not a fast writer, and preparing chapters was a slow, determined process. I offer my thanks yet again to my family for challenging me from the outset to find appealing ways to communicate information and to tell my stories with lively prose. Susan especially offered valuable insights and suggestions along the way – even digging through boxes of pictures and files in the basement to unearth long-forgotten treasures.

Grant Listings

A book about grantmaking over a long period cannot, in my view, end without at least providing lists of the recipients that I thought, and the RBF board agreed, were worthy and promising. The following brief sections, organized by chapters (with the exception of a final list devoted to grants that did not fit within the structure of the book), offer such information.

Each grant list is preceded by a couple of paragraphs designed to supplement the perspective taken in that particular chapter. I wish I could have included more information about each entry in these lists, but time and space did not allow me to do so. I take comfort in the fact that it is quite easy to Google most, if not all, of the grantees mentioned, should readers want more information about these organizations and how they have evolved since the stories told in this book. I should also note the possibility that a few grant recipients could, sadly, have been overlooked, as I prepared nearly 1,000 grant recommendations during 40 years. I apologize if this turns out to be the case.

I was fortunate to be entrusted with the opportunity to recommend the use of more than $50 million during the course of my four decades at the RBF.* In current money terms (2014), that amount would be equivalent to far more than $100 million. This might not seem like a big number,

---

* Information about total numbers and total amounts of grants relating to specific chapters are noted in those chapters.

at a time when we often hear about billion-dollar projects and expenses. Nevertheless, I stand by the assertion in this book – that relatively modest resources can be allocated in thoughtful ways to produce lasting good.

Chapter Three
The Importance of Collaboration
Africa, 1968 to mid-1980s

Chapter 3 described how the RBF's Africa program evolved from a focus on East Africa in 1968, when I joined the Fund, to a concentration on southern Africa – a region troubled by war and by the persistence of apartheid in South Africa – and on Francophone West Africa, including countries that ranked among the poorest of the poor: a region that was not receiving much attention. The chapter also told the story of how the RBF seized the opportunity to devote time and resources to the southern African nation of Botswana, where a multiracial society, solid political leadership, and a functioning education system were already in place. Our grantmaking in Africa illustrated the importance (and challenge) for donors of finding ways to collaborate with local people in developing countries.

The list below reflects these features of our grantmaking. But it also includes a major grantee and partner, the African American Institute (AAI) in New York City, that is barely mentioned in the chapter. The Fund viewed the AAI as a critical ally because of its ability to bring people together – in the US and abroad – to discuss important Africa-related issues and its proactive roles in helping to organize efforts to address these challenges. In addition, the list below includes a set of grants to organizations in East Africa that I took over from Jim Hyde when I arrived, and a set of grants to organizations in West Africa that I recommended in the mid-1970s. Neither cluster of grants received sufficient attention in chapter 3; it simply was not possible to discuss every grant, however worthy!

Africa News Service
Durham, NC

African Wildlife Husbandry Development Association
Ouagadougou, Burkina Faso

African Wildlife Leadership Foundation
Washington, DC

The African-American Institute
New York, NY

Africare
Washington, DC

**American Friends
Service Committee**
New York, NY

Botswana, Republic of
Gaborone, Botswana

Botswana Society
Gaborone, Botswana

Council on Foreign Relations
New York, NY

**Food and Agriculture
Organization of the
United Nations**
Rome, Italy

**Foundation for International
Conciliation**
Windsor, United Kingdom

**International Union for
Conservation of Nature and
Natural Resources**
Gland, Switzerland

**International
Voluntary Services**
Washington, DC

**Kanye Brigades
Development Trust**
Kanye, Botswana

Kenya, Government of
Nairobi, Kenya

**Kenya National Parks,
Trustees of**
Nairobi, Kenya

**Kweneng Rural Development
Association**
Molepolole, Botswana

**Lawyers' Committee for Civil
Rights Under Law**
Washington, DC

Legal Resources Trust
Johannesburg, South Africa

Maru A Pula Foundation
Gaborone, Botswana

Middlebury College
Middlebury, VT

**National Council of the
Churches of Christ in the USA**
New York, NY

**National Museum and
Art Gallery**
Gabarone, Botswana

**Ngamiland Youth
Training Centre**
Maun, Botswana

Operation Crossroads Africa
New York, NY

**Partnership for Productivity
Foundation USA**
Washington, DC

Pelegano Village Industries
Gaborone, Botswana

**Phelps-Stokes Fund,
Trustees of the**
New York, NY

**Phillips Brooks House
Association**
Cambridge, MA

Policy Sciences Center
Staten Island, NY

**Private Agencies
Collaborating Together**
New York, NY

School for the Training of Wildlife Specialists
Garoua, Cameroon

Seven Springs Center
Mount Kisco, NY

Smithsonian Institution
Washington, DC

South African Institute of Race Relations
Johannesburg, South Africa

Tanzania National Parks, Trustees of
Arusha, Tanzania

Technoserve
Greenwich, CT

Uganda National Parks, Trustees of
Kampala, Uganda

United States South Africa Leader Exchange Program
Old Greenwich, CT

University of Science and Technology
Kumasi, Ghana

Volunteers in Technical Assistance
Mt Ranier, MD

Waterford School
Mbabane, Swaziland

Woodrow Wilson International Center for Scholars
Washington, DC

University of the Witwatersrand
Johannesburg, South Africa

World Council of Churches
Geneva, Switzerland

Chapter Four
Investing in Individuals
Latin America, 1968 to mid-1980s

When I arrived at the RBF in 1968, the Fund's largest grant recipient in Latin America, the American International Association for Economic and Social Development (AIA), was wrapping up its work after more than 20 years of useful activity in rural economic development, thus freeing up RBF resources for other purposes in the region. Chapter 4 told the story of how we recalibrated our grantmaking to concentrate more on wildlands management and eco-development as strategies for pursuing both conservation and job-creation goals. The central and extended role played by one young American, Kenton Miller, in many of these efforts illustrated the importance of identifying good people to support and work with – and points to some of the questions that are raised for funders by this kind of close collaboration with an individual.

For readers interested in more information about our efforts to advance employment generation between 1968 and the mid-1980s, the list below provides the names of those Latin American and US-based organizations that received RBF support for this purpose – some of which had been grantees since well before 1968.

Acción Comunitaria del Perú
Lima, Peru

ACCION International
Cambridge, MA

American International Association for Economic and Social Development
New York, NY

Americas Society
New York, NY

Amigos de la Naturaleza
San José, Costa Rica

Center for Inter-American Relations
New York, NY

Council on Foundations
Arlington, VA

Food and Agriculture Organization of the United Nations
Rome, Italy

Fundación Luis Muñoz Marín
San Juan, Puerto Rico

Fund for Multinational Management Education
New York, NY

Fundación Nicaragüense para el Desarrollo
Managua, Nicaragua

Inter-American Legal Services Association
Washington, DC

International Union for Conservation of Nature and Natural Resources
Gland, Switzerland

Organization for Tropical Studies
Seattle, WA

Organization of American States
Washington, DC

Overseas Education Fund of the League of Women Voters
Washington, DC

OXFAM America
Boston, MA

Pan American Development Foundation
Washington, DC

Policy Sciences Center
Staten Island, NY

Private Agencies Collaborating Together
New York, NY

Private Agencies in International Development
Washington, DC

Rodale Institute
Emmaus, PA

Simón Bolívar Foundation
New York, NY

Smithsonian Institution
Washington, DC

SOLIDARIOS
Guatemala City, Guatemala

Survival International
London, United Kingdom

Technoserve
Greenwich, CT

Tropical Agriculture Center for Research and Training
Turrialba, Costa Rica

University of Michigan, Regents of the
Ann Arbor, MI

Venezuelan Federation of Private Foundations
Caracas, Venezuela

Volunteers for International Technical Assistance
Schenectady, NY

Volunteers in Technical Assistance
Mt Ranier, MD

Chapter Five

A Willingness to Take Reasonable Risks

Caribbean Islands, mid-1970s to late 1980s

In the 1960s and early 1970s most of the islands in the Caribbean became independent countries – mini-states with relatively few resources, persistent social/ethnic tensions, and high unemployment. Thanks to conversations with Laurance Rockefeller, who had large investments in the region, and to meetings Jim Hyde and I attended in New York City about the challenges facing these small, young countries, we became increasingly concerned about the unmet needs so close to us. When the RBF board (which Laurance then chaired) encouraged staff to examine whether we should allocate resources for these neglected island states, I jumped at the chance. Chapter 5 described the evolution, outcomes, and lessons learned from this program.

Among the organizations and programs listed below, there are many that endeavored to blend environmental and economic considerations in what we then called an 'eco-development' approach. I am proud that we were such early funders in the sustainable development arena, although our terminology never caught on.

ACCION International
Cambridge, MA

American Jewish Committee
New York, NY

Antigua-Caribbean Training Institute
St John, Antigua

Association of Caribbean Transformation
Port of Spain, Trinidad

Association of Caribbean Universities and Research Institutes Foundation
Coral Gables, FL

CADEC
Bridgetown, Barbados

Caribbean Agro-Economic Society
Bridgetown, Barbados

Caribbean Conservation Association
Gainesville, FL

Dominica Community High School
Roseau, Dominica

Environmental Research Projects
Charleston, SC

Foundation for PRIDE
Miami, FL

Fund for Multinational Management Education
New York, NY

Good Hope School
St Croix, Virgin Islands

Harvard College, President and Fellows of
Cambridge, MA

Island Resources Foundation
St Thomas, Virgin Islands

King's Hill Youth Group
Roseau, Dominica

Meals for Millions/Freedom from Hunger Foundation
New York, NY

National Association of the Partners of the Alliance
Washington, DC

Organization for Rural Development
St Vincent, West Indies

Partners for Livable Communities
Washington, DC

Partnership for Productivity Foundation USA
Washington, DC

Quebec-Labrador Foundation
Ipswich, MA

SERVOL
Port of Spain, Trinidad

Sierra Club Foundation
San Francisco, CA

Trinidad and Tobago Development Foundation
Port of Spain, Trinidad

Turks and Caicos Development Trust
Grand Turk, Turks and Caicos

University of Michigan, Regents of the
Ann Arbor, MI

Volunteers in Technical Assistance
Mt Ranier, MD

Chapter Seven

The Convergence of Opportunity and Strategy

Central and Eastern Europe, 1980s

Chapter 7 focused on the first decade of the RBF's work in CEE, during which we funded a number of creative academic as well as practical initiatives to address sustainability challenges and promote East–West contact. The RBF was active in the region at a critical juncture, despite uncooperative and often hostile governments.

A centerpiece of chapter 7 was the story of the RBF's involvement in the creation of the Foundation for the Development of Polish Agriculture (FDPA) – the first independent foundation to be established in Poland since the Second World War. The story of the FDPA reveals a great deal about what it can mean to be an engaged grantmaker, with the RBF supporting the negotiations with communist government officials as well as the planning and launch of the FDPA. Grants for these purposes were made through a US-based NGO, Economic Perspectives, with one of its principals playing a key role in the process.

While a list of grants cannot reveal very much about the bold steps taken by the RBF in a new geographic arena, this list does suggest some of the creative ways in which a private American foundation, functioning below the radar, could be helpful in delicate political situations.

AFS International/ Intercultural Programs
New York, NY

Alerdinck Foundation
Amsterdam, Netherlands

American Association for the International Commission of Jurists
New York, NY

American Center for International Leadership
Baltimore, MD

American Council of Learned Societies
New York, NY

American Trust for Agriculture in Poland
McLean, VA

Biokultúra Egyesület
Budapest, Hungary

Budapest University of Economic Sciences
Budapest, Hungary

Colorado Outward Bound School
Denver, CO

Council on Foreign Relations
New York, NY

**East West
Management Institute**
New York, NY

Economic Perspectives
Whittier, VA

Environmental Law Institute
Washington, DC

European Cooperation Fund
Amsterdam, Netherlands

**Fondation pour une Entraide
Intellectuelle Européenne**
Paris, France

Friends of WWB/USA
New York, NY

**Fund for Private Assistance in
International Development**
Washington, DC

Green Library
Berkeley, CA

**H J Coolidge Center for
Environmental Leadership**
Cambridge, MA

**Hungarian Academy
of Sciences**
Budapest, Hungary

**Hungarian Institute of
International Affairs**
Budapest, Hungary

Institute for EastWest Studies
New York, NY

**Institute of
International Education**
New York, NY

**International Executive
Service Corps**
Stamford, CT

**International Federation of
Institutes for Advanced Study**
Toronto, Canada

**International Foundation for
Development Alternatives**
Nyon, Switzerland

International House, New York
New York, NY

**International Human
Rights Law Group**
Washington, DC

**International Institute for
Environment and Development**
London, United Kingdom

**International Network of
Resource Information Centers**
Durham, NH

**International Union for
Conservation of Nature and
Natural Resources**
Gland, Switzerland

INTERPHIL USA
Alexandria, VA

ISAR
Washington, DC

**Lawyers' Committee for
International Human Rights**
New York, NY

National Academy of Sciences
Washington, DC

National Audubon Society
New York, NY

**Natural Resources
Defense Council**
New York, NY

Overseas Development Council
Washington, DC

Pittsburgh, University of
Pittsburgh, PA

Policy Sciences Center
Staten Island, NY

Sabre Foundation
Somerville, MA

Sierra Club Foundation
San Francisco, CA

Sussex, University of
East Sussex, United Kingdom

Universities Field Staff International
Indianapolis, IN

University of Minnesota Foundation
Minneapolis, MN

Wharton Econometric Forecasting Associates
Washington, DC

Woodrow Wilson International Center for Scholars
Washington, DC

Winrock International Institute for Agricultural Development
Little Rock, AR

World Resources Institute
Washington, DC

Chapter Eight

Harnessing Optimism and Creative Energy through Cooperative Action

Central and Eastern Europe, 1990 to 1995

During the 1980s I had become acquainted with a number of impressive young leaders of the environmental movements in Poland, Czechoslovakia, and Hungary. The RBF had made some early grants to support their fight against the disgusting environmental degradation in communist-controlled countries. We were thus poised to begin a responsive sustainable resource use program in CEE immediately after the historic changes of 1989; and the Environmental Partnership for Central Europe (EPCE) was a central part of the story. It was a project in which the RBF, the German Marshall Fund of the United States, the Charles Stewart Mott Foundation, and other funders pooled their resources. We initially made grants through the German Marshall Fund to create the EPCE's locally managed programs of small grants, technical assistance, and training for NGOs and municipal governments.

The Fund had long maintained a program designed to strengthen the non-profit sector in the United States, which in the early 1990s was extended to CEE. A wonderful colleague, Nancy Muirhead, joined me

and took a leading role in developing and implementing that new program, which became a productive and enjoyable collaboration into the
new century.

Alerdinck Foundation
Amsterdam, Netherlands

**American Center for
International Leadership**
Baltimore, MD

**American Committee for
Aid to Poland**
McLean, VA

**American Council of
Learned Societies**
New York, NY

**American-Latvian Association
in the United States**
Dix Hills, NY

Beneficial to the Public Fund
Liptovský Hrádok, Slovakia

Biokultúra Egyesület
Budapest, Hungary

**Charitable Fund 'Carpathian
Euroregion'**
Debrecen, Hungary

**Case Western Reserve
University**
Cleveland, OH

Center for Clean Air Policy
Washington, DC

**Center for Environmental
Public Advocacy**
Poniky, Slovakia

**Center for Environmental
Studies Foundation**
Budapest, Hungary

**Center for International
Environmental Law**
Washington, DC

**Central and East European
Publishing Project**
Oxford, United Kingdom

**Central Connecticut State
University**
New Britain, CT

Council on Foundations
Arlington, VA

**Czechoslovak Management
Center Foundation**
Čelákovice, Czech Republic

**East European Environmental
Research Foundation**
Budapest, Hungary

**Eastern European Independent
Environmental Foundation**
Budapest, Hungary

**Eisenhower Exchange
Fellowships**
Philadelphia, PA

Environmental Law Institute
Washington, DC

**Environmental Management
and Law Association**
Budapest, Hungary

European Cooperation Fund
Amsterdam, Netherlands

**European Natural Heritage
Fund**
Rheinback/Bonn, Germany

Foundation for a Civil Society
New York, NY

Foundation for Social Innovations–USA
San Francisco, CA

Foundation for the Development of Polish Agriculture
Warsaw, Poland

Friends of the Earth International (France)
Villamblard, France

German Marshall Fund of the United States
Washington, DC

Goncol Foundation
Vác, Hungary

Greenways-Zelené Stezky
Prague, Czech Republic

Harvard University: Graduate School of Business Administration
Boston, MA

Harvard University: John F Kennedy School of Government
Cambridge, MA

Hudson Institute
Indianapolis, IN

Hungarian Foundation for Self-Reliance
Budapest, Hungary

Hungarian-American Enterprise Fund
Washington, DC

Institute for EastWest Studies
New York, NY

Institute for Environmental Policy
Prague, Czech Republic

Institute for Human Sciences
Vienna, Austria

Institute for Sustainable Communities
Montpelier, VT

Institute for Sustainable Development
Warsaw, Poland

Institute for Transportation and Development Policy
New York, NY

Institute of Sociology
Prague, Czech Republic

InterAction: American Council for Voluntary International Action
Washington, DC

International House, New York
New York, NY

International Management Center Foundation
Budapest, Hungary

Johns Hopkins University – Institute for Policy Studies
Baltimore, MD

Junior Achievement
Colorado Springs, CO

Kentucky Coalition
Charlottesville, VA

Michael Fields Agricultural Institute
East Troy, WI

Ministry of Agriculture of the Czech Republic
Prague, Czech Republic

Mirosław Dzielski Institute of Industry and Commerce
Kraków, Poland

National Forum Foundation
Washington, DC

Panos
London, United Kingdom

Policy Sciences Center
Staten Island, NY

Polish Ecological Club – Mazovian Branch
Warsaw, Poland

Portland State University Foundation
Portland, OR

Project for Public Spaces
New York, NY

Quebec-Labrador Foundation
Ipswich, MA

Resources Development Foundation
New York, NY

Rutgers, the State University of New Jersey
New Brunswick, NJ

Tides Foundation
San Francisco, CA

Veronica
Brno, Czech Republic

Voluntary Sector Research Project in Eastern Europe
Lost River, WV

Woodrow Wilson International Center for Scholars
Washington, DC

World Wildlife Fund
Washington, DC

Chapter Nine
Taking Stock and Refining Strategies
Central and Eastern Europe, 1996 to 2004

During these years, we focused on supporting initiatives in community revitalization, land stewardship, and transportation/energy that helped local people understand and mobilize around fresh strategies for promoting more sustainable resource use. Chapter 9 highlighted the challenge of protecting and maintaining public transportation systems.

In the non-profit sector arena, we built on progress made in order to enhance the organizational capacity and self-sufficiency of promising NGOs – by supporting efforts to improve the legal and fiscal frameworks within which non-governmental organizations operated, for example, and by funding the development of local resource centers that could continue to train and advise NGO leaders. Much of this grantmaking was managed by my experienced and thoughtful colleague Nancy Muirhead. This important work was in addition to the grants I managed, which are listed below.

I invite interested readers to Google any or all of the grantees on these lists, to see what they are doing today and what is said about them. I was gratified to find through my informal research that a large percentage of our grantees are still doing important work in our two main issue areas: sustainable development and civic engagement/democratic practice.

A Rocha-Christians in Conservation
Husinec, Czech Republic

A-Projekt
Liptovský Hrádok, Slovakia

Air and Waste Management Association
Pittsburgh, PA

American Trust for Agriculture in Poland
McLean, VA

Carpathian Foundation
Košice, Slovakia

CEE Bankwatch Network
Prague, Czech Republic

Center for Clean Air Policy
Washington, DC

Center for Environmental Public Advocacy
Poniky, Slovakia

Center for Environmental Studies Foundation
Budapest, Hungary

Centre SOS Prague
Prague, Czech Republic

Clean Air Action Group
Budapest, Hungary

Conservation Fund
Arlington, VA

Council on Foundations
Arlington, VA

Czech Eco-Counselling Network
Brno, Czech Republic

Czech Environmental Partnership Foundation
Brno, Czech Republic

Ecologists Linked for Organizing Grassroots Initiatives and Action
Middlebury, VT

Environmental Management and Law Association
Budapest, Hungary

European Centre for Ecological Agriculture and Tourism, Poland
Stryszów, Poland

European Natural Heritage Fund
Rheinback/Bonn, Germany

European Roma Rights Center
Budapest, Hungary

Foundation for a Civil Society
New York, NY

Foundation for Organic Agriculture
Prague, Czech Republic

Foundation for the Development of Polish Agriculture
Warsaw, Poland

Foundation for the Support of Ecological Initiatives
Kraków, Poland

International Coalition to Protect the Polish Countryside
Małopolska, Poland

Foundation Institute of Public Affairs
Warsaw, Poland

Friends of the Carpathian Foundation–United States
Washington, DC

Friends of the Earth International
Amsterdam, Netherlands

Friends of the Earth International (France)
Villamblard, France

German Marshall Fund of the United States
Washington, DC

Green Federation
Kraków, Poland

Greenways-Zelené Stezky
Prague, Czech Republic

Indiana University Foundation
Indianapolis, IN

Institute for EastWest Studies
New York, NY

Institute for Environmental Policy
Prague, Czech Republic

Institute for Human Sciences
Vienna, Austria

Institute for Sustainable Communities
Montpelier, VT

Institute for Sustainable Development
Warsaw, Poland

Institute for Transportation and Development Policy
New York, NY

International Coalition to Protect the Polish Countryside
Małopolska, Poland

International House, New York
New York, NY

International Institute for Energy Conservation–Europe
London, United Kingdom

International Network of Resource Information Centers
Durham, NH

International Youth Foundation
Washington, DC

ISAR
Washington, DC

Oživení
Prague, Czech Republic

Pocantico Conferences
Sleepy Hollow, NY

Polish Ecological Club, Mazovian Branch
Warsaw, Poland

Polish Environmental Partnership
Kraków, Poland

Prague Mothers
Prague, Czech Republic

Project for Public Spaces
New York, NY

Quebec-Labrador Foundation
Ipswich, MA

Rails to Trails
Washington, DC

Research Foundation of the State of New York
Albany, NY

Rožmberk Society
Třeboň, Czech Republic

Rural Organization for Community Activities (VOKA)
Banská Bystrica, Slovakia

Via Foundation
Prague, Czech Republic

World Resources Institute
Washington, DC

Chapter Ten
Last Stop
Western Balkans, 2000 to 2007

How could a modest-sized foundation such as the RBF make a difference in Serbia, Montenegro, and Kosovo in 2000, when so many wounds from the ethnic fighting of the 1990s were still open and hurting? Economic development was a key concern in all three places; many people understood the fundamental importance of managing natural and cultural resources wisely; and courageous citizens and citizen groups were tackling daunting social problems. During my eight years in charge of the Western Balkans program, the Fund's grantmaking guidelines focused on these basic needs: (1) building democratic capacity; (2) grappling with questions of national identity and challenges of ethnic reconciliation; and (3) developing sustainable communities.

During this last phase of my career at the RBF, as described in chapter 10, I had more regular, direct contact with national government leaders than at any other time in my 40 years of grantmaking. As the list below suggests, we made a conscious and determined effort not only to reach out to civic groups, NGOs, academic institutions, and business groups at all levels but also to help new government structures in the Western Balkans operate in as effective, even-handed, and honest a fashion as possible.

Artspace Projects
Minneapolis, MN

Association People's Parliament
Leskovac, Serbia

Balkan Community Initiatives Trust
Belgrade, Serbia

Balkans Youth Link Albania
Tirana, Albania

Belgrade Fund for Political Excellence
Belgrade, Serbia

Brown University
Providence, RI

Center for Civil Society Development – Protecta
Niš, Serbia

Center for Development of Non-Governmental Organizations
Podgorica, Montenegro

Center for Multicultural Education
Preševo, Serbia

Center for Regionalism
Novi Sad, Serbia

Center for the Living City
New York, NY

Center for the Protection and Research of Birds
Podgorica, Montenegro

Centre for Free Elections and Democracy
Belgrade, Serbia

Centre for Political and Social Research
Pristina, Kosovo

Citizens Action – Center for Community Organizing
Banská Bystrica, Slovakia

Citizens' Association for Democracy and Civic Education – Civic Initiatives
Belgrade, Serbia

Civic Association Kuda.Org
Novi Sad, Serbia

Columbia University in the City of New York, Trustees of
New York, NY

Community Center–Bar
Bar, Montenegro

Council of Europe
Strasbourg, France

Crisis Management Initiative
Helsinki, Finland

Development School
Ghent, Belgium

East West Management Institute
New York, NY

Expeditio
Kotor, Montenegro

European Foundation Centre
Brussels, Belgium

European Stability Initiative
Berlin, Germany

Film Video Arts
New York, NY

Forum for Ethnic Relations
Belgrade, Serbia

Foundation for a Civil Society
New York, NY

Foundation for Democratic Initiatives
Gjakova, Kosovo

Fund for an Open Society (Yugoslavia)
Belgrade, Serbia

G-17 Institute
Belgrade, Serbia

German Marshall Fund of the United States
Washington, DC

Green Home
Podgorica, Montenegro

Green Network of Vojvodina
Novi Sad, Serbia

Human Rights Committee Vranje
Vranje, Serbia

Institute for EastWest Studies
New York, NY

Institute for Sustainable Communities
Montpelier, VT

Institute for Sustainable Development
Warsaw, Poland

International Center for Transitional Justice
New York, NY

International Ecotourism Society
Washington, DC

Johns Hopkins University – Paul H Nitze School of Advanced International Studies
Washington, DC

Humanitarian and Charitable Society of Kosova – Mother Theresa
Pristina, Kosovo

Kosovar Institute for Policy Research and Development
Pristina, Kosovo

Media and Reform Centre Niš
Niš, Serbia

Multiethnic Children and Youth Peace Centre
Mitrovica, Kosovo

Nansen Dialogue Center Montenegro
Podgorica, Montenegro

Natura
Kolašin, Montenegro

Network for the Affirmation of the NGO Sector
Podgorica, Montenegro

New Horizon
Ulcinj, Montenegro

New Vision
Prijepolje, Serbia

New York Foundation for the Arts
Brooklyn, NY

Non-Governmental Organization Group for Changes
Podgorica, Montenegro

Novi Sad Faculty of Law
Novi Sad, Serbia

Project for Public Spaces
New York, NY

Project on Ethnic Relations
Princeton, NJ

Quebec-Labrador Foundation
Ipswich, MA

Thomas Jefferson Institute for the Study of World Politics
Washington, DC

Tides Center
San Francisco, CA

TRAIL Association
Niš, Serbia

United Nations Development Programme
New York, NY

Wars of 1991–1999 Documentation Center
Belgrade, Serbia

Youth Initiative for Human Rights
Belgrade, Serbia

Grants not included in chapter lists

In my experience it is good to have surprises at the end of a long process – or a long book! For those readers who have taken the time and shown the special interest required to review the grant lists on the preceding pages, I offer one more list – of grants that did not fit into the framework of this book but were part of my portfolio during my tenure at the Fund. These grants – about 170 of them, totaling nearly $10 million over 40 years – deserve attention too! Some of this grantmaking falls under the heading of 'international cooperation,' which was a theme, to varying degrees, throughout my four decades. Other RBF interests are reflected in the lists below as well.

Since none of these grants are discussed at any length in the book, I will say a few things here. First, I wish to note that my participation in workshops and study sessions offered by several of these organizations was an important part of my 'continuing education' about a range of international issues. Second, I note the inclusion here of several groups that provide international exchange opportunities – often unheralded but important programs in promoting cooperation and mutual understanding among nations and peoples. Third, this list includes half a dozen organizations that work on international human rights. This is a subject dear to my heart, and I was excited to manage the RBF's grantmaking in this area in the late 1970s and early 1980s. Finally, while the arts were not an ongoing focus of my work, the Fund's involvement in one initiative listed here, Arts International, gave me a very exciting opportunity to collaborate with an RBF board member, Nancy Hanks (who had been the second chair of the National Endowment for the Arts), Alistair Cooke (longtime BBC journalist), and others to promote international cultural and arts activities – another important means of improving international understanding and encouraging international cooperation.

American Association for the International Commission of Jurists
New York, NY

American Council for Emigres in the Professions
New York, NY

American Council for Nationalities Service
New York, NY

American Field Services
Washington, DC

Arts International
New York, NY

Atlantic Council of the United States
Washington, DC

Atlantic Institute for International Affairs
Paris, France

Brookings Institution
Washington, DC

Canadian Institute of International Affairs
Toronto, Canada

Carnegie Endowment for International Peace
Washington, DC

Columbia University in the City of New York, Trustees of
New York, NY

Council on Foreign Relations
New York, NY

Council on Foundations
Arlington, VA

Foreign Policy Association
New York, NY

Friends of Women's World Banking/USA
New York, NY

Friendship Force International
Atlanta, GA

Hospitality Committee for the United Nations Delegations
New York, NY

Human Rights Internet
Washington, DC

Institute of International Education
New York, NY

International Federation of Institutes for Advanced Study
Toronto, Canada

International Federation of Institutes for Advanced Study (Sweden)
Solna, Sweden

International House, New York
New York, NY

International League For Human Rights
New York, NY

International Social Service, American Branch
New York, NY

Overseas Development Council
Washington, DC

Overseas Education Fund of the League of Women Voters
Washington, DC

Procedural Aspects of International Law Institute
Washington, DC

Project Orbis
New York, NY

Salzburg Seminar in American Studies
Cambridge, MA

Save the Children Federation
Westport, CT

Survival International
London, United Kingdom

Travelers Aid–International Social Service of America
New York, NY

Trilateral Commission (North America)
New York, NY

United Nations
New York, NY

United Nations Association of the United States of America
New York, NY

United Service Organizations
New York, NY

University of Sussex
Brighton, United Kingdom

Worldwatch Institute
Washington, DC

Yale University
New Haven, CT

Index

This index includes only those grantees that are treated at some length in the book. Other grantees, including those that are mentioned or briefly discussed in the text, can be found in the Grant Listings on pages 280–300, which are organized by chapter.